Pizza, Focaccia, Filled and Flat Breads

FROM YOUR BREAD MACHINE—
Perfect Every Time

Pizza, Focaccia, Filled and Flat Breads

FROM YOUR BREAD MACHINE—
Perfect Every Time

LORA BRODY
with Lynne Bail, P. J. Hamel, and Cynthia Salvato

WILLIAM MORROW AND COMPANY, INC.

NEW YORK

Library of Congress Cataloging-in-Publication Data

Brody, Lora, 1945–
Pizza, focaccia, flat and filled breads from your bread
machine : perfect every time / Lora Brody with Lynne Bail,
P. J. Hamel, and Cynthia Salvato. — 1st ed.
p.   cm.
Includes index
ISBN 0-688-13752-0
1. Bread.   2. Automatic bread machines.   I. Bail, Lynne.
II. Hamel, P. J.   III. Salvato, Cynthia.   IV. Title.
TX769.B797   1995
641.8'15—dc20   94-26833
                                      CIP

Printed in the United States of America

FIRST EDITION

3 5 7 9 10 8 6 4 2

BOOK DESIGN BY MARYSARAH QUINN

June 12, 1994

To Harriet and Charlie,

Love is all around you

Acknowledgments

Once again I am in the happy position of being able to publicly thank the women (my treasured friends) who helped me write this book. Lynne Bail, P. J. Hamel, and Cindy Salvato took this project on with their usual unbridled creativity and enthusiasm. The results reflect it. I suspect there won't be much time for our ovens to cool down before the next project starts heating up once again. Rest up, I'll be ready as soon as I finish off this piece of pizza. Thanks guys, you are the greatest.

Thanks and love as well to my editor (the joyously newly married) Harriet Bell, for her unending support, and for her forbearance in not strangling me every time I call to say "I've just had the greatest idea . . ."

The-Double-Cheese-Pizza-with-Everything Award gets delivered from the oven to my beloved agent Susan Ginsburg. Anna, Rachel, Aaron, and Josh; do you know your mom is really Wonder Woman?

Contents

Filled Breads, Braids, Twists, and Sandwiches 95

Deep-Dish Pies 151

Flatbreads, Crackers, and Breadsticks 185

Rolls, Muffins, Scones, and Pancakes 231

Sweet Breads, Dumplings, Biscotti, and Other Desserts 269

Introduction

The inspiration for this book hit me like a bolt of lightning the very last time I shelled out twelve bucks for pizza at our local pizza emporium. I couldn't help noticing the brand-new red Corvette parked right out in front. Then I saw that Apollo, the owner of the place, was wearing a very spiffy red sweater with a little Corvette emblem where the alligator usually goes. Putting two and two (or six and six) together, I realized just how much of a profit margin there was in this pizza business. Not only was Apollo making out like a bandit, he wasn't even giving good value for my money. His crusts were too thick (too many uneaten smiles of unsauced edges were tossed away by kids who liked only the covered parts), the sauce was uninspired at best, and the cheese had no flavor whatsoever. Hey, I could make better pizza than that—and for a fraction of the price.

And now you can as well. The bread machine makes it so easy to make world-class pizza dough that you will be forever spoiled. From the most basic pizza with red sauce to the ultimate in designer pizza—all are possible, and tastier—in record time. And the news gets better; other classic breads are just a push of a button away. You can make hundreds of filled breads, braids, and twists, not to mention that new shining star on the food block: focaccia. The bread machine will open up a whole new world of flatbreads. Wait until you see how easy it is to make your own crackers, pitas, and lavosh. You'll find yourself inviting company over just to wow them with your interesting breadsticks.

There is another very important reason to start making not only your own pizzas and focaccias but all your bread as well. Now that you have a bread machine, you are in complete charge of the kinds and quality of the ingredients you feed yourself, your family, and friends. By using unbleached, unchemically treated flours, grains, nuts, fruits, vegetables, herbs, and spices grown without pesticides and not treated with dangerous preservatives, you have a leg up in the nutrition game. By adding nonfat dry milk to your doughs, and low-fat dairy products to your toppings and fillings, you get a major calcium boost. By combining foods such as legumes (in the form of cooked chick-peas or puréed black beans) with the complex carbohydrates in the flour, you create a bread with nearly perfect protein, which, when combined with a salad or plate of steamed dark green leafy vegetables, makes a balanced meal. Add some bran or whole wheat flour and you've got your fiber for the day. You can turn any of the recipes here into vegetarian recipes by omitting, or substituting tofu for, the meat.

If you like to get your hands in the dough, and make great-tasting bread and pizza almost from scratch, then these recipes will satisfy that urge. Let the bread machine make the dough; you do the rolling or forming and baking by hand. It's a perfect combination of talents. And don't forget to stash away all the money you've saved by making your own pizzas. I think a red Corvette would look great parked in front of your place as well.

Using Your Bread Machine as a Dough Maker

All of the recipes in this book were tested on a large (1½ pound) machine. **All the recipes can be used in ALL 1½ pound machines.** Market surveys show that 90 percent of bread machine owners have the large models, and that trend is continuing. This does not mean you cannot use the recipes in a small machine, but some adjustments are necessary. You have two choices: Reduce the ingredients called for in the recipe by one third or make the full amount, watching carefully that the dough doesn't rise up and overflow the pan. If it threatens to do this, simply remove it to a well-oiled or buttered bowl, cover it with plastic wrap, and continue the rise for the remainder of the time indicated on the machine.

All bread machines come with a Dough cycle. Sometimes it's called Manual or Basic Dough. What it means is that the machine kneads the dough and then allows it to rise (depending on the brand of machine, this happens once or twice). At the end of the final cycle, the machine will signal that the dough is ready. You can then remove the dough and prepare to form it into bread.

Many recipes here instruct you to place the finished dough on a work surface, cover it with clean towel or plastic wrap, and let it rest for a few minutes. The act of deflating, or "punching down," the dough, activates the gluten (protein) and makes the dough tense and therefore difficult to roll out. A short rest allows the gluten to relax and renders the dough more manageable.

You can refrigerate doughs after you deflate them. I store my doughs either in an oiled bowl, covered with plastic, or in a heavy-duty plastic freezer bag. It's important to use oversized bags, as the dough will continue to rise in the refrigerator. Doughs without perishable ingredients (eggs, milk, etc.) can be refrigerated for up to six days. Those with perishable ingredients should not be kept more than three days. You can freeze both kinds of dough that come out of the machine at the end of the dough cycle. I freeze my doughs for up to three months in 1-gallon heavy-duty plastic freezer bags. You can defrost them (still in the bag) either in the refrigerator (this is best for doughs with perishable ingredients) or at room temperature.

Many of the finished recipes in this book taste best when enjoyed hot from the oven, or at least while they are still warm. This is certainly true of pizza, although you couldn't prove that by my kids, who think leftover pizza for breakfast is one of the world's great treats. Storage at room temperature is infinitely preferable to refrigeration, which robs the bread of moisture and allows other food smells to seep in. If you plan to freeze breads they should be completely cooled before being wrapped in plastic or placed in a plastic freezer bag. Defrost frozen breads while they are still wrapped so the moisture will collect on the outside of the bag, not on the bread. You can reheat or refresh breads in a moderate (350°F) oven for ten to fifteen minutes. Wrap them loosely in foil and place them right on the rack, which allows hot air to circulate around them. If a bread is sliced, it is helpful to separate the slices slightly before reheating.

A toaster oven is perfect for reheating (and/or toasting) slices of bread as well as rolls and scones. A microwave is less successful, since bread tends at first to get soggy, then turn hard as a rock. If you don't mind soggy pizza crust, then reheat it in a microwave. I'll stick to my toaster oven.

If you do not see freezing or reheating directions in a recipe, it's because we felt the bread didn't stand up to it.

There are a few things that contribute greatly to success in baking regardless of whether you use a bread machine to make your dough or do it totally by hand. They are the kind and quality of ingredients, the pans used for baking, and the oven temperature.

Ingredients

The order in which manufacturers instruct you to put ingredients into the machine varies from machine to machine. I have found that with the exception of the Dak or Welbilt it makes no difference at all *if you are going to be making dough right away.* The Dak and Welbilt seem to perform best when the yeast goes in first. If you are programming the machine to make dough at a later time, then follow the order specified by your machine's manufacturer. Remember, just as it is unsafe to place perishable ingredients in the machine and program for baking at a later time, it's not a good idea to leave finished dough in the machine more than a few hours after the final cycle ends. It is an especially bad idea to leave doughs with perishable ingredients (butter, milk, eggs) in the machine for any time after the final cycle. Some recipes here call for an extra-long rise after the final cycle, though it's usually no more than two hours.

Some bread machine manufacturers call for ingredients to be at room temperature before being added to the machine. Even though my machine has a warming cycle, I still like to have my ingredients at room temperature. The reason is simple: The key to success in using a bread machine is to watch the dough being formed for the first five to ten minutes of the kneading process. This way you will know whether or not you have to add more liquid, or flour, as the case may be. If you add cold ingredients, the machine can take up to fifteen minutes to warm them before actually starting to knead. Meanwhile, you've become occupied with more important things than staring into a machine in which nothing exciting is happening. You wander away, and when the kneading cycle starts, you're busy in the garden or writing the great American novel instead of watching to see if your dough is too wet or too dry. Having ingredients at room temperature puts less strain on the machine as well.

You'll notice that many of these recipes call for a certain amount of flour or water plus an additional amount if needed. Flour absorbs moisture from the atmosphere. Thus, if you live in Florida you'll typically need less liquid in your dough than someone in Arizona. The machine is smart, but not smart enough to tell you if there is not enough or too much liquid in your dough. Most of the common problems bread machine owners have can be eliminated by disregarding the place in the manual that says not to open the bread machine after you put in the ingredients. **It is imperative not only to open the machine, but to feel comfortable adding additional ingredients to achieve the consistency of dough described in the recipe.**

If you've never made pizza or played with pizza dough, and you don't have a clue what the dough is suppose to look like, go to the supermarket and buy some frozen pizza dough. Take it home and let it defrost. Sprinkle a little flour on a work surface and get your hands into the dough. See how soft and silky it is? See how it stretches and is pliable? Notice how after you've played with it for a while the dough becomes less willing to stretch? This is because you've activated the gluten (protein), which can be thought of as elastic bands running through the dough. The yeast fills these bands with pockets of carbon dioxide, pushing the dough up. Baking cements the bands so that the bread stays up after it cools. Cover the dough with a clean towel and let it rest on the counter for 10 minutes. You'll notice then that the gluten has relaxed and the dough can be stretched once more.

Ninety-nine percent of the recipes in this book call for all-purpose flour either by itself or in addition to other kinds of flour. This means flour made from hard wheat that has a protein content of between thirteen and fifteen grams per cup. This gives enough gluten to get the rise you need to make successful bread. We used King Arthur Flour to create and test these recipes. If you wish to use King Arthur and cannot find it in your store, you can call (800) 827-6836 to either get the location of a store near you that carries it or to order it by mail. No matter what flour you use, make sure that it is neither bleached nor chemically treated with bromates. This information will appear on the package.

Another flour commonly called for is King Arthur's White Wheat, a new variety of wheat that combines the fiber and nutritional benefits of whole wheat and the sweeter, lighter taste and appearance of all-purpose flour. If you cannot find this, you can substitute a like amount of regular whole wheat flour. The result will be a heavier, denser bread. Whole wheat flour should be kept in a cool place to keep it from becoming rancid. I store mine in the freezer in a large plastic bucket.

Difficult-to-find flours, such as rye and buckwheat, are sold in health food stores. Remember that flours and grains not treated with preservatives or grown without pesticides are easily subject to meal moths, which can infest your kitchen quicker than you can say cereal killer. Take care to buy those products in small quantities. Place the bags in a large heavy-duty plastic freezer bag and store the bags in the refrigerator or freezer. Cornmeal should also be stored there as well as seeds, nuts, and ingredients such as flaked unsweetened coconut.

Yeast is the second critical ingredient in making bread. We used Red Star Dry Active Yeast and Red Star Bread Machine Yeast in testing these recipes. (Several recipes for crackers and flatbreads in this book, though, are made without yeast.) I strongly recommend staying away from those individual envelopes of yeast. Bulk yeast is far more economical, far easier to use, and more accurate to measure. Four-ounce and seven-ounce jars of yeast are available in some supermarkets. Store yeast in glass or plastic containers with tightly sealed lids in the refrigerator or freezer. Take care to use only a clean, dry measuring spoon when scooping yeast to measure. You can use yeast directly from the freezer.

Sourdough starters can be made at home from the recipe in this book (page 20) or they can be mail-ordered (page 301). You can also make a sourdough starter from a powdered mix called Gold Rush. It is available in gourmet and specialty food stores. Remember that you have to feed your starter twelve to twenty-four hours before you want to make your dough.

Nonfat dry milk along with other dairy products is a great source of calcium. It also relaxes the dough and gives it the ability to stretch. Since it also serves to soften the crumb and crust of the finished bread, nonfat dry milk will result in a soft rather than crisp crust.

Salt acts as a yeast retardant. You don't want your yeast to do all its work in the first few minutes. You want it to work throughout the making of the dough. Without salt, the finished bread will be overraised and will lack character and taste. Too much salt will stop the yeast dead in its tracks and you'll end up with a hockey puck.

Sugar, as well as honey, molasses, corn syrup, and maple syrup act along with flour as a yeast food. In many breads these sweeteners give the yeast a little jump-start for the rising process. Too much sugar will cause the yeast to stop working completely.

Fats in the form of butter, margarine, oil, egg yolks, cheese, and other dairy products give breads and crusts tenderness, flavor, and a refined crumb and a crisp crust as well as lengthening their shelf life. Those breads made without fat tend to become stale a very few hours after baking. This is not to say that breads made without fat have no merit. Many flatbreads and crackers have great taste and texture and will keep a long time after baking. Pizza crusts and focaccie call for a small amount of oil which gives them the crispness associated with and expected of such breads. Brioche and coffee cakes, on the other hand, depend on butter to deliver their classic rich texture and taste.

Olive oil has a distinctive taste that sets it apart from vegetable oil. To my mind, there are few things as pleasing as really good cold-pressed extra virgin olive oil. Because of its assertive flavor, you don't need a lot, and because of the price, I would suggest using it only on the top of pizzas and focaccie and using a less expensive type for the dough. There has been a flurry of really great flavored oils on the market. You can choose among garlic, chili, basil, rosemary, red pepper, porcini, and probably dozens of other kinds of oil. And don't ignore oils that have been around a long time, such as sesame, walnut, hazelnut, almond, and apricot kernel. You can mail-order these oils (page 301) or pick them up in a gourmet or natural foods store. Store them, tightly covered, in a cool place; after being opened, the nut oils should be stored in the refrigerator.

In many recipes you can substitute one fat for another: vegetable oil for olive oil, margarine for butter, and egg substitute for fresh eggs. Bear in mind, however, that the taste and texture of the finished bread and the appearance of the crust will not be the same as if you used the fat specified in the recipe.

Liquids can be more than the obvious ones: water, milk, wine, beer, fruit and vegetable juice. Anything that melts during the baking process is considered a liquid: cheese, yogurt, sour cream, and cream cheese, for example. A fantastic source of vitamins and flavor are vegetable juices that are either purchased or made in a juicer. If you use a juice you have made, try throwing in some of the leftover solids or pulp since they are a great source of fiber. Foods that have been soaked before going into the dough (even though most of the liquid has been pressed out or drained off) also account for moisture in the bread. A perfect example is the dried mushrooms in the Porcini Pizza on page 31. The recipe calls for slightly less liquid than usual which makes the dough appear dry during the first part of kneading. However, once the water is squeezed out of the mushrooms the dough becomes smooth and soft.

In recipes that call for milk, you may substitute nonfat dry milk, or powdered buttermilk, or even powdered goat's milk, plus the same amount of water as the amount of milk designated in the recipe.

Many of these recipes call for seeds and/or nuts. Be sure to use care when buying and storing these ingredients. The oil in nuts and seeds can become rancid when they are stored incorrectly. The best place is in the freezer in either plastic freezer bags or tightly sealed plastic containers. Defrost at room temperature before adding to the bread machine.

On the subject of nuts, the best way to bring out the flavor in nuts is to toast them before adding them to your recipe. Spread them in a single layer on a heavy-rimmed baking sheet and place it in a preheated 300°F oven for about 10 minutes, or until you can smell them. Check frequently to make sure they do not burn. Remove the nuts when they are a light golden brown and cool them in the pan before using the nuts in cooking. It makes sense to toast a quantity of nuts, then save some in the freezer for the next time you need them. Flaked unsweetened coconut can be toasted the same way.

My first bread machine book called for specific sizes of eggs. This was crucial since most of the breads were baked in the machine and the margin for error was less. The doughs in this book are much more flexible and forgiving. If you're making a recipe that calls for large eggs but you have only medium, you can make up the difference with water. Just add the number of eggs specified in the recipe, let the machine go through the first couple of minutes of the knead cycle, then add a few tablespoons of water until the dough is smooth and soft. Naturally the opposite is true; if you have jumbo eggs and the recipe calls for extra-large, you can add more flour, a tablespoon at a time, after the first few minutes of the knead cycle.

Herbs and spices give flavor and spark to many of these recipes. While it's great when you can use fresh herbs, dried herbs that are not stale (and have not lost their flavor) make a good substitute. If you find a recipe that appeals to you with the exception of some herbs or spices, feel free to substitute those that are to your liking. The same is true for toppings and sauces. If you can't find or can't stand the taste of pesto, fennel, sausage, or goat cheese, top the pizza with something that you do like or have on hand.

Equipment

Next to your bread machine your most important piece of equipment is your oven. Many of the recipes in this book call for oven temperatures of 400°–500°F. This high temperature delivers the very best pizza crust. When you turn your oven up this high, any leftover spills from previous baking will start to burn and smoke. This will give your pizza or focaccia an unpleasant taste—not to mention smelling up your house. So, much as you might hate to do it, you better clean the oven before you fire it up.

Next thing you need is a kitchen timer—the kind that clips to your apron or hangs on a cord so you can wear it around your neck. As much as I cook (and believe me, it's a lot), I always use a timer, and I usually set it to go off five minutes before the time suggested in the recipe—just in case.

Some people use pizza stones or tiles in place of pans. The stone or tiles made of unglazed ceramic material are placed directly on the oven rack or floor. They are heated during the preheating of the oven and the pizza or focaccia, which has been formed on a wooden paddle called a peel, is slid off (this is made easy by sprinkling the peel with cornmeal) directly onto them. The benefit here is that your pizza or focaccia will have a wonderfully crisp bottom from having been cooked directly on the stone. The downside of pizza stones is that they are very heavy and for some people are hard to haul around and hard to store. Tiles are slightly more convenient, but the cornmeal can sift through the cracks onto the oven floor. I wouldn't want to discourage anyone from using a stone; I have one in my oven and use it for all kinds of baking. However, there have been times when I've forgotten that it's there and preheated my oven in order to cook something that couldn't be baked on a stone. There I was, stuck with a twenty-pound hot potato, too hot and heavy to lift out of the oven. If you choose to use a stone, you should also invest in a long wide metal spatula for lifting the cooked pizza from the stone back onto the peel, as well as a wide brush for sweeping the cornmeal off the stone.

There are excellent alternatives to stones and tiles. Look for pizza pans (both round and rectangular) with perforated bottoms. I have seen them in

8-inch, 12-inch, 14-inch, and 16-inch as well as 17 × 11-inch sizes. The holes allow steam to escape and heat to get in—no more soggy bottoms. Just remember in recipes that call for dusting the pan with cornmeal, you'll want to oil your pan or spray it with nonstick vegetable spray.

Toward the end of writing this book I discovered the innovative trick of rolling pizza dough right onto the bottom of an overturned sheet pan that has been oiled or sprayed with nonstick vegetable spray. I used my jelly roll pans (which measure 17 × 11 inches) for this. You can make the most wonderfully thin pizza crust this way. The only real challenge is getting the pan to stay still while you roll. Try laying a thick, damp towel under the pan or asking a friend to hold it in exchange for the first piece of pizza.

Deep-dish pizza can be made in any number of pans, my favorite being the above jelly roll pan, but this time turned right side up. If you are going to buy a pan, make sure to buy the heavy-duty kind, since the cheap kind warp and buckle in a very hot oven and the result is uneven cooking and a tidal wave of sauce spilling into one corner of the pan.

There are a few recipes that call for special pans, notably, Quitza Lorraine (page 172). I made up this recipe in an attempt (successful, I think) to cross pizza with quiche. My favorite pan for this job is made by Kaiser, in their La Forme series, and it is called a conical springform. Basically it's a round deep-dish pizza pan with sides that tilt outward and a bottom that releases so you don't have to serve your beautiful Quitza in the pan. It comes in 12- and 13-inch sizes.

If a recipe calls for a pan of a size that you don't own, use the one you have closest in size. You may have to use only part of the dough, or make two batches. Crackers, especially, can be made in quick batches. Just let the pan cool slightly, or run cold water over it and dry it, before rolling out the next piece of dough.

A pizza cutter is a sharp round wheel attached to a handle that cuts as it rotates through dough or crust. Not only is it perfect for slicing wedges of pizza and focaccia, it's great for cutting cracker dough and strips for breadsticks. If you're buying a pizza wheel, buy one that has a large enough blade: $2\frac{1}{2}$ or 3 inches in diameter. Marie Huntington, owner of Codes and Company, in Columbus, Indiana, showed me the great trick of using a heavy cleaver to cut pizza—try it—it works.

Another great implement is a good bread knife. The serrated blade should be a minimum length of 8 inches. This does not go in the dishwasher or get tossed in a drawer along with other kitchen utensils.

Unless you are incredibly coordinated and fearless as well, give up fantasies of throwing a glob of dough up in the air and having it come down in a flat round pizza crust–like disk. The most straightforward way to roll out pizza and other doughs is with a rolling pin. The heavier the rolling pin and the higher you position your upper body above the work surface, the more leverage you'll have and the easier it will be to roll out the dough. If you're vertically challenged, stand on a phone book or low stool.

On the subject of work surfaces, smooth and cool is what you're looking for. Formica, marble, granite, and wood can make fine work surfaces as long as they are large enough to enable you to roll out the dough. The surface should be absolutely clean and perfectly dry. If you want to use a large dense plastic cutting board, make sure to anchor it in place by slipping a thick bath towel underneath. This will keep it from slipping around on the counter while you roll.

You can keep your dough from sticking to the work surface either by sprinkling a small amount of flour (or even finely ground cornmeal) on it, or rubbing on a small amount of vegetable oil or spraying it with nonstick vegetable oil. Different people feel more comfortable with one technique or the other. Try both, then stick (or unstick) with what works for you. Take care not to overflour the dough during the rolling process. Use only enough to keep the dough from sticking, brushing away any excess that accumulates on the dough.

A bowl scraper (also called a bench knife) is another invaluable tool. Made either of hard plastic or metal, it is a wide blade that can be used not only to scrape away flour, crumbs, and scraps left over after you roll out and cut the dough, but also to rotate and turn the dough to keep it from sticking during rolling.

Secrets for Success—Perfect Every Time

Having made hundreds of pizzas, crackers, flatbreads, and filled breads for this book, the team came up with several great tips that make it easier to get glorious results. I hope you'll use them, plus make a mental note of tricks you discover. Better yet, make a written note and pass it on to me at 831 Beacon Street, Newton Centre, Massachusetts 02159—I'd love to hear about your successes and will be happy to give you a hand with problems.

Pizza Sauces and Bread Fillings

Less is definitely more when it comes to pizza sauces and bread fillings. Try to hold back that urge to pour a thick layer of sauce over the dough. It makes for a soggy, uncooked crust. If you really love a generous helping of sauce, spread on half the amount (leaving off the cheese), bake the pizza for 10 minutes, then add the rest of the sauce and the cheese and continue baking until done. Thin, watery sauces and fillings also make for soggy crusts and soggy interiors. A good trick is to empty these kinds of sauces or fillings into a fine-mesh strainer and press down gently with the back of a large spoon to press out any liquid before topping the pizza or filling the bread. Remember, sauce isn't always necessary (is that how focaccia came to be?). I love to roll out pizza dough really thin and top it with olive oil and fresh scallions and a sprinkling of freshly grated Parmesan cheese.

Grated Cheese

Don't ever mistake the stuff in the cardboard tube on the grocery shelf for the real thing. Treat yourself to a wedge of fresh Parmigiano-Reggiano or pecorino or Romano. You can buy whole pieces in a deli or cheese store and grate them either with a hand grater or in a food processor, or have the store do it. Keep the grated cheese in a sealed plastic container in the freezer. No need to defrost it before using it.

Long, Slow, Cold Rises for Rich Doughs

We have found that rich yeasted doughs made with butter and eggs, such as those used to make brioche and croissants, benefit greatly from a long, slow, cold rise in the refrigerator after the final cycle in the machine is completed. Try this, and the texture and taste of these breads will amaze and delight you. I place these doughs in a gallon-size plastic freezer bag, then wipe out the bag and use it for the next dough.

Cold Oven Starts

I was having trouble with my braided breads. They would "explode" in the oven, strands tearing away and the middle pushing out. P. J. Hamel came up with the solution of placing the braids in a cold oven, then turning it on to heat it. This works perfectly not only with braids but with filled breads that have perishable fillings (such as the salmon-filled Coulibiac on page 168). You don't want to let these doughs rise very long at room temperature and risk having the filling spoil. A short rise outside the oven and then a gradual warming (and subsequent rise) in the oven while it heats does the trick.

Microwave Proof Box

One of my students gave me this great idea: If you lack a warm, draft-free place to let your formed dough rise (but happen to have a microwave), fill a 4-cup glass measure half full with very hot water. Place the measure in the microwave and set it for 3 minutes on high. Let the water come to a rapid boil (your microwave may take longer). Quickly pull the glass measure out and put the dough pan in. Close the door and let the dough rise in the nice steamy warm proof box. Don't open and close the door to check on it too often (use the microwave light, if there is one), as this diminishes the heat.

No Rise

Don't panic if you can't find directions for rising in some of these recipes. Many doughs do not rise at all but are formed or rolled out and baked immediately. Even some of those that contain yeast.

Oven Timing

All these pizzas and breads were tested in calibrated ovens. Chances are your oven is not exactly the same temperature as mine even though both dials are set the same. This fact and altitude will alter baking times, as will the length of time you have had your oven on and the number of times you've opened the door. Always set the timer for five minutes less than the minimum amount of cooking time suggested in the recipe, then extend it if need be. You can always bake the bread longer; once you've burned it the best you can do is scrape away the black parts.

Covering the Dough

Most doughs and many formed breads need to be covered either with a clean towel (a dish towel is fine) or plastic wrap (sprayed with nonstick vegetable spray) during the rising process to keep a dry crust from forming on top. It is this crust that can split in an unattractive way when the bread is actually baked. Another way to prevent a dry crust is to paint the top of the formed dough with an egg glaze made either with one egg white or one whole egg mixed with one tablespoon of water, milk, or cream. Breads that are glazed will brown much faster during baking, and will need a loose layer of foil placed on top halfway through the baking to prevent burning.

Preparing Ahead

This last tip is true for whatever kind of cooking you undertake. Assemble all the ingredients ahead of time. Place them on the counter in the order they are called for in the recipe. After you use an ingredient, place it somewhere else or put it away. This way you'll never wonder "Gee, did I put in the yeast . . . ?" You get one hell of a rise from a bread with too much yeast.

Pizzas

Sam's Pizza

My son Samuel likes his pizza the old-fashioned way: crust not too thin, not too thick; traditional red sauce and extra cheese. He used to prefer frozen pizza until I came up with a recipe that approximates the store-bought kind.

With an eye toward nutrition, I use nonfat dry milk and an amount of whole wheat flour for the crust. While Sam doesn't taste any difference, he does get a calcium and fiber boost, and the dry milk makes the crust easier to roll out.

You can make the dough up to three days in advance and store it in a plastic bag in the refrigerator. And you can cook the entire pizza, cool it at room temperature, and then freeze it, wrapped in plastic wrap. To reheat it, put it partially defrosted in a 350°F oven for fifteen minutes.

MAKES ONE 14-INCH PIZZA

FOR THE DOUGH

1	tablespoon yeast
2	cups all-purpose flour
1	cup whole wheat flour or White Wheat flour (page 5)
3	tablespoons cornmeal
1½	teaspoons salt

3	tablespoons olive oil
1	cup water, plus up to an additional ⅓ cup or more to make a smooth dough after the first few minutes of kneading

Place all the ingredients in the machine, program for Dough, Basic Dough, or Manual, and press Start. At the end of the final cycle, remove the dough to a lightly oiled work space, cover it with a clean towel, and let it rest 10 minutes.

TO FINISH THE PIZZA

1	cup (8 ounces) pizza sauce, homemade or commercially prepared
1	generous cup (about 4 ounces)

grated mozzarella cheese (whole or skim-milk)

Preheat the oven to 475°F with the rack or pizza stone or tiles in the center position. Sprinkle a pizza pan, baking sheet, or pizza peel with cornmeal. Roll the dough out to a 14-inch circle and place it on the prepared pan. Spread the sauce in a thin layer over the dough, leaving a very small unsauced edge, about ½ inch. Sprinkle on the cheese.

Slide the pan into the oven, or the pizza from the peel onto the pizza stone, and bake for 15 to 17 minutes, or until the crust is golden brown and the cheese is melted.

Serve hot, warm, or at room temperature.

Mystic Pizza

Did you see the movie? If not, rent it to eat with this version of the pizza it inspired. There's nothing like sharing a great pizza meal with Julia Roberts.

MAKES ONE 11-INCH PIZZA

FOR THE DOUGH

2	teaspoons yeast		1	teaspoon salt
2¹/₂	cups all-purpose flour		1	teaspoon olive oil
1	teaspoon sugar		³/₄	cup plus 3 tablespoons water

Place all the ingredients in the machine, program for Dough, Basic Dough, or Manual, and press Start.

TO FINISH THE PIZZA

2	tablespoons olive oil	1¹/₂	cups tomato or pizza sauce or
	Salt to taste		more if you're an extra-sauce fan
	Freshly ground black pepper	1 to 1¹/₂	cups grated mozzarella cheese
	to taste		

When the dough cycle is completed, transfer the dough to a floured work surface and let it rest for 5 minutes. Preheat the oven to 400°F. Lightly dust a heavy baking sheet with cornmeal and set it aside. Roll out the dough to an 11-inch circle. Transfer the dough onto the baking sheet. Brush the olive oil over the surface of the dough and then shake on salt and pepper. Leaving a 1-inch border, spread the sauce over the surface of the dough and top the sauce with the mozzarella. Bake the pizza for 20 minutes until the crust is a nice golden brown.

Grilled Pizza

"So, where do you like to eat pizza in Boston?" is a typical question I'm asked. "Providence" (as in Rhode Island) is always the answer. Johanne Killeen and George Germon welcome old friends and friends-to-be to Al Forno with equal parts warmth, charm, and exuberance. They celebrate both New England and Italian food with flair and success that other restaurateurs can only dream of.

My idea of heaven is George and Johanne's grilled pizza: wafer-thin, crisp as a tuxedo shirt. Imbued with the just-right light smoky taste from the fire, this is one pizza I won't share—everyone else at the table knows enough to order their own.

Grilling your own pizza takes a little patience and practice. This recipe, inspired by the one in George and Johanne's book Cucina Simpatica *(Harper-Collins, 1991), has been adapted for the bread machine. This dough can be made up to three days ahead, stored in a large plastic bag in the refrigerator, or frozen for up to three months, then defrosted still wrapped.*

SERVES 2 TO 3

FOR THE DOUGH

2	teaspoons yeast	2	tablespoons olive oil
3	cups all-purpose flour	1	cup water, plus 3 or more
¼	cup finely ground cornmeal		additional tablespoons if necessary
2	teaspoons salt		

Place all the ingredients in the machine, program for Dough, Basic Dough, or Manual, and press Start, adding the extra water if necessary to make a soft dough that forms a relaxed yet discrete ball.

TO FINISH THE PIZZA

3	tablespoons olive oil	¼	cup grated Parmesan cheese
2	garlic cloves, minced	6	oil-packed sun-dried tomatoes, cut
½	cup mixed fresh herbs, such as		into quarters
	basil, thyme, oregano, and chervil		
½	cup shredded soft cheese, such as		
	fontina		

Preheat a gas grill or start a charcoal fire. Place the rack 3 to 4 inches above the coals.

At the end of the final cycle, transfer the dough to a lightly oiled work surface and use your hands to push and flatten the dough into a rough 10- to 12-inch circle without a lip. Or divide the dough in half and make 2 smaller circles. This is a free-form pizza(s)—don't make yourself crazy trying to get the circle(s) perfectly round. An even thickness is more important than an even edge.

Lay the dough on the grill and let it cook for 1 minute, or until it puffs slightly and the underside stiffens and grill marks appear. Use a wide spatula or tongs to turn it over and place it on the side of the grill (off the direct heat). Quickly brush the top with half the oil and distribute the garlic, herbs, and cheeses over the top. Add the sun-dried tomatoes and finally drizzle on the remaining oil. Slide the pizza back to the middle of the grill and continue cooking while you rotate it to assure even cooking. The pizza is done when the cheese has melted, about 5 to 6 minutes. Serve immediately.

HINT: *You can grill almost any pizza dough as long as it is rolled out very thin. Be sure to have your toppings ready and your fire hot.*

Sourdough Chèvre Pizza

The perfect marriage of a slightly tangy, chewy crust with a creamy goat cheese and thyme topping makes a pizza inspired by the French countryside. Since your milkman probably doesn't deliver goat's milk to your door, you can find either fresh goat's milk or the powdered version in your local health food store. The starter must be made the day before you plan to make the pizza.

MAKES ONE 15-INCH PIZZA

FOR THE STARTER   MAKES 1¹/₂ CUPS

³/₄ cup fresh goat's milk or 3 tablespoons powdered goat's milk dissolved in ³/₄ cup water

1 teaspoon yeast
³/₄ cup rye flour

Heat the goat's milk to 90°F and stir in the yeast. When the yeast dissolves, stir in the flour, mixing well. Cover with plastic wrap and keep in a warm place for 12 hours, then refrigerate for 12 hours.

FOR THE DOUGH

3 cups all-purpose flour
1¹/₂ teaspoons salt
1 cup starter

¹/₄ cup olive oil
²/₃ cup water

Place all the ingredients in the machine, program for Dough or Manual, and press Start. The dough will be extremely wet and will not form much of a ball. At the end of the final knead, turn the dough out onto a floured work surface and knead it briefly, adding only enough flour to form the dough into a very soft ball. Cover it with a clean cloth and let it rest on the work surface while you prepare the topping.

TO FINISH THE PIZZA

12 ounces goat cheese, crumbled
1 teaspoon dried thyme or 1 tablespoon fresh thyme, chopped into very small pieces

2 to 3 tablespoons olive oil
Freshly ground black pepper

Preheat the oven to 475°F with the rack in the center position. Since this dough is so very loose, it's easier to bake it on a pizza pan or baking sheet rather than letting it rise on a paddle and transferring it to a pizza stone. Select a large (16-inch) pizza pan or baking sheet and roll or stretch the dough to a 15-inch circle, pushing outward from the middle to make it thinner in the center and slightly thicker around the rim.

Sprinkle the dough with the goat cheese and thyme, then drizzle it with the oil, and finally sprinkle it with pepper. Bake the pizza for 15 to 18 minutes, or until the rim is crusty and brown and the cheese is bubbling.

Serve hot or at room temperature.

HINTS: *If you want a milder taste, use a plain pizza crust (page 17) or substitute cream cheese for the goat cheese.*

Try adding small pieces of sun-dried tomatoes or oil-cured olives to the topping for a more Mediterranean flavor.

Vidalia Onion–Chèvre Pizza

Sweet Vidalia onions appear in grocery stores in early spring. They are also available by mail order (page 301). The onions in this recipe must be caramelized before they go on the pizza and the very easiest way to do this is in a slow cooker (for twelve hours). If you don't have one, you can cook the onions on the stove top or in the oven (for four hours) (recipes follow). This can be done several days before you plan to make the pizza. The sweet onions combine with the tangy goat cheese to create a marvelous tapestry of flavors and textures. This crust is seasoned with dehydrated onions which are added to the dough. Spanish onions can be substituted if you can't find Vidalias.

SERVES 8 TO 10

FOR THE ONIONS

6	Vidalia or Spanish onions (approximately 2½ pounds), about 3 inches in diameter, peeled and left whole	1	stick (4 ounces) unsalted butter
		1	13-ounce can chicken, beef, or vegetable broth

Place the onions, butter, and broth in a slow cooker and cook on low 12 hours until the onions are golden brown and very soft. Or place the onions, butter, and broth in a heavy pan, cover, and set over *very* low heat (or on a flame tamer). Every half hour or so, remove the cover and spoon some of the butter over the onions. Cook the onions for about 4 hours, or until they are golden brown and very tender. Alternatively, you can place the onions, butter, and broth in a covered baking dish and bake in a 225°F oven for 4 hours, or until the onions are golden brown and very tender. When they are cool enough to handle, slice the onions into quarters from root end to stem end. Reserve the butter and cooking liquid to use in a soup or stew.

Store the onions in a covered container in the refrigerator. Bring them to room temperature before you place them on the pizza either by removing them from the refrigerator 1 hour before you roll out the dough, or by placing them in a microwave for 60 seconds.

FOR THE DOUGH

2	teaspoons yeast	4	tablespoons nonfat dry milk
¼	cup rye flour	1	teaspoon salt
1¾	cups all-purpose flour, plus an additional 2 to 3 tablespoons if necessary	2	teaspoons dehydrated onion
		3	tablespoons olive oil
		¾	cup water

Place all the ingredients in the machine, program for Dough or Manual, and press Start. The dough will be quite moist at first, but do not add any more flour until after the first 3 to 5 minutes of kneading; then add only enough to form a discrete ball.

TO FINISH THE PIZZA

6	ounces goat cheese, either plain, peppered, or herbed, crumbled	Prepared Vidalia onions

At the end of the final cycle, preheat the oven to 450°F. If you're using a pizza stone, or tiles, lay them in the oven before preheating. Adjust the rack to the center position.

On a lightly floured surface, pat and stretch the dough or use a rolling pin to form a 14- to 16-inch circle approximately ⅛ inch thick and place it on a baking sheet, pizza pan, or pizza paddle lightly dusted with cornmeal.

Immediately after rolling out the dough, sprinkle the cheese over the dough, leaving a 1½-inch border. Place the onion quarters over the cheese. Slide the baking sheet into the oven or the pizza onto the stone or tiles and bake for 12 to 15 minutes, or until the crust is crisp and browned and the cheese is melted.

Serve immediately or cool and serve at room temperature.

Pizza Bianca

Red sauce move over. What makes this pizza so special is the combination of flavors and textures in the topping, which consists of caramelized onions, chicken breast, mushrooms, artichoke hearts, and mascarpone. If you wish to make this a meatless pizza, omit the chicken.

MAKES ONE 12-INCH PIZZA

FOR THE DOUGH

1½	teaspoons yeast		1	teaspoon salt
2	cups all-purpose flour		1	teaspoon sugar
¼	teaspoon freshly ground black pepper		¾	cup water
			1	tablespoon olive oil

Place all the ingredients in the machine, program for Dough, Basic Dough, or Manual, and press Start.

FOR THE TOPPING

1	large onion, sliced		1	6-ounce jar artichoke hearts, drained and quartered
6	tablespoons olive oil		8	ounces mushrooms, sliced
4	garlic cloves, minced			
½	pound boneless, skinless chicken breast, cubed			

In a large skillet, sauté the onion slices in the olive oil and cook them over medium heat until they are golden brown, then add the garlic and the chicken and continue cooking until the chicken is cooked. Add the artichoke hearts and mushrooms and continue cooking until the mushrooms begin to wilt. Remove from the heat and cool.

TO FINISH THE PIZZA

Olive oil	½	pint mascarpone (available in specialty cheese shops or Italian markets)
Salt		
Freshly ground black pepper		

When the dough cycle is finished, transfer the dough to a lightly floured work surface and let it rest for 5 minutes.

Preheat the oven to 400°F with the rack or a pizza stone in the center position. Roll out the dough to a 12-inch circle and transfer it onto a cookie sheet or pizza peel that has been dusted with cornmeal. Rub the surface of the dough with olive oil and sprinkle it with salt and pepper. Leaving a 1-inch border, spread the onion topping over the dough. Then drop the mascarpone by the spoonful onto the pizza. Bake the pizza for 20 to 25 minutes, or until the top is bubbling and the crust is a golden brown. Serve hot, warm, or at room temperature.

An Italian Trio: Pesto, Sun-dried Tomato, and Garlic Pizzas

If you have trouble deciding between three great flavors, then this recipe is for you. It's sort of "have your pizza and eat it too." I offer you a basic dough to which you add a flavor (pesto, tomato, or garlic) and then form your choice of either pizza or focaccia or a rustic loaf. Or, for a really big splash, the three flavors of dough can be braided together to form a magnificent tricolor braid (page 29). As pizza, while you may use virtually any sauce or topping that you choose, my favorite way to top this is with a generous layer of freshly grated Parmigiano-Reggiano cheese. In the hot oven this cheese develops a crunchy gold filigree that perfectly complements the crust.

The doughs can be made up to thirty-six hours ahead, placed in lightly oiled bowls, covered with oiled plastic wrap, or stored in heavy-duty plastic bags and refrigerated until ready to be formed.

Pesto, sun-dried tomato, and garlic pastes, which come in toothpaste type tubes and can be found in many supermarkets and most specialty food stores, are the secret ingredients in this pizza. These are added to the basic pizza dough to give each one its own distinctive color and taste. Store open tubes in the refrigerator.

The technique for forming this dough was inspired by Todd English, chef extraordinaire. In his restaurant Figs, in Charlestown, Massachusetts, the pizzas are rolled out and cooked on the bottom of a large overturned baking sheet. The result is a thin, crisp crust—a most perfect pizza, if you ask me.

MAKES 2 LARGE THIN-CRUST PIZZAS

FOR PESTO DOUGH

1 tablespoon yeast	⅓ cup olive oil or garlic oil
1½ teaspoons salt	1¼ cups water or more to form a
½ cup cornmeal	smooth ball
3 cups all-purpose flour	2 tablespoons pesto paste

FOR SUN-DRIED TOMATO DOUGH

1 tablespoon yeast	1¼ cups water or more to form a
1½ teaspoons salt	smooth ball
½ cup cornmeal	2 tablespoons sun-dried tomato
3 cups all-purpose flour	paste
⅓ cup olive oil or garlic oil	4 to 5 oil-packed sun-dried tomatoes,
	cut into thirds

FOR GARLIC DOUGH

1	tablespoon yeast	$^1/_3$	cup olive oil or garlic oil
$1^1/_2$	teaspoons salt	$1^1/_4$	cups water or more to form a
$^1/_2$	cup cornmeal		smooth ball
3	cups all-purpose flour	2	tablespoons garlic paste

Place all the ingredients in the machine, program for Dough or Manual, and press Start. The dough will be on the soft side at first, but it will become firmer as the gluten develops through the kneading process.

TO FINISH THE PIZZAS

Sauce or topping of your choice or
$^1/_2$ cup (4 ounces) freshly grated
Parmigiano-Reggiano cheese

Preheat the oven to 500°F with the rack in the center position. Spray the under side of a large heavy-duty (17 × 11-inch) sheet pan (the kind with a rim that goes all the way around) with nonstick vegetable spray. Cut the dough in half and cover one half with a clean towel. Place the other half on the prepared pan and (you'll have to either anchor the pan with a wet bath towel to keep it from sliding around, or have a friend hold the pan in place) use a rolling pin to roll the dough evenly in the pan, reaching as far toward the edges as you can. Don't worry about making the edges even—this is a free-form pizza.

Spread with sauce or sprinkle with cheese and bake immediately for 8 to 10 minutes, or until the crust is golden and crisp and the cheese is melted. You can serve this pizza right off the pan (the way they do at Figs). Use a pizza cutter to cut it into squares.

Fresh Mozzarella, Plum Tomato, and Basil Pizzettes

This universal combination is fantastic on a thin-crusted pizzette. Use either buffalo mozzarella or fresh mozzarella.

MAKES 4 INDIVIDUAL PIZZETTES

FOR THE DOUGH

1	teaspoon yeast		2	tablespoons olive oil
1½	cups all-purpose flour		1	pinch freshly ground black pepper
1	teaspoon sugar		1	teaspoon salt
½	cup water			

Place all the ingredients in the machine, program for Dough or Basic Dough, and press Start. The dough will be firm and pull away from the machine while mixing. While the dough is rising, you can prepare the topping.

TO FINISH THE PIZZETTES

1	pound mozzarella cheese			Olive oil for brushing
¾	pound (4 large) plum tomatoes			Salt
3	tablespoons olive oil			Freshly ground black pepper
1	garlic clove, minced		⅓	cup chopped fresh basil leaves

At the end of the final cycle, transfer the dough to a lightly floured work surface, cover with a clean towel, and let it rest for 5 minutes. Preheat the oven to 450°F with the rack in the center position. Lightly flour 2 baking sheets and set them aside.

Drain the mozzarella, cut each ball into thin slices, and lay the slices on paper towels for extra draining. Slice the tomatoes into thin slices and set aside. Mix together the 3 tablespoons olive oil and minced garlic.

Cut the dough into 4 pieces and on a lightly oiled work surface, roll each piece out to a 7-inch circle. Transfer the circles to the prepared baking sheets. Brush the surface of each with the garlic and oil mixture. In a spiral, starting ¾ inch in from the edge, alternate the cheese and tomato slices. Place a slice of cheese and a slice of tomato in the center. Brush the top of the cheese and tomatoes with olive oil. Sprinkle with salt and pepper and bake for 12 minutes. The cheese will be slightly runny. Remove the pizzettes from the oven and immediately sprinkle on the freshly chopped basil and serve immediately.

Vicki Caparulo's Tricolor Braid

New Jersey cooking teacher and food writer Vicki Caparulo was generous enough to share her innovative and dramatic braided bread with me. The braid is made with a rope of pesto dough, a rope of sun-dried tomato dough, and a rope of garlic dough. The three dough recipes used are enough to make two large braids, or you can make one braid and three pizzas or focaccie.

This dough freezes beautifully, so you can save some for a later time. I like to freeze dough in a large heavy-duty plastic bag (making sure there is ample room for rising), then defrost the dough in the bag either at room temperature or in the refrigerator.

This bread is started in a cold oven to keep it from overrising and "exploding," which sometimes happens from the oven "spring" which occurs when bread goes into a hot oven.

MAKES 2 LARGE BRAIDS, EACH SERVING 8 TO 10

1   recipe Pesto Dough (page 26)
1   recipe Sun-dried Tomato Dough
    (page 26)

1   recipe Garlic Dough (page 27)
1   egg beaten with 1 tablespoon
    water

Cut each ball of dough in half and reserve the other half to make a second braid, pizza, or focaccia, or freeze it. Select a heavy-duty baking sheet or baking pan at least 14 inches long. Line it with foil and spray the foil lightly with nonstick vegetable spray. Form each piece of dough into a 22-inch rope. The easiest way to do this is by gently pulling and squeezing it with your hands. Pinch the ropes together at one end, braid them, then pinch the other ends together. Place the braid on the prepared baking sheet and cover with a piece of plastic wrap that has been sprayed with nonstick vegetable spray. Repeat with the remaining dough if desired.

Place the braid(s) in a warm place to rise until slightly less than doubled in bulk, about 45 minutes.

Brush the top of the braid(s) with the egg glaze and place in a cold oven on the middle rack. Set the oven at 425°F and bake for 20 minutes. Reduce the oven to 350°F and continue baking another 20 to 25 minutes, or until the top is golden brown and when you lift the end of the braid(s) with a metal spatula, the underside is browned as well. Cool the braid(s) on a wire rack before slicing.

Double Pesto Pizza

After you have tried the pesto crust with grated cheese, go one step further and add a thin topping of pesto and then some grated Parmesan cheese. The results celebrate the bounty of the summer garden. While you can use store-bought pesto, homemade is ever so much more delicious, and a food processor makes it easy to whip up in minutes (recipe follows).

SERVES 6 TO 8

1	recipe Pesto Dough (page 26)	Olive oil or basil oil (available in
⅔	cup Pesto	gourmet shops or by mail order,
	Freshly grated Parmesan cheese	page 301)

If you like thin crust, preheat the oven before you roll out the dough, follow the rolling and baking instructions on page 27, and bake the dough immediately. Spread the pesto in a *very* thin layer over the dough, leaving a 1-inch border unsauced, and sprinkle with cheese before baking.

If you want a thick crust, roll and pat the dough into a 14-inch circle and place it on a cornmeal-dusted pizza pan or pizza peel. Spread the dough with the pesto, leaving a 1-inch border unsauced. Sprinkle with cheese and allow to rise, uncovered, in a warm place for 20 to 30 minutes, or until nicely puffed. Preheat the oven to 450°F with the rack or a pizza stone in the center position. Bake the pizza for 17 to 20 minutes, or until the crust is deep golden brown and the cheese has melted. Drizzle with olive oil.

Pesto

Since this sauce freezes beautifully, make extra so you will have it on hand for next time. Store it in small plastic containers in the freezer and defrost it at room temperature or in a microwave.

MAKES ABOUT 1¼ CUPS

3	cups basil leaves, stems removed, very well rinsed	½	cup freshly grated Parmesan cheese
2 to 3	garlic cloves, peeled and cut into large pieces	½	teaspoon freshly ground black pepper
⅓	cup toasted pine nuts (page 267)	½	teaspoon salt (optional)
½	cup olive oil		

Rip the larger basil leaves into thirds and place them along with the garlic and pine nuts in a food processor or blender. Process or blend to a purée, then add the oil, cheese, and pepper, blending or processing just to mix. Taste before adding salt, as the cheese is quite salty.

Porcini Pizza

I promise you've never tasted a pizza quite like this one. The crust is made from the Porcini Focaccia dough, rolled very thin and topped with sautéed mixed mushrooms and freshly grated Parmesan cheese. What could be better?

This dough is too fragile to be transferred from a pizza paddle to tiles, so bake it on a pan.

SERVES 6 TO 8

1 pound assorted fresh mushrooms, such as portobello, cremini, shiitake, domestic, or cèpes	1 recipe Porcini Focaccia Dough (page 70)
¼ stick (1 ounce) unsalted butter Salt to taste Freshly ground black pepper to taste	¼ to ⅓ cup freshly grated Parmesan cheese

Clean the mushrooms, trim any woody stems, and cut (caps with stems still attached) into generous slices, about ¾ inch thick. Melt the butter in a large skillet and sauté the mushrooms over medium heat until they are wilted and have given up their liquid. This is important, otherwise the pizza will get soggy. Drain off the liquid and reserve it for another use (soup or stew or pasta sauce). Season with salt and pepper.

Roll the dough out to either one large 16-inch circle or two 8-inch circles or a 17 × 11-inch rectangle. Place the dough on either a pizza pan or a 17 × 11-inch jelly roll pan that has been lightly dusted with cornmeal. Distribute the cooked mushrooms over the pizza and sprinkle with the cheese.

Bake the pizza for 15 to 17 minutes for the large version and 13 to 14 minutes for the smaller version. Serve hot.

Tricolor Roasted Pepper Pizza

Bell peppers are now available in all designer colors (and prices), so create your own trilogy or use the colors below.

MAKES ONE 10-INCH PIZZA

FOR THE DOUGH

1½	teaspoons yeast		1	tablespoon olive oil
2	cups all-purpose flour		¾	cup water
1	teaspoon salt			

Place all the ingredients in the machine, program for Dough or Basic Dough, and press Start.

While the dough is rising you can roast the peppers.

FOR THE PEPPERS

1	large yellow bell pepper		1	large red bell pepper
1	large green bell pepper			

TO FINISH THE PIZZA

2	tablespoons olive oil		½	cup tomato sauce
	Salt		3	scallions, chopped
	Freshly ground black pepper		½ to ¾	cup grated mozzarella cheese

Preheat the oven to 400°F. Lightly sprinkle a cookie sheet with cornmeal.

When the dough cycle has finished, transfer the dough to a lightly floured work surface and let it rest for 5 minutes. Roll out the dough to a 10-inch circle. Brush the olive oil over the surface of the dough and then sprinkle with salt and pepper. Leaving a 1-inch border, spread the tomato sauce over the dough, arrange the roasted peppers on it, sprinkle on the scallions, and top with the grated cheese. Bake the pizza for 20 to 25 minutes.

To Roast Peppers

Preheat the broiler to high with the rack in the highest position. Line a rimmed baking sheet with foil.

Cut the peppers in half lengthwise. Remove the cores and seeds. Place the peppers cut side down on a work surface and push down with your hand to flatten them—they will rip, but that's okay.

Place the peppers cut side down on the baking sheet and broil them until the skins turn black. They won't be an even black, there will be brown spots as well. Use tongs to place the hot peppers in a heavy-duty plastic bag. Seal the bag and allow the peppers to cool, then slip off the skins.

You now have roasted peppers! Slice the peppers lengthwise into 1-inch strips. Toss them together and set them aside.

Double Anchovy Pizza

Now the anchovy lovers in your life won't have to do without—they can have a pizza of their very own, loaded with the flavor of those salty little devils that the rest of the world has not yet learned to appreciate. This thin-crusted pizza is a cross between a cracker and flatbread that you top with anchovies only. If you want something a little more complex, try Pizza Forianna (page 36). The dough is made with equal parts whole wheat flour and white flour. I like to use King Arthur's White Wheat in this recipe, which gives the sweet taste of whole wheat without the brown color. The pizza is lighter as a result.

This pizza should be enjoyed the day it is made—preferably right out of the oven. Anchovies don't make great leftover food.

SERVES 8 TO 10

FOR THE DOUGH

1	tablespoon yeast	1⅓	cups water or more to make a smooth ball
½	teaspoon salt		
½	cup cornmeal	2	tablespoons anchovy paste
1½	cups White Wheat flour (page 5) or regular whole wheat flour	2	teaspoons coarsely ground black pepper
1½	cups all-purpose flour	1	tablespoon dried parsley
⅓	cup olive oil or garlic oil	2	tablespoons capers, drained
			Finely grated zest of 1 large lemon

Place all the ingredients except the capers and lemon rind in the machine, program for Dough or Manual, and press Start. At the end of the final cycle, add the capers and lemon rind, restart the machine, and allow it to knead only until the final ingredients are mixed in, about 2 to 3 minutes.

TO FINISH THE PIZZA
1   2-ounce tin flat anchovies in oil

Preheat the oven to 475°F with the rack in the center position. Select either two 8- or 9-inch pizza pans or one 16-inch pizza pan (preferably with a perforated bottom). Spray the pan(s) lightly with nonstick vegetable spray. Remove the dough from the machine and sprinkle it with just enough flour to keep the dough from sticking to your hands. Form it into a ball and place it in the center of the pizza pan. Use your hands (lightly dusted if necessary) to push the dough out evenly to the rim of the pan. The dough should be quite thin.

Place the anchovies on the dough, leaving a 1½-inch border. Drizzle the anchovy oil over the dough and use your fingers or a pastry brush to spread it all over the surface. Bake the pizza 15 to 18 minutes, or until the crust is crisp. Serve hot or at room temperature.

HINT: *This makes a splendid snack to serve with cock-tails, wine, or beer. Cut the pizza into thin wedges or squares spread with a little softened cream cheese.*

Pizza Forianna

Ciro and Sal's Restaurant in Provincetown, Massachusetts, serves a pasta that people travel miles to enjoy. According to Ciro, Forianna, a dish made with pine nuts, walnuts, parsley, raisins, lemon juice, and anchovies, comes from the island of Ischia, near Capri. For the record, I traveled to Ischia in search of other wonderful dishes and found that I shouldn't have bothered making the trip—the food at Ciro's is far more delicious.

SERVES 8 AS AN APPETIZER; 6 AS A MAIN COURSE

FOR THE TOPPING

²/₃ cup olive oil	1 teaspoon dried oregano
4 garlic cloves, minced	¹/₄ teaspoon red pepper flakes
12 anchovy fillets, patted dry with paper towels	¹/₂ teaspoon freshly ground black pepper
¹/₂ cup (3 ounces) walnuts, broken into pieces	¹/₂ cup coarsely chopped fresh Italian parsley leaves
¹/₂ cup pine nuts	Juice of 1 lemon
¹/₂ cup raisins	

Heat the oil in a deep skillet. Add the garlic and anchovies and cook over medium heat, stirring with a fork to mash the anchovies, until the garlic has just started to turn golden and the anchovies are dissolved. Add the nuts, raisins, oregano, and peppers, and cook for 4 minutes, stirring occasionally. Add the parsley and lemon juice, stirring to combine.

TO FINISH THE PIZZA

1 recipe anchovy pizza dough (page 34)

Preheat the oven to 450°F with the rack or a pizza stone or tiles in the upper position and roll out the pizza crust. Spread the sauce over the crust, leaving a 1-inch border, and bake for 15 to 18 minutes, or until the crust is golden brown. Serve hot or room temperature.

Pissaladière Niçoise

A specialty of the French Riviera, this tart is made using pizza dough. We've decided to jazz up the dough with a few egg yolks and butter. If you're an anchovy lover, this one's for you.

SERVES 8

FOR THE DOUGH

1½	teaspoons yeast		¼	stick (1 ounce) unsalted butter
2½	cups all-purpose flour		2	egg yolks
½	teaspoon salt		¾	cup water
1	teaspoon sugar			

Place all the ingredients in the machine, program for Dough or Basic Dough, and press Start.

FOR THE TOPPING

1	very large Spanish onion, thinly sliced		4 to 5	tablespoons olive oil
			2	large garlic cloves, minced

Sauté the onion slices in the olive oil over medium heat until they turn a light golden brown and are tender. Remove them from the heat and stir in the minced garlic, strain any excess oil from the onions, and set aside.

TO FINISH THE PISSALADIÈRE

1	tablespoon olive oil, for the pizza dough		1	2-ounce can anchovy fillets, drained
2	plum tomatoes, seeded and chopped		2	teaspoons parsley flakes
16	large "real" (not canned) black olives, pitted and cut in half			

When the dough cycle is completed, transfer the dough to a lightly floured work surface and let it rest for 5 minutes.

Preheat the oven to 425°F with the rack in the center position.

Lightly dust a cookie sheet with cornmeal and set aside. Roll out the dough to a 12-inch circle and transfer it to the prepared cookie sheet. Brush the tablespoon of oil over the surface of the dough. Spread the onion slices over the surface of the dough, leaving a ¾-inch border. Spread the tomatoes on over the onions and then the black olives. Lay on the anchovies. Finally, sprinkle the parsley over the top.

Bake the pissaladière for 20 minutes. The crust should be a rich golden brown. Serve hot or warm, cut into wedges.

Red Clam Sauce Pizzettes

Soppressata is a very special dry Italian sausage in the salami family. If Soppressata is not available in your neck of the woods, you can use hard salami or pepperoni. If fresh littleneck clams are not available, you can use canned or defrosted frozen chopped clams.

MAKES 4 INDIVIDUAL PIZZETTES

FOR THE DOUGH

1½	teaspoons yeast	1	teaspoon salt
2½	cups all-purpose flour	2	tablespoons sour cream
1	teaspoon sugar	¾	cup plus 3 tablespoons water

Place all the ingredients in the machine, program for Dough, Basic Dough, or Manual, and press Start. While the dough is rising you can prepare the sauce.

FOR THE SAUCE

1	cup chopped onions	1	teaspoon crushed red pepper
5	tablespoons olive oil		flakes
1	tablespoon chopped garlic	1	tablespoon fresh chopped parsley
5	large plum tomatoes, peeled, seeded, and chopped	2	teaspoons salt
3	tablespoons red wine	½	teaspoon freshly ground black pepper
⅛	pound (3 to 4 slices) Soppressata		
10	littleneck clams (not steamers), cleaned and sand-free		

In a nonstick frying pan over medium heat, cook the onions in the olive oil until tender. Add the garlic, tomatoes, red wine, and Soppressata and continue cooking over low heat for 15 minutes. Add the littlenecks, red pepper flakes, parsley, salt, and pepper. Cover the pan and cook the littlenecks until the shells open, approximately 5 minutes. After the shells have opened, remove the pan from the heat and let the sauce cool. After the sauce has cooled, remove the clams from the shells and stir the clam meat into the sauce. Discard the shells.

TO FINISH THE PIZZETTES

Preheat the oven to 400°F and lightly sprinkle a baking sheet with cornmeal and set aside.

When the dough cycle is completed, transfer the dough to a lightly floured work surface and let it rest for 5 minutes. Divide the dough into 4 pieces and roll each piece out to a 6-inch circle and transfer the circles onto the prepared baking sheet. Spread the sauce out over the dough and bake for 15 minutes. Cut into wedges and serve hot.

Four Vegetarian Pizzas

Pizza is swiftly becoming the favorite quick and easy vegetarian meal. Topping a whole wheat crust with fresh vegetables and herbs gives a high-fiber, low-calorie, easy-to-fix entrée that will leave you pleased not only with the taste of your meal, but also that you made it from scratch and had complete control over the quality of the ingredients you used.

This crust is made from a combination of whole wheat and white flour. I find crusts made entirely with whole wheat flour too heavy and raw-tasting. In keeping with the nutritional focus of these recipes, it's important to use flour that is unbleached and not chemically treated. I have added nonfat dry milk to the crust for two reasons: It provides extra calcium and it helps relax the dough to make it easier to roll out. This ingredient can be omitted if you wish.

The dough can be made up to forty-eight hours ahead. Dust it with flour and store it in a large plastic bag in the refrigerator or freezer. Defrost it, covered, either in the refrigerator or at room temperature.

MAKES ONE 14-INCH PIZZA

FOR THE DOUGH

1	tablespoon yeast	3	tablespoons nonfat dry milk
1½	cups whole wheat flour	2	tablespoons olive oil
1½	cups all-purpose white flour	1	cup water or more to make a
2	teaspoons salt		smooth ball

Place all the ingredients in the machine, program for Dough or Manual, and press Start. The dough should be soft and slightly moist at first, but then will form a discrete ball within the first minutes of kneading.

TO FINISH THE PIZZA
Vegetarian topping of your choice

At the end of the final cycle, either refrigerate the dough for use later or stretch or roll it out to a 14-inch circle and place it on a lightly oiled or cornmeal-dusted pizza pan or baking sheet. Cover the dough with one of the four toppings (recipes follow), leaving a 1-inch border, and allow it to rise for 20 minutes in a warm place.

Bake the pizza in a 425°F oven for 15 to 20 minutes, or until the crust is deep brown and the topping is bubbling hot. Serve hot or at room temperature.

Eggplant, Zucchini, and Plum Tomato Topping

1 medium eggplant, cut into ¼-inch slices	1 to 2 tablespoons olive oil
1 large zucchini, cut into ¼-inch slices	1 tablespoon red wine vinegar Salt to taste
4 plum tomatoes, cut into ½-inch slices	Freshly ground black pepper to taste

Place the vegetables in a mixing bowl. Add the olive oil, vinegar, salt, and pepper and toss to coat the vegetables. Arrange the vegetables on top of the dough.

Greek Salad Topping

1¼ pounds fresh spinach, washed, spun dry, and the stems removed	1 egg
1 cup (8 ounces) feta cheese, crumbled	½ teaspoon freshly ground black pepper
½ cup oil-cured black olives, pitted and halved	

Cook the spinach by steaming it or placing it in a microwavable bowl with ¼ cup water. Cover with plastic and microwave on high for 4 to 5 minutes until it is wilted. Cool it slightly, then squeeze out as much moisture as possible. In a mixing bowl, combine the spinach with the cheese, olives, egg, and pepper. Mix to combine, then spread over the dough.

Fennel, Radicchio, and Endive Topping

3 tablespoons olive oil	2 medium endives, root end trimmed, cut into ½-inch slices
1 small fennel bulb, top and root end trimmed, cut into ½-inch slices (about 1 cup)	Salt to taste Freshly ground black pepper to taste
1 small head radicchio, cut into eighths	

Heat the oil in a large skillet and quickly cook the vegetables over high heat, stirring or shaking the pan frequently. Cook just until the vegetables begin to wilt, about 4 to 5 minutes, then spoon the vegetables and the pan juices onto the dough and sprinkle with salt and pepper.

Portobello Mushroom Topping

1   pound portobello mushrooms, wiped clean, stems trimmed, cut into ½-inch slices

3   tablespoons olive oil

1   teaspoon dried rosemary or 2 tablespoons fresh rosemary leaves, chopped

½   teaspoon salt

½   teaspoon freshly ground black pepper

½   cup freshly grated Parmesan cheese

In a mixing bowl, toss together the mushrooms, olive oil, rosemary, salt, and pepper. Scatter the mixture over the dough, then sprinkle with the cheese.

Fried Eggplant
Sicilian-Style Pizza

If you are a fan of eggplant Parmigiana, then this is the pizza for you. If you have a one-pound bread machine, cut the recipe in half.

MAKES 1 LARGE SHEET-STYLE PIZZA, SERVING 8 TO 10

FOR THE DOUGH

2½	teaspoons yeast		1	teaspoon sugar
4	cups all-purpose flour		3	tablespoons olive oil
2	teaspoons salt		1½	cups water

Place all the ingredients in the machine, program for Manual, Dough, or Basic Dough, and press Start. The dough will be firm and pull away from the sides of the machine. While the dough is rising, you can fry the eggplant.

PREPARE THE EGGPLANT

1	medium eggplant		2	cups corn oil or canola oil
4	cups breadcrumbs			for frying
4 to 6	large eggs			

Peel and slice the eggplant into ¼-inch rounds and set aside. Pour the bread-crumbs into a flat dish or pie pan. Whisk the eggs in a bowl large enough for dipping.

Set up a paper bag or paper towels on a cookie sheet to drain the eggplant after frying. Heat the corn oil in a large heavy skillet to 300°F. Dip each eggplant round in the egg and then in the breadcrumbs. After you have coated 6 to 8 rounds, begin frying them, 2 at a time, in the hot oil. Turn the slices over once the top side is a rich brown and the crust is crunchy. Remove the eggplant rounds from the pan and let them drain on the paper bag or paper towels. Repeat this until all the rounds are fried. Set them aside at room temperature until the dough is ready.

TO FINISH THE PIZZA

3	tablespoons olive oil	1½ to 2 cups grated mozzarella cheese	
1½	cups tomato sauce (homemade or store-bought)		

Preheat the oven to 425°F with the rack in the upper position. Sprinkle cornmeal over the surface of an 18 × 12-inch baking sheet.

When the dough cycle is completed, transfer the dough to a lightly floured work surface and let it rest for 5 minutes. Roll out the dough to an 18 × 12-inch rectangle and transfer it to the prepared baking sheet. Brush the olive oil over the surface of the dough. Spread on the tomato sauce, leaving a ½-inch border. Lay out the eggplant over the sauce and sprinkle the mozzarella over the eggplant. Bake the pizza for 30 to 35 minutes until the cheese has melted and turns a beautiful golden brown.

Tuscan White Bean Pizzettes
with Asiago Cheese

This classic Italian open-faced tart is prepared with cannellini beans, fresh thyme, and Asiago cheese. If Asiago is not available, you can use Parmesan or Romano.

FOR THE DOUGH

1	teaspoon yeast	³/₄	cup water
2	cups all-purpose flour	1	tablespoon molasses
1	teaspoon salt		

Place all the ingredients in the machine, program for Manual, Dough, or Basic Dough, and press Start. The dough will be firm and silky. While the dough is rising, prepare the topping.

FOR THE TOPPING

4	tablespoons olive oil	2	garlic cloves, minced
1	medium onion, peeled and chopped (¹/₂ cup)	¹/₄	cup canned chicken broth
1	celery stick, leaves trimmed, finely chopped	1	20-ounce can cannellini beans (white kidney beans), drained
1	small carrot, peeled and finely chopped		

In a nonstick pan set over medium heat, heat the olive oil and sauté the onion, celery, and carrot until tender. Stir in the garlic and chicken broth and cook for an additional 2 minutes. Add the beans and continue cooking, stirring constantly until the beans begin to break down, for an additional 5 minutes. The beans will be partially mashed when they are done. Set them aside and let them cool.

TO FINISH THE PIZZETTES

2 to 3	plum tomatoes, cut into 16 thin slices		Salt to taste
2	tablespoons fresh thyme or 2 teaspoons dried thyme		Freshly ground black pepper to taste
		¹/₂	cup grated Asiago cheese

Preheat the oven to 425°F and lightly flour 2 cookie sheets and set them aside. When the dough is completed, transfer it to a lightly floured work surface, cover it with a clean towel, and let it rest for 5 minutes. Divide the dough into 4 pieces and roll each piece to an 8-inch circle; the dough will be thin. Transfer the circles to the prepared cookie sheets. Divide the beans among the circles and spread them out, leaving a slight border. Lay 4 tomato slices on each circle. Sprinkle on the thyme, salt, and pepper. Bake the pizzettes for 15 minutes, remove them from the oven, sprinkle on the Asiago, and serve immediately.

Potato and Onion Sourdough Pizza

Roasted potatoes and golden brown onions—especially when they are sitting atop a crispy, thin-crusted sourdough pizza—are foods of the gods. You can use either caramelized or uncooked Spanish onions in this recipe. I made my pizza with sweet Yukon Gold potatoes. If you can't find them, use russets. Leave the peels on—they are a great source of iron.

The only leavening in this pizza crust comes from the starter. For information about sourdough starters, see page 6.

SERVES 6 TO 8

FOR THE DOUGH

1   cup sourdough starter
1½   teaspoons salt
2½   cups all-purpose flour

²/₃   cup water, plus 1 to 2 additional tablespoons if necessary to make a soft, slightly tacky dough

Place all the ingredients in the machine, program for Dough or Manual, and press Start. Add more water if necessary to make a soft, slightly tacky dough. At the end of the final cycle, remove the dough to a lightly floured work space. The dough will still be quite soft. Knead it by hand for a few minutes, adding only enough flour to make it form a smooth, soft ball. Cover it with a cloth and let it rest on the work surface for 30 minutes.

TO FINISH THE PIZZA

3   caramelized Vidalia onions (page 22), cut in half, layers separated, or 2 large Spanish onions, peeled and very thinly sliced
1   pound Yukon Gold or russet potatoes, scrubbed, very thinly sliced (¼ inch), parboiled for 5 minutes, then well drained and patted dry with paper towels

¼   cup olive oil
Coarse salt
Freshly ground black pepper

Preheat the oven to 475°F with the rack in the center position. Stretch or roll the dough out to a 15- or 16-inch circle and place it on a perforated-bottomed or regular pizza pan. Layer it first with the onions, leaving a 1-inch border, then top with a layer of potatoes. Drizzle on the oil and sprinkle with salt and pepper.

Bake the pizza for 20 to 25 minutes, or until the crust is well browned and the potatoes are soft. Remove the pizza from the oven and place the broiler on high with the rack in the center position. Broil the pizza for 3 to 4 minutes until the potatoes are golden brown and crisp. Serve hot or at room temperature.

Greek-Style Pizzettes

This pizza dough is spiced with oregano and lemon. The topping includes baby spinach leaves, Kalamata olives, and feta cheese. In short, this pizza is better than the salad.

MAKES 4 INDIVIDUAL PIZZETTES

FOR THE DOUGH

1¹/₂	teaspoons yeast
2³/₄	cups all-purpose flour
1	teaspoon salt
1	cup water
1	teaspoon honey

¹/₂	teaspoon grated lemon rind
¹/₄	teaspoon freshly ground black pepper
1	teaspoon oregano

Place all the ingredients in the machine, program for Manual, Dough, or Basic Dough, and press Start. After the first 5 minutes of kneading the dough will be firm and pull away from the sides of the machine. While the dough is rising you can prepare your topping.

TO FINISH THE PIZZETTES

¹/₄	stick (1 ounce) unsalted butter
¹/₄	pound baby spinach leaves, rinsed and dried
1	garlic clove, minced
12 to 14	Kalamata olives, pitted and cut in half

¹/₂	cup feta cheese, crumbled
2	tablespoons chopped parsley
	Salt to taste
	Freshly ground black pepper to taste
2 to 3	tablespoons olive oil

In a sauté pan, heat the butter over low heat and cook the spinach long enough for it to wilt, about 2 minutes. Remove the pan from the heat and stir in the garlic. Set the mixture aside until you assemble the pizzettes.

Preheat the oven to 425°F with the rack in the center position. Lightly flour 2 baking sheets and set them aside. When the dough cycle is completed, transfer the dough to a lightly floured work surface, cover it with a clean towel, and let it rest for 5 minutes. Divide the dough into 4 even pieces and roll each piece out to a 6-inch circle. Transfer the circles to the prepared baking sheet. Distribute the spinach over the circles followed by the olives and feta cheese. Sprinkle on the chopped parsley, salt, and pepper. Drizzle a small amount of olive oil over the top of each. Bake for 20 minutes, or until the crust is deep golden brown and the top is starting to brown as well. Serve 1 whole pizza per person, hot, warm, or at room temperature.

Salsa Pizza with Black Bean Crust

While you should feel free to spread salsa on top of any pizza crust that you find in this book, my guess is that you won't find a better match than this one made with refried beans and chili powder. This is my idea of a Southwest deep-dish pizza. The beans, which can be made from scratch, come from a can, or reconstituted from a mix, give the crust a moist and earthy, yet still light and airy quality that is perfectly suited to the spicy topping with its load of melted cheese.

This pizza is great cold, if there is any left over to get cold . . .

SERVES 6 TO 8

FOR THE DOUGH

1	tablespoon yeast		1	cup (10 ounces) refried beans
½	cup yellow cornmeal		¼	cup vegetable oil
3	cups all-purpose flour		1	extra-large egg
1½	teaspoons salt		1	tablespoon honey
2	teaspoons chili powder		⅔	cup water

Place all the ingredients in the machine, program for Dough or Manual, and press Start. The dough will be quite moist but should form a discrete ball. At the end of the final cycle, punch down the dough and place it on a lightly floured work surface to rest for 5 minutes.

TO FINISH THE PIZZA

- 2 cups (16 ounces) chunky salsa
- 1 cup (4 ounces) shredded Cheddar cheese or Monterey Jack cheese

Preheat the oven to 475°F.

On a lightly floured work surface, roll the dough out to a 17 × 11-inch rectangle. If you have a jelly roll pan that has slightly different dimensions, roll the dough to fit it. Lightly oil the pan and place the dough into the pan, stretching it with your hands so that it covers the surface up to the edges.

Spread the dough with the salsa, leaving a 1-inch border, and sprinkle with the cheese. Place the pizza in a warm place to rise for 30 minutes, then bake it for 17 to 20 minutes, or until the crust is deep brown and the cheese is bubbling. Serve hot or at room temperature.

> HINT: *This dough can be prepared up to 24 hours ahead and stored, covered with plastic wrap, in an oiled bowl or plastic bag in the refrigerator. Roll it out and proceed as above when you're ready to cook.*

Bengal Pizza

Traditional curry spices flavor this delicate flaky crust which is topped with curry paste or a combination of curry paste and ground lamb. Toasted chick-pea flour, made from ground toasted chick-peas and available in health food stores, gives this extra-thin crust an ethereal lightness. It is important to bake the pizza at a very high temperature as soon as it is rolled out.

SERVES 6

FOR THE DOUGH

1	tablespoon yeast
1	cup toasted chick-pea flour
2	cups all-purpose flour, plus 2 to 3 additional tablespoons if necessary
1½	teaspoons salt
½	teaspoon ground ginger
½	teaspoon ground turmeric

½	teaspoon ground cumin
½	teaspoon chili powder
⅓	cup garlic oil or ⅓ cup olive oil plus ½ teaspoon garlic powder
¾	cup water or more to make a smooth ball

Place all the ingredients in the machine, program for Manual or Dough, and press Start. After 3 minutes of kneading if there is still a film of dough on the bottom of the pan, add 1 to 2 tablespoons of flour until a discrete ball forms.

At the end of the final knead, place the dough in a large plastic bag or in an oiled bowl and cover it with plastic wrap. Refrigerate for at least 2 hours or as long as 12 hours.

TO FINISH THE PIZZA

8	ounces ground lamb, browned and drained of all liquid (optional)

4	tablespoons curry paste (available in speciality food stores)

Prepare the lamb if desired. Select a 16-inch perforated pizza pan or large heavy-duty baking sheet. Preheat the oven to 475°F with the rack in the center position. Place the dough on a cold unfloured work surface and use a heavy rolling pin to roll it to one large 16-inch circle or two 8- to 9-inch circles. The dough should be as thin as possible—no more than ⅛ inch thick. Immediately roll the dough back around the rolling pin and unroll it onto the pan.

Spread a thin layer of curry paste onto the dough and top it with the lamb if desired. Place the pizza in the oven and bake for 16 to 18 minutes, or until the crust is very brown and crisp. Serve immediately.

> HINTS: *You can substitute ground turkey for the lamb. Serve this with cucumber yogurt or mulligatawny soup.*

Mexican Pizzettes

In this zesty creation all your favorite Mexican flavors are baked onto a delicious cornmeal crust. Remember to use a thick salsa, which makes for a hearty, salsifying topping. A recipe for homemade salsa follows, or you can use your favorite store-bought brand.

MAKES 4 INDIVIDUAL PIZZETTES

FOR THE DOUGH

1¼	teaspoons yeast		¾	cup water
2	tablespoons cornmeal		2	tablespoons sour cream
2½	cups all-purpose flour		¼	teaspoon crushed red pepper
1	teaspoon salt			flakes
1	teaspoon sugar			

Place all the ingredients in the machine, program for Manual, Dough, or Basic Dough, and press Start. The dough will be firm and pull away from the sides of the bowl. While the dough is rising you can prepare the topping.

FOR THE SALSA

4	plum tomatoes, peeled, seeded, and chopped		1	tablespoon fresh cilantro or 1 teaspoon dried cilantro
½	cup your favorite salsa (mild, medium, or spicy as you wish)		¼	teaspoon freshly ground black pepper
1	garlic clove, minced		¼	teaspoon salt
⅓	cup chopped red onion			

In a mixing bowl, blend together all the ingredients. Refrigerate until you're ready to assemble the pizzettes.

TO FINISH THE PIZZETTES

2	avocados, peeled, pitted, and cut into thin slices		⅛	cup sliced jalapeño peppers (optional)
1	cup sour cream			
⅓	pound grated Monterey Jack cheese			

Preheat the oven to 400°F with the rack in the center position. Lightly dust 2 baking sheets with cornmeal and set aside.

When the dough cycle is completed, transfer the dough to a lightly floured work surface, cover it with a clean towel, and let it rest for 5 minutes. Divide the dough into 4 equal pieces and roll out each piece to an 8-inch circle. Transfer the

circles to the prepared baking sheet. Spread the salsa on each circle, leaving a
$\frac{1}{2}$-inch border. Lay on the avocado slices and then spoon on the sour cream.
Sprinkle with the cheese and top with the peppers if desired. Bake for 20 minutes
until the topping is bubbly and the crust is deep brown.

Serve 1 per person, hot, warm, or at room temperature.

Individual Smoked Chicken and Asparagus Pizzettes

Top-quality smoked chicken is available in most delis. Request thick (¹/₂-inch) slices and cut them into ¹/₂ × 2-inch strips before putting them on the pizza. These little pizzettes are delicious, especially if you can find pencil-thin asparagus.

MAKES 4 INDIVIDUAL PIZZETTES

FOR THE DOUGH

1	teaspoon yeast		¹/₂	teaspoon sugar
2³/₄	cups all-purpose flour		1	cup water
¹/₂	teaspoon salt		1	tablespoon olive oil

Place all the ingredients in the machine, program for Manual, Dough, or Basic Dough, and press Start. The dough will form a soft ball and pull away from the sides of the machine after the first few minutes of kneading.

TO FINISH THE PIZZETTES

1 pound smoked chicken breast, cut into 1-inch × ¹/₂-inch slices

2 plum tomatoes, sliced

¹/₂ pound fresh thin asparagus, trimmed, cut in half, and sautéed in ¹/₄ stick (1 ounce) unsalted butter for 3 to 4 minutes

¹/₂ pound fresh mozzarella, sliced into ¹/₄-inch slices

Preheat the oven to 425°F with the rack in the center position. Sprinkle cornmeal over the surface of 2 baking sheets.

When the dough cycle is completed, transfer the dough to a lightly floured work surface, cover it with a clean towel, and let it rest for 5 minutes. Cut the dough into 4 equal pieces. Roll out each piece to a 6-inch circle. Transfer the circles to the prepared pans.

Distribute the chicken over the 4 circles and lay 3 tomato slices on top of each. Distribute the asparagus over the tomato slices and finally lay the mozzarella on the tops. Bake for 20 minutes until the cheese is melted and bubbling and the crust is golden brown. Serve hot or warm.

Ploughman's Pizza

A ploughman's lunch is an English specialty consisting of a slice or two of crusty bread, a hunk of Cheddar cheese, a dab of chutney, some pickled onions, and sweet pickles. These ingredients are combined to make this unusual but absolutely delicious pizza.

Be sure to let the dough rise so you get a thick crust.

MAKES ONE 14-INCH PIZZA

FOR THE DOUGH

1	tablespoon yeast
3½	cups all-purpose flour
2	teaspoons salt
1	cup water, plus up to an additional ⅓ cup if necessary to form the dough

⅓ cup Cheddar cheese, coarsely shredded

Place all the ingredients in the machine, program for Dough, Basic Dough, or Manual, and press Start. Add more water, a little at a time, if the dough is dry and crumbly after the first few minutes of kneading. The dough should form a soft, discrete ball.

TO FINISH THE PIZZA

8 slices aged Cheddar cheese, approximately 4 × 2 × ½ inches each

1 cup (8 ounces) mango chutney

20 pickled onions

8 medium-sized pickles (sweet or sour depending on your taste), sliced ¼ inch thick

When the machine has completed the final cycle, remove the dough and form it into a 14-inch circle. Place the dough on a lightly oiled pizza pan or a pizza peel that has been sprinkled with cornmeal. Cover it with a clean cloth and allow it to rise in a warm place for 30 minutes.

Preheat the oven to 400°F with the rack or a pizza stone in the center position. Distribute the slices of cheese on top of the dough, then add dabs of chutney, the onions, and finally the pickles. Cook the pizza for 15 minutes at 400°F, then lower the oven to 375°F and continue cooking for another 10 to 12 minutes, or until the crust is very brown and the cheese has melted. Serve immediately or cool and serve at room temperature.

Pear, Rosemary, and Goat Cheese Tarts

This is a very special yeasted tart and is a treat to serve as an appetizer along with a bowl of marinated olives. It also makes a superb brunch offering.

SERVES 6 TO 8

FOR THE DOUGH

½	teaspoon yeast		½	tablespoon grainy mustard
2¼	cups all-purpose flour		2	tablespoons olive oil
¾	teaspoon salt		¾	cup water

Place all the ingredients in the machine, program for Dough or Basic Dough, and press Start.

TO FINISH THE TARTS

3	large pears (Anjou are the best for this tart)		3	tablespoons dried rosemary leaves
3 to 4	tablespoons olive oil, plus additional oil for brushing the dough		1	3½-ounce log plain goat cheese (domestic goat cheeses are milder than imported ones)

Peel the pears, cut them into quarters, and remove the seeds and cores. Heat a nonstick skillet and sauté the pears in the olive oil until they are a light golden brown and tender. Be careful not to overcook them; you want the pears to still have some body. Remove the pears from the skillet, drain them on a paper towel, and let them cool.

When the dough cycle is finished, transfer the dough to a lightly floured surface and let it rest for 5 minutes. Divide the dough into 2 pieces and roll each piece out to an 8-inch circle. Transfer the circles onto a lightly greased cookie sheet.

Preheat the oven to 475°F with the rack in the center position.

Brush the circles with olive oil and place the pears in a concentric circle on each, leaving about an inch between each pear. Sprinkle the circles with the rosemary and finally break up the goat cheese and sprinkle it over them. Let the tarts rest for 10 minutes, then bake them for 15 minutes. Cut in wedges and serve hot or warm.

Sweet Potato Tarts with Bacon, Scallions, and Goat Cheese

Sparkling with flavor and boasting a kaleidoscope of textures, these tarts are a winner in the personality department. You will find green peppercorns packed in brine in the gourmet section of your supermarket or in specialty food stores. Drain off the brine before chopping them either by hand or in a food processor, and take care not to grind them to mush.

MAKES 4 INDIVIDUAL TARTS

FOR THE DOUGH

1¹/₂	teaspoons yeast	³/₄	cup water or more to make a smooth, firm ball
2¹/₂	cups all-purpose flour		
2	teaspoons sugar	1	tablespoon olive oil
1	teaspoon salt		Pinch of freshly ground black pepper

Place all the ingredients in the machine, program for Manual, Dough, or Basic Dough, and press Start. The dough will be firm and will pull away from the sides of the bowl. While the dough is rising you can prepare the topping.

TO FINISH THE TARTS

1	pound sweet potatoes, cooked and mashed (1¹/₄ cups) or an equal amount of canned sweet potatoes	8	slices lean bacon, cooked until crisp and coarsely chopped
1	tablespoon unsalted butter	2	ounces goat cheese, crumbled
2	tablespoons whole milk or light cream	2	tablespoons green peppercorns, drained of brine and ground
5	scallions (both green and white parts), trimmed and cut on an angle into 1-inch slices		

Mix the mashed sweet potatoes with the butter and milk. Set aside. Preheat the oven to 425°F. Lightly flour a baking sheet and set it aside.

When the dough cycle is completed, transfer the dough to a lightly floured work surface and let it rest for 5 minutes. Divide the dough into 4 pieces and roll each out to a 6-inch circle. The dough will be thin. Transfer the circles to the prepared baking sheet. Divide the sweet potatoes among the 4 circles and spread them out, leaving ¹/₂-inch borders. Sprinkle on the scallions and bacon and then the goat cheese and ground peppercorns. Bake for 25 minutes until the crust is a rich brown. Serve hot, warm, or at room temperature.

Shrimp, Scallop, and Fresh Fennel Pizza

This is a winner if you're a seafood lover. Try to use the tiny bay scallops since they add such a nutty sweetness to this pizza.

MAKES ONE 12-INCH PIZZA

FOR THE DOUGH

2	teaspoons yeast		1	teaspoon sugar
2½	cups all-purpose flour		1	tablespoon olive oil
½	teaspoon salt		¾	cup water

Place all the ingredients in the machine, program for Dough or Basic Dough, and press Start.

FOR THE TOPPING

1	cup fresh fennel, well rinsed, dried, then sliced crosswise in ¼-inch pieces		¼	pound bay scallops
				Juice of 1 medium lemon
2	teaspoons olive oil, plus additional oil for brushing			Salt to taste
				Freshly ground black pepper to taste
½	pound small shrimp, shelled and deveined			

Toss together the fennel and olive oil. Set aside.

Combine the remaining ingredients and let them marinate for 5 to 10 minutes, drain them thoroughly, and refrigerate them until you are ready to assemble the pizza.

TO FINISH THE PIZZA

When the dough cycle is completed, transfer the dough to a lightly floured work surface and let it rest for 5 minutes. Preheat the oven to 425°F. Sprinkle a small amount of cornmeal on a cookie sheet and set it aside. Roll out the dough to a 12-inch circle and transfer it onto the cookie sheet. Brush the dough with a small amount of olive oil and lay the fennel out on the surface, leaving a ¾-inch border. Spread out the shrimp and scallops over the fennel. Sprinkle with salt and pepper. Bake the pizza for 20 minutes. The crust should be a nice golden brown; the shrimp and scallops will be cooked.

Smoked Salmon Pizzettes

Tired of the same old lox and bagels every Sunday morning? Try this new and tasty twist. You can make the dough the day before and refrigerate it until you are ready to make the pizzettes.

MAKES 8 INDIVIDUAL PIZZETTES

FOR THE DOUGH

2	teaspoons yeast		2	teaspoons dried dillweed
3	cups all-purpose flour		1/4	cup vegetable oil
1 1/2	teaspoons salt		1	cup water
1/2	teaspoon freshly ground black pepper			

Place all the ingredients in the machine, program for Dough or Manual, and press Start. At the end of the final cycle, remove the dough to an oiled work surface and divide it into 8 pieces. Cover the dough with a clean towel and allow it to rest for 10 minutes.

TO FINISH THE PIZZETTES

8	ounces whipped cream cheese (plain or flavored)		8	sprigs of fresh dill
8	slices (10 to 12 ounces) smoked salmon or lox			

Preheat the oven to 475°F with the rack in the center position. Roll each piece of dough as thin as possible into a free-form shape and place it on a baking sheet sprinkled with cornmeal (you'll need 2 baking sheets). Work fast so the dough does not have a chance to rise—you want the pizzettes as thin and crisp as possible. Bake the pizzettes for 7 to 10 minutes, reversing the baking sheets once halfway through the baking. Remove the pizzettes to a rack to cool for 10 minutes before spreading each with cream cheese and topping with the smoked salmon. Garnish each with a sprig of dill and serve immediately.

Pizza Benedict

Don't you love eggs Benedict? But when you're serving a crowd, it's a pain in the neck to have to split, toast, and butter all those English muffins, slice and cook the ham, poach the eggs, blah blah blah. Here's a simple way to serve eggs Benedict with just a fraction of the work: Pizza Benedict. Whole eggs, cradled by a chewy "English muffin bread" pizza dough, cook under a layer of ham as the dough bakes. Make Hollandaise Sauce while the pizza's in the oven, and when it's done you'll have it on the table within five minutes. And all without having to poach one egg!

SERVES 8

FOR THE DOUGH

1	tablespoon yeast		$1/3$	cup water
3	cups all-purpose flour		$1/4$	cup vegetable oil
1	tablespoon sugar		$1/4$	teaspoon baking soda dissolved
$1\frac{1}{2}$	teaspoons salt			in 1 tablespoon water
1	cup buttermilk, either fresh or			
	reconstituted from powder			

Combine all the ingredients in the machine except the baking soda dissolved in water, program for Manual, Dough, or Basic Dough, and press Start. Check the dough 10 minutes before the end of the second kneading cycle; it should be smooth and supple, not at all tacky. Adjust the consistency with flour or water as necessary.

When the machine has completed its cycle, cancel it and add the baking soda dissolved in water. Program for Manual, Dough, or Basic Dough and press Start. Let the machine knead until the baking soda and water mixture is incorporated into the dough, about 2 minutes. Cancel the machine and transfer the dough to a lightly oiled work surface. Let the dough rest, covered with a damp towel or plastic wrap, for 10 minutes.

Pat the dough into a 14-inch round deep-dish pizza pan, making sure the edges are higher than the center. Let the dough rest for 15 minutes. Preheat the oven to 400°F with the rack in the center position.

TO FINISH THE PIZZA

8	large eggs		$1/2$	pound ham, thinly sliced
	Salt to taste			
	Freshly ground black pepper			
	to taste			

Gently break the eggs onto the dough. Sprinkle with salt and pepper to taste (keeping in mind the saltiness of the ham you're using). Lay the ham slices on top of the eggs, covering them completely.

Bake the pizza for 20 minutes, or until it's golden brown. Serve with hollandaise sauce.

Hollandaise Sauce

2 egg yolks
2 tablespoons cold water
Pinch of salt
1½ sticks (6 ounces) unsalted butter, melted and kept hot

1½ teaspoons lemon juice
Dash of Tabasco Brand Hot Sauce

In a small saucepan set over very low heat, whisk together the egg yolks, water, and salt for 45 seconds, or till foamy. Dribble in the butter in a steady stream, whisking continuously. Continue whisking for about 1 minute after you've added all of the butter, or until the sauce thickens. If it doesn't seem to be thickening, turn the heat up, but just a tiny bit; you don't want to curdle the eggs. When the sauce has thickened, add the lemon juice and Tabasco sauce. Serve each slice of pizza with a couple of tablespoons of the sauce.

Caspian Pizzas

Okay, we're talking major indulgence here. Caviar lovers suspected this the moment they saw the title of this recipe. They know that real caviar comes from sturgeon that spawn and swim in the landlocked sea bound by Iran and countries of the former Soviet Union. If you simply can't justify the expense of the "real thing," you'll get a very nice result using American salmon roe which is a fraction of the price of the imported version. Whichever one you choose to top this heavenly delight, be sure to have a glass of champagne with it.

This recipe calls for a small amount of buckwheat flour which is the ingredient that gives blini (the small yeasted pancakes traditionally served with caviar) their unique flavor.

SERVES 8

FOR THE DOUGH

1½	teaspoons yeast	2	tablespoons olive oil
2	cups all-purpose flour	1⅓	cups water, plus up to an
1	cup whole wheat flour		additional ¼ cup to make a
⅓	cup buckwheat flour		smooth ball of dough after the first
2	teaspoons salt		5 minutes of kneading
1	tablespoon sugar		

Place all the ingredients in the machine, program for Dough or Manual, and press Start. At the end of the final cycle, remove the dough to a lightly oiled work surface and divide it into 6 pieces. Cover the dough with a clean towel and allow it to rest for 10 minutes.

TO FINISH THE PIZZAS

1½	cups (12 ounces) mascarpone cheese (available in Italian and specialty food stores)	100	grams caviar

Preheat the oven to 475°F with the rack as close to the center position as possible. Roll each piece of dough as thin as possible into a free-form shape and place it on a baking sheet sprinkled with cornmeal (you'll need 2 baking sheets). Work fast so the dough does not have a chance to rise—you want the pizzas as thin and crisp as possible. Spread the mascarpone over the dough, leaving a ½-inch border. Prick the dough with a fork and bake for 7 to 10 minutes, reversing the baking sheets once halfway through the baking.

Remove the pizzas to a cooling rack and allow to cool for 5 minutes. Top each pizza with a generous dollop of caviar and serve immediately.

Gluten-Free
Wheat-Free Pizza Crust

Thanks to baking wizard Beth Hillson, folks with gluten and wheat allergies can enjoy pizza and bread. Beth, whose Gluten-Free Pantry (see page 301) supplies baking mixes for bread machines, has generously given me the recipe she developed for pizza crust. Use your favorite toppings on it or pick some from the many in this book. A lot of these ingredients are available both in health food stores and by mail order from King Arthur (page 301).

MAKES TWO 12-INCH CRUSTS

FOR THE DOUGH

4	teaspoons yeast		1	tablespoon sugar
2	cups white rice flour		1	teaspoon salt
1/2	cup potato starch		1	egg, slightly beaten
1/2	cup cornstarch		2	tablespoons olive oil
1	tablespoon gum xanthan (optional)		1 1/3	cups warm water or milk

Place all the ingredients in the machine, program for Dough, Basic Dough, or Manual, and press Start.

TO FINISH A PIZZA

At the end of the final cycle, preheat the oven to 425°F with the rack in the lowest position. Oil or spray 2 pizza pans with nonstick vegetable spray. Oil one side each of two 14-inch pieces of plastic wrap. Divide the dough in half and sandwich one piece between the 2 oiled sides of the pieces of plastic wrap. Roll the dough out to a 12-inch circle about 1/4 inch thick. Remove the plastic wrap and place the rolled-out dough on one of the prepared pans. Reuse the plastic wrap to repeat this with the other piece of dough.

Top the dough with sauce or topping of your choice and bake for 12 to 15 minutes, or until the edges are brown. Serve hot.

Focaccie

Rustic Sourdough Focaccia

I owe a big debt of thanks to Joe Ortiz, California's gentle Bread Giant whose kind heart and gentle touch make miracles out of flour, water, and yeast. I was determined to learn to make rustic focaccia with a great crust and a chewy crumb studded with big, irregular holes. WET DOUGH and A LONG, SLOW, COLD RISE were Joe's words of wisdom and voilà! Success! There is a recipe for Sourdough Starter on page 20. It can also be ordered by mail (page 301).

This very wet dough, which is leavened with a sourdough starter and just a little yeast, is kneaded and has a rise in the machine, then the pan is removed (if you have a pan with a hole in the bottom, you'll have to transfer the dough to an oiled bowl) and refrigerated for at least twelve hours. The formed dough gets yet another long, slow rise in a cool place.

The results are definitely worth the wait—a crusty, gutsy loaf that you'll be proud to hold up against any store-bought focaccia. Buon appetito!

The focaccia is best eaten the day it is made.

SERVES 8

FOR THE DOUGH

¹/₂	teaspoon yeast
3	cups plus 1 tablespoon all-purpose flour
1¹/₂	teaspoons coarse salt
1	cup sourdough starter

1¹/₂	cups water, plus up to an additional
¹/₄	cup if necessary to make a very wet dough that does not form a discrete ball

Place all the ingredients except the tablespoon of flour in the machine, program for Dough or Manual, and press Start. After the first 3 to 4 minutes of kneading, add more water if necessary to form a very wet dough that barely holds its shape and does not leave the bottom of the pan.

At the end of the final cycle, remove the pan from the machine or remove the dough to a lightly oiled bowl. Sprinkle the top of the dough with the 1 tablespoon flour, cover the top of the pan or bowl with plastic wrap, and place it in the refrigerator. Refrigerate at least 12 hours and up to 18 hours.

TO FINISH THE FOCACCIA

2	tablespoons olive oil	1 to 2	teaspoons coarse salt

Place the dough on a lightly floured work surface. Punch it down and form it into an 11-inch disk, then place it on a baking sheet or pizza pan or wooden paddle that has been lightly sprinkled with cornmeal. Cover the dough with a clean towel and place it back in the refrigerator for 4 hours. At the end of that time, take it out of the refrigerator and leave it, still covered, at room temperature until it rises to almost double in bulk. This may take up to 2 hours.

Preheat the oven to 475°F with the rack or a pizza stone or tiles in the center position. Just before baking, lightly press your fingertips into the dough to make gentle indentations in the surface. Drizzle with the olive oil and sprinkle with salt. Slide the pan into the oven, or slide the dough onto the pizza stone or tiles, and bake for 18 to 22 minutes, or until the top is crusty and a rich golden brown color. Eat hot, warm, or at room temperature.

HINTS: *This focaccia makes wonderful sandwiches. My favorite is smoked turkey, Stilton cheese, watercress, and scallions. Don't forget the beer—this one will make you thirsty.*

Leftover focaccia is perfect for making croutons. Cut the bread into 1-inch cubes and sauté them in garlic oil until brown and crisp. Drain on paper towels.

Sun-dried Tomato Focaccia

You can save a lot of money by buying sun-dried tomatoes in bulk and packing them in oil yourself. Place the tomatoes in a large strainer set in a mixing bowl. Pour enough white vinegar over the tomatoes to give them a thorough soaking. Let the tomatoes sit in the vinegar for several minutes, then remove the strainer and shake out the vinegar by tapping the strainer on the sink. Place the tomatoes in a glass or plastic container and fill the container with olive oil. Store the tomatoes in a cool place. You can store them in the refrigerator, but the olive oil will solidify. When this happens, run the container under hot water to soften the oil before using the tomatoes. The oil is great for making salad dressing.

SERVES 6 TO 8

1	recipe Sun-dried Tomato Dough (page 26)	1 to 2 teaspoons coarse salt
2	tablespoons oil from sun-dried tomatoes	

Pat and stretch the dough to a 9-inch disk and place it on a lightly oiled pizza pan or a pizza paddle dusted with cornmeal. Cover the dough with a clean towel and place it in a warm place to rise until doubled in bulk.

Preheat the oven to 475°F with the rack or a pizza stone in the center position. Just before placing the dough in the oven, use your fingertips to make indentations in the surface. Drizzle with the oil and sprinkle with the salt. Bake the focaccia for 18 to 20 minutes, or until the top is golden brown. Cool slightly before slicing. Eat warm or at room temperature.

Pesto Focaccia

Pesto seems to be everyone's flavor of choice these days. And with good reason. You can serve homemade or store-bought pesto along with this focaccia as a dipping sauce. Use the focaccia as a snack or an accompaniment to a meal, or split it and make sandwiches.

SERVES 6 TO 8

1   recipe Pesto Dough (page 26)
2   tablespoons olive oil or pesto-
    infused olive oil (available in
    gourmet stores)

1 to 2   teaspoons coarse salt

Pat and stretch the dough to a 9-inch disk and place it on a lightly oiled pizza pan or pizza paddle dusted with cornmeal. Cover the dough with a clean towel and place it in a warm place to rise until doubled in bulk.

Preheat the oven to 475°F with the rack or a pizza stone in the center position. Just before placing the dough in the oven, use your fingertips to make indentations in the surface. Drizzle with the oil and sprinkle with the salt. Bake the focaccia for 18 to 20 minutes, or until the top is golden brown. Cool slightly before slicing. Eat warm or at room temperature.

Red Pesto Focaccia

The red pesto for this amazing focaccia was inspired by Patricia Wells's red pesto in her book Trattoria. *Both the dough and the pesto in this lively, ruby-hued loaf contain sun-dried tomatoes. It's important to buy the kind that come packed in oil, since the oil is also an ingredient in the pesto, or you can reconstitute dried tomatoes (which are more economical in price) by soaking them for two to three minutes in white vinegar (to remove some of the salt) and then packing them in olive oil in a clean, lidded jar. Let them soak for one to two days before using.*

SERVES 6 TO 8

FOR THE DOUGH

1¼	teaspoons yeast		4 to 5	oil-packed sun-dried tomatoes, drained
2½	cups all-purpose flour			
1	teaspoon salt		1	cup water
1	teaspoon sugar			

Place all the ingredients in the machine, program for Dough, Basic Dough, or Manual, and press Start. If the dough appears sticky, add up to ⅓ cup additional flour, 1 tablespoon at a time. While the dough is rising you can prepare the Red Pesto.

FOR THE RED PESTO

6	garlic cloves		¼	teaspoon freshly ground black pepper
15	oil-packed sun-dried tomatoes, plus 2 tablespoons of the oil			Pinch of salt
2	teaspoons dried rosemary leaves			

Place all the ingredients in a food processor and process for 10 to 15 seconds. The red pesto should be coarse and not smooth, so be careful that you do not overprocess.

TO FINISH THE FOCACCIA
3 tablespoons olive oil

Preheat the oven to 450°F with the rack in the center position. Brush the olive oil over a heavy cookie sheet and set it aside.

Transfer the dough to a lightly floured work surface and let it rest for 5 minutes. Roll out the dough to a 12-inch circle and transfer it to the prepared cookie sheet. Spread the pesto over the surface of the dough. Bake the focaccia for 15 minutes, or until it is crisp and golden brown, then cut in wedges and serve hot or warm.

Hummus Focaccia

Toasted chick-pea flour (available in health foods stores and by mail order, page 301) combined with light whole wheat flour gives this flat bread a wholesome nutty taste. Sesame seeds, both ground (tahini) and whole, add a sweetness and crunch.

The complementary combination of a legume flour (chick-pea) and a whole wheat flour creates a perfect protein which needs only a salad to make a nutritious meal.

SERVES 8 TO 10

FOR THE DOUGH

1	tablespoon yeast	$^1/_2$	teaspoon coarsely ground black pepper
1	cup toasted chick-pea flour		
1	cup White Wheat flour (page 5)	$^1/_3$	cup tahini
1	cup all-purpose flour	1	extra-large egg
$1^1/_2$	teaspoons salt	$^3/_4$	cup plus 2 tablespoons water or more to serve a slightly sticky dough
$^1/_2$	teaspoon garlic powder		

Place all the ingredients in the machine, program for Manual or Dough, and press Start. This dough is sticky but should form a discrete ball. If it looks dry and crumbly after the first 3 minutes of kneading, add 1 to 2 additional tablespoons water.

TO FINISH THE FOCACCIA

1	egg beaten with 1 tablespoon water	3	tablespoons sesame seeds

At the end of the final knead, use your hands or a rolling pin to form the dough into a 9-inch disk. Brush the top with half of the egg glaze and then sprinkle it liberally with sesame seeds. Drizzle the remaining half of the egg glaze over the sesame seeds. Place the dough, uncovered, in a warm place to rise until almost doubled in bulk, 30 to 40 minutes.

Preheat the oven to 425°F with the rack in the center position. Just before you place the dough in the oven, gently press the surface with your fingertips to make light indentations. Bake the focaccia for 20 to 24 minutes until the underside is lightly colored and the sesame seeds are golden brown.

Serve hot or at room temperature.

> HINT: *Slice the cooled focaccia in half and make sandwiches of thinly sliced red onion, feta cheese, and red leaf lettuce.*

Porcini Focaccia

If you love the dark, deep-woods flavor of porcini mushrooms, then this double-barrel loaf is for you. It's a glorious deep mushroom color, perfumed with porcini, and set off by tiny flashes of caraway. The inside is moist and tender and the top is lightly crusted with coarse salt. You can also use this dough to make a porcini pizza crust (page 31).

Dried porcini mushrooms and porcini oil are available in supermarkets and specialty food shops and also by mail order (page 301).

The focaccia can be frozen in a heavy-duty plastic freezer bag after it is thoroughly cooled; defrost it at room temperature still in the bag. The dough can be frozen after the final rise. Form it into a nine-inch disk and place it in a heavy-duty plastic freezer bag. Defrost it either at room temperature or in the refrigerator, still wrapped, then place it on a pan and allow it to rise, following the directions below.

SERVES 8

FOR THE DOUGH

1 ounce ($^3/_4$ cup) dried porcini mushrooms	$^1/_3$ cup cornmeal
1$^3/_4$ cups boiling water	1$^1/_2$ teaspoons salt
1 tablespoon yeast	1 tablespoon sugar
2 cups less 2 tablespoons all-purpose flour	1 teaspoon coarsely ground black pepper
1 cup whole wheat flour	$^1/_3$ cup porcini oil
2 tablespoons buckwheat flour	1 tablespoon caraway seeds

Place the mushrooms in a small bowl, cover them with the boiling water and allow them to soak for 10 to 15 minutes, or until they are very soft. Set a fine-mesh sieve over a glass 2-cup measure and drain off the liquid, pressing the mushrooms gently to squeeze out as much excess liquid as possible. Reserve the liquid.

Place all the ingredients and 1 cup of the reserved mushroom liquid in the machine, program for Dough or Manual, and press Start. If after the first 30 to 40 minutes of kneading the dough appears dry and crumbly, add 1 to 2 more tablespoons of the mushroom liquid until the dough forms a slightly sticky but discrete ball.

2	tablespoons porcini oil	2	teaspoons coarse salt

At the end of the final knead, form the dough into a 9-inch round and place it on a baking sheet or pizza pan lightly dusted with cornmeal. Cover it with a clean cloth and allow the dough to rise in a warm place until almost doubled in bulk. This will take about 1 hour because buckwheat and whole wheat flour have very little gluten. Preheat the oven to 425°F with the rack in the center position. Use your fingertips to make light indentations in the top of the dough. Drizzle the top with the oil and sprinkle with the salt. Bake for 20 to 25 minutes, or until the top is deep brown and the underside is dry and browned as well.

Serve hot or at room temperature.

HINT: *Split the porcini focaccia and layer it with crumbled goat cheese and very thinly sliced red onions. Place it under the broiler until the cheese melts for a fantastic open-faced sandwich.*

Potato Caraway Focaccia

*This soft-crusted, mellow high-rising loaf looks, and tastes, like a work of art.
A slight hint of cumin brings a golden taste to the velvety soft crumb. Hot from
the oven, it's my idea of the perfect loaf of bread. While you can make this with
instant mashed potatoes, I prefer the taste of the real thing. It is one of the best
ways to use up leftover cooked potatoes.*

SERVES 8 TO 10

FOR THE DOUGH

2½	teaspoons yeast	1	cup (8 ounces) mashed potatoes
1½	teaspoons salt		made from scratch, or from
1	cup rye flour		"instant" mashed potatoes
2	cups all-purpose flour	¼	cup garlic oil or olive oil
½	teaspoon ground cumin	⅔	cup water
½	teaspoon freshly ground black pepper		

Place all the ingredients in the machine, program for Dough or Manual, and
press Start. The mixture will be very dry and crumbly at first. Do not add
more water until the potatoes give up their cooking liquid—about 5 minutes into
the first kneading cycle. Then add just enough to make a firm ball. At the end of
the final cycle, remove the dough, which will be quite tacky and soft, to a lightly
floured work space. Sprinkle the dough with flour and knead briefly by hand,
adding only enough flour to form a soft ball of dough.

TO FINISH THE FOCACCIA

2	tablespoons olive oil	1	tablespoon caraway seeds

Place the ball of dough either on a wooden pizza paddle sprinkled with cornmeal or on a cornmeal-dusted baking sheet. Cover with a clean cloth and let
the dough rise for 30 minutes in a warm place.

Preheat the oven to 450°F with either the rack or a pizza stone or tiles in the
center position. Just before placing the dough in the oven, indent the top of it
with your fingertips, pushing down rather aggressively to deflate it, not completely but by about a third. Drizzle it with the olive oil and sprinkle with the
caraway seeds. Slide the pan into the oven or the dough onto the pizza stone or
tiles. Bake for 10 minutes at 450°F, then lower the oven to 375°F and bake an

additional 5 to 7 minutes, or until the top is deep golden brown and the bottom is browned as well. (Use a wide metal spatula to lift up a corner and take a peek.)

Serve hot, warm, or at room temperature.

HINT: *Slice the cooled focaccia in three layers, spread one layer with mayonnaise and greens and another with oil-packed canned tuna that has been puréed with a little oil from the can, capers, and lemon juice. Replace the layers to make a triple-decker sandwich. Or coat one layer with grainy mustard and lay on pieces of thinly sliced Cheddar cheese and another with mustard and sliced turkey breast, replacing the layers to make a triple-decker sandwich.*

Rosemary Mustard Focaccia

Grainy mustard lends a distinctive flavor to this fragrant loaf. Try to use fresh rosemary when it is available since the taste is far superior to dried, and the leaf-studded focaccia is so pretty. King Arthur White Wheat Flour is available in supermarkets or by mail order (page 301), or you can substitute regular whole wheat flour, although the texture of the focaccia will not be as delicate.

SERVES 6 TO 8

FOR THE DOUGH

1	tablespoon yeast		1	cup water, plus an additional 1 to 2 tablespoons if necessary
1	cup White Wheat flour			
2	cups all-purpose flour		1/3	cup grainy mustard such as Pommery
1/3	cup yellow cornmeal			
2	teaspoons salt		1/4	cup fresh rosemary leaves or 1 1/2 tablespoons dried rosemary
1/4	cup olive oil			

Place all the ingredients in the machine, program for Dough or Manual, and press Start. Add just enough extra water until the dough forms a relaxed yet discrete ball. At the end of the final cycle, shape the dough into a 10-inch disk and place it either on a pizza peel or baking sheet that has been sprinkled with cornmeal. Cover the dough with a clean cloth and allow it to rise in a warm place until doubled in bulk.

TO FINISH THE FOCACCIA

Preheat the oven to 450°F with the rack or a pizza stone in the center position. Just before baking, use your fingertips to make 1/2-inch dimples in the top of the dough. Slide the pan into the oven or the dough onto the stone and bake for 17 to 20 minutes, or until crusty and golden brown. Cool the focaccia slightly before cutting it into wedges. Or cool it completely, slice it in half horizontally, fill it with cheese and/or meat, then cut it into wedges to make sandwiches.

Green Peppercorn Focaccia

Want to add a little spice to your life? Wait until you see how adding a few tablespoons of green peppercorns to a simple focaccia can jazz things up. Great on its own, and extraordinary when split and slathered with goat cheese, this green peppercorn focaccia stands out from the rest.

Green peppercorns come in small cans and can be found in specialty food shops and many supermarkets. They come in brine which should be drained off before you use them. Leftover peppercorns should be transferred to a nonmetal covered container and stored in their brine in the refrigerator, where they will keep for many months. Try using them in salad dressings and on grilled fish and chicken.

SERVES 8 TO 10

FOR THE DOUGH

1	tablespoon yeast	3	tablespoons garlic oil or 3 tablespoons olive oil plus 1 large garlic clove, minced
1	cup whole wheat flour		
2	cups all-purpose flour		
3	tablespoons cornmeal	2	tablespoons green peppercorns, drained of brine
1½	teaspoons salt		
1¼	cups water		

Place all the ingredients except the peppercorns in the machine, program for Dough or Manual, and press Start. At the end of the final knead, add the peppercorns and restart the machine, kneading just until the peppercorns are incorporated but not pulverized.

TO FINISH THE FOCACCIA

2 tablespoons olive oil or garlic oil
Coarse salt

Freshly ground black pepper

Form the dough into a 10-inch disk and place it either on a pizza peel that has been dusted with cornmeal, or on a pizza pan that has been oiled or sprayed with nonstick vegetable spray. Allow the dough to rise, uncovered, for 1 hour in a warm place.

Preheat the oven to 475°F with the rack or a pizza stone in the center position. Just before baking, use your fingertips to make indentations in the surface of the dough. Drizzle on the oil and sprinkle with salt and pepper. Bake for 15 minutes, or until well browned. Enjoy hot, warm, or at room temperature.

Roasted Garlic
and Olive Focaccia

This focaccia is for serious garlic and olive lovers! There are a few baking secrets that enhance the quality of this bread. First, start with BIG cloves of garlic. Second, use REAL olives, not the tinny-tasting canned ones. Third, use a good-quality olive oil. A nice item to keep around the kitchen is a bottle of olive oil infused with fresh rosemary and garlic, which is very special for making any type of focaccia or pizza.

SERVES 8 TO 10

FOR THE DOUGH
1¼ teaspoons yeast
2 cups all-purpose flour
½ teaspoon salt

¾ cup water
2 tablespoons olive oil

Put all the ingredients in the machine, program for Dough, Basic Dough, or Manual, and press Start.

TO FINISH THE FOCACCIA
2 tablespoons olive oil
Salt to taste
Freshly ground black pepper to taste
12 garlic cloves, roasted (see page 77)

½ cup pitted olives: black colossal, green Spanish, Kalamata, or Italian or Greek oil-cured

Preheat the oven to 400°F.
When the dough cycle is completed, transfer the dough to a lightly floured working surface and let it rest for 5 minutes. Roll the dough to a 10-inch circle, then transfer it to a lightly floured cookie sheet. Brush the surface of the dough with the olive oil and then sprinkle with the salt and pepper. Lay out the garlic and olives over the top and let the dough rise for an additional 5 minutes. Bake for 20 minutes, or until lightly browned. Serve hot, warm, or at room temperature, cut into wedges.

To Roast Garlic Cloves

Separate the cloves from the bulb and do not peel the skin away from them. Toss the cloves in a small amount of olive oil. Place the cloves in a heavy ovenproof pan (cast-iron is ideal) and roast them for about 20 minutes in a 350°F oven. Remove the pan from the oven and cool the cloves; once they are cool enough to handle, remove their skins and they are ready to use.

Alternatively, you can use a garlic roaster, which is a terra-cotta container available in gourmet shops and by mail order (page 301).

Fresh Rosemary Onion Focaccia

Now that most markets carry fresh herbs year-round, there is no excuse to wait to make this bread. This is classic focaccia at its best: sweet onions, the country scent of fresh herbs, a hearty crust punctuated with bits of browned onions, moist chewy bread—in short, perfection.

You can serve this rustic loaf hot from the oven, or at room temperature slathered with goat cheese, or you can use it to make crostini, Italian grilled sandwiches.

While focaccia is best eaten the day it's made, it's fine toasted the next day. The trick is to keep it at room temperature, not in the refrigerator. If you wish to freeze this focaccia, cool it first, then wrap it airtight in plastic wrap—you can freeze it for six months. Defrost it while still wrapped.

This dough can be made up to forty-eight hours ahead of time. Place it in a large well-oiled bowl, cover with oiled plastic wrap, and refrigerate until you're ready to roll it out and bake it. Or, you can roll out the dough, cover it with oiled plastic wrap, and refrigerate it for its final rise, or even overnight.

SERVES 6 TO 8

FOR THE DOUGH

1 large Spanish onion (about 10 ounces), peeled, cut into eighths, and cooked in 2 tablespoons olive oil (see the Hint)	3 cups all-purpose flour
	2 teaspoons salt
	1/3 cup olive oil
1 tablespoon yeast	1 1/4 cups water
1/2 cup cornmeal	1/3 cup fresh rosemary leaves

Place all the ingredients except the cooked onion in the machine, program for Dough or Manual, and press Start. At the end of the final knead, add the onion (but not the liquid) to the machine. Restart and knead only until the onion is roughly mixed in. The dough will be wet and the onion will remain in clumps, sticking out of the dough. Turn the dough out on a well-floured board and knead briefly by hand to form a ball. This is peasant bread, and the dough will reflect that.

Oil a pizza pan or baking sheet. Place the dough on the prepared pan and pat it into a 12-inch disk. Coat the top of the dough with the onion juices. Cover with plastic wrap and let it rise either at room temperature until doubled in bulk, or in the refrigerator overnight. A long cold rise in the refrigerator will result in a more flavorful bread with a heartier interior.

TO FINISH THE FOCACCIA

1 to 2   tablespoons olive oil or garlic oil   Freshly ground black pepper
          Coarse salt

Preheat the oven to 450°F with the rack in the center position. Just before baking the dough, use your fingertips to gently make indentations in the surface. Drizzle on the oil and then sprinkle with salt and pepper. Bake for 10 minutes, then reduce the oven to 350°F and bake for another 12 to 15 minutes, or until the focaccia is golden brown.

Serve hot or at room temperature.

HINT: *You can prepare the onion either in a microwave or on the stove top. In a microwave: Place the onion and oil in a microwavable bowl. Cover the bowl with plastic wrap and microwave for 8 to 12 minutes, or until the onion is very soft and has just started to turn golden. Let the onion stay in the covered dish to cool. On the stove top: Heat the oil in a skillet. Add the onion and sauté over medium heat, stirring occasionally, until the onion is very soft and has just started to turn golden. Allow the onion to cool in the pan. When the onion is cooled, strain off the cooking liquid into a small bowl, pressing down on the onion to release as much liquid as possible.*

Carrot, Sweet Potato, and Ginger Focaccia

So, you bought a juicer before you bought your bread machine. Haul it out and whip up a loaf of the most healthful, tastiest (not to mention prettiest) bread you've ever had. If you don't have a juicer, look no further than your local health food store for carrot juice. You can use fresh or canned sweet potatoes in this recipe, but if you do use canned, buy the unseasoned variety.

This gaily colored focaccia is best eaten the day it is made; however, it can be frozen and eaten at another time. Cool it completely, then wrap it airtight in plastic wrap—it can be frozen for up to six months. Defrost it wrapped, then refresh it in a 300°F oven for fifteen minutes.

SERVES 8

FOR THE DOUGH

1	tablespoon yeast		1	cup (8 ounces) carrot juice
2⅓	cups all-purpose flour		2	tablespoons minced fresh
1	cup whole wheat flour			gingerroot
1½	teaspoons salt		1	tablespoon honey
4	tablespoons nonfat dry milk		¼	cup vegetable oil
1	cup (9 ounces) cooked, mashed sweet potatoes, fresh or canned			

Place all the ingredients in the machine, program for Dough or Manual, and press Start. The dough will be extremely wet. At the end of the final knead, turn the dough out onto a moderately floured work space and knead it briefly to form a ball. Place the dough in a lightly oiled bowl, cover with lightly oiled plastic wrap, and refrigerate for at least 1 hour or as long as overnight.

TO FINISH THE FOCACCIA

1 to 2 tablespoons mild toasted sesame oil
Coarse salt to taste

Freshly ground black pepper to taste

Oil or spray with nonstick vegetable spray a 12-inch pizza pan. Place the dough in the center of the pan and use your hands to press it out to a 12-inch circle. Cover the dough with a clean cloth and place it in a warm place to rise until doubled in bulk.

Preheat the oven to 450°F with the rack in the center position. Just before placing the dough in the oven, use your fingertips to make indentations in the surface. Drizzle with the sesame oil and sprinkle with the salt and pepper.

Bake 10 minutes at 450°F, then lower the oven to 350°F and bake an additional 15 minutes, or until the top is a deep golden color. Serve hot or at room temperature.

HINT: *Split the focaccia to make sandwiches with grilled vegetables, or toast it and spread it with herbed cream cheese.*

Classic Roasted Potato and Onion Focaccia

This beautiful focaccia is the perfect thing to serve with creamed soup on a cold, blustery day, and equally good toted along on a picnic, where it teams up well with salad and cheese. Roasting brings out the natural flavor in vegetables, and nowhere is it more evident than in this intensely flavored mixture of new potatoes and sweet onions.

SERVES 12

FOR THE DOUGH
2	teaspoons yeast	1	cup lukewarm water
2½	cups all-purpose flour	¼	stick (1 ounce) unsalted butter
1	tablespoon sugar	¼	cup olive oil
1½	teaspoons salt		

Place all the ingredients in the machine, program for Manual, Dough, or Basic Dough, and press Start. Check the dough 10 minutes before the end of the second kneading cycle; it should be a smooth, sticky ball. Adjust the consistency with flour or water as necessary.

FOR THE TOPPING
2	medium-to-large onions (5 to 6 ounces each)	¼	cup olive oil
1½	pounds small new potatoes (red or white)		

Peel the onions and cut them into 1-inch chunks; separate the layered pieces. Steam the potatoes till barely tender; the amount of time this takes will depend on the size of the potatoes.

Pour the olive oil into the bottom of an 18 × 13-inch sheet pan or other large pan with 1-inch sides. Place the potatoes and onions into the pan in one layer, and use a spatula to toss them in the oil. Place the pan in a preheated 375°F oven and bake for 50 minutes to 1 hour, turning once, or until the potatoes and onions are golden brown but not at all burned.

TO FINISH THE FOCACCIA

3	tablespoons olive oil		1/2	teaspoon coarsely ground black
1/2	teaspoon coarse salt			pepper
1	teaspoon rosemary			

When the machine has completed its cycle, transfer the dough to a lightly floured work surface. Roll or pat it into a rectangle that will fit into a large 18 × 13-inch sheet pan or a pan with an equivalent area. Pour 2 tablespoons of the olive oil into the bottom of the pan and transfer the dough to the pan. Rub the remaining 1 tablespoon olive oil onto the dough and let it rest for 20 minutes. Gently place the potatoes and onions onto the dough. Sprinkle with the salt, rosemary, and pepper. Let the dough rest for an additional 20 minutes while you preheat your oven to 425°F.

Bake the focaccia for 15 minutes, or until it's golden brown all over. Remove the pan from the oven and transfer the focaccia to a wire rack to cool (if you leave it in the pan it'll get soggy).

You may notice an example of "the incredible shrinking dough" when you put the dough into the pan. A well-developed dough—one in which the gluten has really been "exercised" by vigorous kneading, such as occurs in the bread machine—has a tendency to shrink back to its original shape after it's been rolled out. When you put the dough onto an oiled surface, as you do here, the oil "greases the skids," as it were, and the dough shrinks before your very eyes. To counteract this shrinking act, roll the dough out a bit larger than the size you actually want, then let it sit for 10 minutes before putting it in the pan. It'll shrink all it wants to during that 10 minutes and be ready to behave when you put it in the pan.

Mediterranean Roasted Vegetable Focaccia

You know how the vegetables in your garden all ripen at once, and you've got a million things to do, and you feel so guilty you can almost hear the beans and zucchini calling "Pick us, we're dying!" Or every morning at work there's another brown grocery bag from someone else's garden, filled with peppers and tomatoes, labeled "Free, take me"? Ah, that's the time to make this focaccia, with its incredible oven-roasted melange of intensely flavored onions, peppers, tomatoes, carrots, potatoes—whatever is presently overflowing from the earth.

Oven roasting—a slow, steady, lengthy cooking—evaporates most of the liquid from vegetables, leaving only their often-sweet and always intense essence. Vegetables prepared in this way are wonderful eaten exactly as is, with perhaps the merest hint of salt, but you may also bake them atop focaccia, thereby adding a delightfully crunchy-chewy base to what is already a sublime dish.

SERVES 12

FOR THE DOUGH

2 teaspoons yeast	1½ teaspoons salt
2½ cups all-purpose flour	1 cup lukewarm water
1 teaspoon sugar	6 tablespoons olive oil

Place all the ingredients in the machine, program for Manual, Dough, or Basic Dough, and press Start. Check the dough 10 minutes before the end of the second kneading cycle; it should be a smooth, sticky ball. Adjust the consistency with flour or water as necessary.

FOR THE TOPPING

½ cup olive oil	1½ pounds onions, cut into 1-inch pieces
2½ pounds cherry or plum tomatoes; cherry tomatoes cut in half, plum tomatoes cut into ½-inch slices	
1½ pounds green bell peppers or a mixture of green and sweet red peppers, cut into 1-inch pieces	

Divide the olive oil between 2 large flat baking pans. Place the vegetables, in a single layer, in the 2 prepared pans. Put the pans in a preheated 300°F oven and bake the vegetables for 1½ to 2 hours, or until they're golden brown but haven't yet begun to turn black (you'll need to watch the onions more closely than the tomatoes or the peppers). Remove the pans from the oven and allow the vegetables to cool to lukewarm.

TO FINISH THE FOCACCIA

1	teaspoon dried basil	1	tablespoon olive oil
¼	teaspoon salt		

When the machine has completed its cycle, transfer the dough to a lightly oiled work surface. Roll or pat it into a large rectangle, about 17 × 12 inches or the equivalent. Transfer the dough to a large, lightly greased cookie sheet or other flat pan. Let it rest for 10 minutes, then pat it back to its original shape and size if it's shrunk.

You should have about 4 cups of oven-dried vegetables; layer them evenly on the dough. Sprinkle them with the basil and salt, then drizzle with the olive oil. Drape the dough gently with lightly greased plastic wrap and allow it to rise for 40 minutes, or until it's puffy.

Bake the focaccia in a preheated 425°F oven for 15 minutes, or until the crust is golden brown. Remove it from the oven, transfer it from the pan to a wire rack, and allow it to rest for 10 minutes, or until it's cool enough to handle. Cut it into 4 × 4-inch squares and serve.

The ideal tool for cutting chunky focaccia—focaccia laden with big pieces of vegetables—is a clean pair of scissors. Not short-bladed kitchen scissors, but a good, big pair of shears. Lift one corner of the focaccia and begin to cut; the scissors allow you to maneuver around the bigger vegetable chunks much more easily than a knife or even a rolling pizza wheel does.

Smoked Fish and Red Onion Focaccia

Good-quality smoked fish—firm, moist, and flavorful—is always a welcome addition to an appetizer spread. But it doesn't have to be offered solely with crackers. These thin focaccie, baked quickly in a very hot oven, provide a cracker-like but more substantial base for smoked fish, which we team up here with red onion, horseradish, and cream. Bring on the wine!

SERVES 12 TO 16 AS AN APPETIZER; 8 AS A MAIN COURSE

FOR THE DOUGH

2	teaspoons yeast	1½	teaspoons salt
2	teaspoons sugar	1	cup lukewarm water
2½	cups all-purpose flour	¼	cup olive oil

Place all the ingredients in the machine, program for Manual, Dough, or Basic Dough, and press Start. Check the dough 10 minutes before the end of the second kneading cycle; it should be smooth and soft, though able to hold its shape. Adjust the consistency with flour or water as necessary.

FOR THE TOPPING

12	ounces smoked fish	⅔	cup heavy cream
1	medium red onion (about 5 ounces)	⅛	teaspoon salt
		1	tablespoon prepared horseradish

Chop or tear the fish into 1-inch pieces. Peel the onion, cut it into ⅛-inch-thick slices, and separate the slices into rings. In a small bowl, stir together the cream, salt, and horseradish.

TO FINISH THE FOCACCIA

2 tablespoons olive oil

When the machine has completed its cycle, transfer the dough to a lightly oiled work surface and divide it into 2 pieces. Working with 1 piece at a time, roll the dough to a 12-inch round and transfer it to a pizza pan or cookie sheet. Brush each round with 1 tablespoon olive oil and cover with lightly oiled plastic wrap. Set the dough aside to rest for 15 minutes while you preheat your oven to 450°F.

Bake the focaccie for 5 minutes, then remove them from the oven. Top each focaccia with half of the fish and half of the onions, then drizzle with half of the horseradish cream. Return the focaccie to the oven and bake for an additional 5 minutes, or until they're golden brown. Remove them from the oven and transfer them to a wire rack to cool slightly before cutting and serving.

You may also make this focaccia with smoked shellfish, such as oysters or mussels. Even if you're not a fish or shellfish fan, screw up your courage and try some of the smoked variety; it's an entirely different and wonderful taste treat.

Stuffed Rosemary Focaccia

Just when you thought things couldn't get better bread-wise, along comes a whole new concept: two layers of rosemary-scented dough surrounding a savory filling of oil-cured olives, sun-dried tomatoes, and cream cheese (or goat cheese if you wish). The cream cheese makes a smooth mild filling while the goat cheese has a more assertive flavor. Think of this as a pizza with hidden filling.

The focaccia dough can be made up to three days ahead, placed in large plastic bag or in an oiled bowl and covered with plastic wrap, and refrigerated. Alternatively, the cooled baked focaccia can be wrapped in plastic and frozen for three months. Defrost the wrapped focaccia at room temperature, then warm it in a 250°F oven for fifteen minutes.

SERVES 8 TO 10

FOR THE DOUGH

1	tablespoon yeast		1	teaspoon dried rosemary or 1
3	cups all-purpose flour			tablespoon fresh rosemary leaves
1½	teaspoons salt		¼	cup olive oil
1	teaspoon coarsely ground black pepper		1¼	cups water

Place all the ingredients in the machine, program for Manual or Dough, and press Start. Add just enough extra water, if necessary, to make a soft, slightly tacky dough. At the end of the final knead, remove the dough from the machine to a lightly floured work space. Knead the dough several times, adding just enough flour to keep it from sticking to the surface. Cover it with a clean cloth while you prepare the filling.

TO FINISH THE FOCACCIA

½	cup oil-packed sun-dried tomatoes, drained and cut into ½-inch pieces		4	ounces cream cheese or goat cheese
⅓	cup black oil-cured olives, pitted and cut in half		2	tablespoons oil from the tomatoes Coarse salt

Spray a 9- or 10-inch springform pan with nonstick vegetable spray or coat it lightly with vegetable oil. Cut the dough in half and stretch or roll one half to a 9- or 10-inch circle. Fit the circle into the bottom of the prepared pan. Sprinkle the dough with the tomatoes, the olives, and finally, pinches of the cream cheese or crumbles of the goat cheese, leaving a 1-inch border of dough around the circumference. Moisten the outer edge of the dough with water.

Roll the remaining dough out to a circle the same size as the first and place it over the filling. Pinch the edges of the 2 pieces of dough to close. Use the point of a knife to cut three $1/2$-inch vent holes in the top piece of dough, cover the pan with a piece of plastic wrap, and set it in a warm place to rise for 30 minutes, or until doubled in bulk.

Preheat the oven to 475°F with the rack in the center position. Just before you place the pan in the oven, press down lightly with your fingertips to make indentations in the top of the dough. Drizzle on the tomato oil and sprinkle with the salt. Bake for 20 to 25 minutes, or until the top is golden brown. Release the springform sides and allow the focaccia to cool for 10 minutes before cutting. Serve hot or at room temperature.

Focaccia with Greens

Cooked greens—escarole, dandelion, chicory, or whatever's fresh—are a favorite part of many Italian meals. Greens can be simply sautéed in olive oil with a bit of salt and pepper, then scooped up with a piece of flat, fried baking powder bread. Or they can be gussied up with other ingredients and presented in a bit fancier fashion—as in this dish, a two-crusted focaccia combining spinach with some other very disparate ingredients.

Serve this warm in thin wedges, as part of a bounteous hot and cold antipasto, or serve it alone, at room temperature, with a glass of light, sweet white wine.

SERVES 8

FOR THE DOUGH

1½	teaspoons yeast	1½	teaspoons salt
1½	teaspoons sugar	1	cup plus 2 tablespoons lukewarm
2	cups all-purpose flour		water
½	cup semolina flour	3	tablespoons olive oil

Place all the ingredients in the machine, program for Manual or Dough, and press Start. Check the dough midway through the second kneading; it should have formed a relaxed ball, soft to the touch.

FOR THE FILLING

4 to 6	garlic cloves (to taste), minced	¼	cup golden raisins
¼	cup olive oil	1	2¼-ounce can sliced pitted black
2	10-ounce packages frozen spinach,		olives, drained, or ½ cup sliced
	defrosted and squeezed dry, or		pitted black olives
	enough fresh spinach or other	4	anchovy fillets, rinsed and finely
	greens, cleaned, coarsely chopped,		chopped
	and steamed, to yield 2 cups	1	teaspoon coarsely ground black
1	tablespoon capers		pepper
¼	cup pine nuts	¼	teaspoon salt

While the machine is preparing the dough, make the filling. In a large frying pan, sauté the garlic in the oil until it just begins to color. Add the remaining ingredients, stirring 2 to 3 minutes, until well blended. Remove the pan from the heat and set aside.

TO FINISH THE FOCACCIA

When the machine has completed its cycle, remove the dough from the pan and punch it down on a lightly oiled work surface. Divide the dough in half.

Using olive oil, lightly oil a 12-inch flat pizza pan. Roll one piece of the dough out to a 13-inch round. Transfer the round to the pizza pan. Spread the filling evenly over the dough, leaving a ½-inch border. Roll the remaining piece of dough out to a 12-inch circle. Place this circle over the filling and fold the edge of the bottom piece over the edge of the top piece, crimping to seal.

Cover the focaccia with lightly oiled plastic wrap and set it aside to rest for ½ hour while you preheat your oven to 400°F.

Bake the focaccia for 25 minutes, or until it's a deep golden brown. Remove the pan from the oven, slide the focaccia off the pan onto a cooling rack, and let it cool for 10 to 15 minutes, or until you can handle it without burning your fingers. Cut it into wedges and serve.

Semolina flour, a light gold flour milled from durum wheat, is most often used to make pasta. Here it gives a slightly golden hue to the focaccia crust. You may use all all-purpose flour if semolina isn't available; or for a fine-textured, softer crust, use all semolina. Semolina flour is available at Italian markets, some health food stores, and through mail-order sources.

Betsy Cunningham's Shredded Wheat Focaccia

Betsy Cunningham of Wellesley, Massachusetts, was kind enough to share this special recipe that comes from her mother. Originally it was a recipe for bread, but I took the liberty of changing a few ingredients to make it into focaccia. The texture and taste are hearty and wholesome—I particularly like to serve this with a thick slice of first-rate Cheddar cheese. I love the contrast it provides with sweet nuggets of raisins, but if you're not wild about raisins, leave them out.

This bread will keep for several days if stored in a plastic bag after cooling. It also freezes quite well, wrapped the same way. Defrost it still wrapped.

SERVES 8 TO 10

FOR THE DOUGH

1	tablespoon yeast	4	tablespoons nonfat dry milk
2	large shredded wheat biscuits, crumbled	2	tablespoons corn oil
1½	teaspoons salt	¼	cup molasses
1	cup whole wheat flour	1⅓	cups water
2½	cups all-purpose flour	½	cup raisins (optional)

Place all the ingredients except the raisins in the machine, program for Dough, Basic Dough, or Manual, and press Start. The dough should be fairly soft and form a discrete ball at the end of 4 minutes of kneading. At the end of the final cycle, add the raisins and start the machine again, allowing it to knead only until the raisins are incorporated.

TO FINISH THE FOCACCIA

	Cornmeal for dusting	1	teaspoon each coarse salt and
2	tablespoons vegetable oil		freshly ground pepper

At the end of the final cycle, remove the dough, flatten it into a 10-inch disk and place it on a pizza paddle or baking sheet that has been lightly dusted with cornmeal. Cover it with a clean cloth and allow it to rise in a warm place until almost doubled in bulk.

Preheat the oven to 425°F with the rack or a pizza stone in the center position. Just before baking, use your fingertips to gently make ¼-inch indentations over the entire surface of the dough, drizzle it with oil, and sprinkle with salt and pepper. Bake the focaccia for 16 to 18 minutes, or until deep brown. Serve hot or at room temperature.

HINT: *This bread is perfect for tuna salad sandwiches. I make mine with Italian olive oil–packed tuna, a few capers, and a squirt of lemon juice.*

Filled Breads, Braids, Twists, and Sandwiches

Zeppole

Zeppole are Italian pastries traditionally served during Christmas, especially on Christmas Eve day while everyone's waiting to go to midnight mass; the afternoon is passed away with coffee, conversation, and something to nibble on. The classic combination of pine nuts, raisins, and anchovies sounds a bit strange, but it's a pretty simple, and tasty, marriage of salt, sweet, and crunchy. (If you're squeamish about the combination, make some zeppole with just anchovies and the others with pine nuts and raisins.)

A plain flour-and-water yeast dough is most traditional, but some cooks add a potato and potato water, milk, butter or margarine, and egg to make a softer, more doughnutlike zeppole. That's the route we've chosen here.

MAKES 32 ZEPPOLE

FOR THE DOUGH

1½	teaspoons yeast
3	cups all-purpose flour
1	tablespoon sugar
1¼	teaspoons salt
1	egg
½	stick (2 ounces) margarine

½	cup potato water (water in which potatoes have been boiled)
1	medium potato (about 5 ounces), riced or mashed (a scant 1 cup)
¼	cup milk

Place all the ingredients in the machine, program for Manual, Dough, or Basic Dough, and press Start. Check the dough 10 minutes before the end of the second knead cycle; it should be soft and supple though not sticky. If it appears hard or lumpy, add an additional tablespoon or 2 of milk or potato water.

TO FINISH THE ZEPPOLE

	Vegetable oil for frying
1	2-ounce can anchovies
3	tablespoons pine nuts

½	cup golden raisins
	Sugar (optional for anchovyless zeppole)

When the machine has completed its cycle, transfer the dough to a lightly oiled work surface. Divide the dough into 4 pieces. Divide each of the 4 pieces into 8 pieces, giving you a total of 32 small pieces of dough.

Pour vegetable oil into a heavy pot or thermostatically controlled frying pan to a depth of 3 inches. (You may also use lard or vegetable shortening if you wish.) Begin to heat the oil over medium-high heat; your eventual frying temperature should be between 365° and 370°F.

Drain the anchovies, rinse them well, and divide each anchovy in half; you should have 32 pieces. If not, divide some of the bigger halves in half again.

Pick up 1 of the pieces of dough, flatten it to a 2- to 2½-inch circle, and place an anchovy piece, 4 pine nuts, and 3 raisins in the middle of the circle. Gather the sides of the circle together and seal; roll the dough between your palms to form a 4-inch log. Repeat until you have 6 to 8 logs, or as many as will comfortably fit into the frying pan.

Line a cookie sheet with newspaper, then with paper towels. Fry the logs for 2 minutes, turn them over, and fry them an additional 2 minutes. Remove them from the pan and set them on the paper to drain. Repeat with the remaining pieces of dough. If you've made any with just raisins and pine nuts, you can roll these in granulated sugar.

Mashed potatoes or potato water, water in which potatoes have been boiled, are often called for as an ingredient in yeast breads. The starch in the potatoes (and their boiling water) acts as a yeast food, helping the bread to rise, and also produces what's called a "moist crumb," the distinctive moist, tender texture found in "potato breads."

Pepperoni Bread

Simple folds create an intricately layered bread filled with pepperoni, onions, mushrooms, and cheese. This bread served warm makes a delicious light supper or luncheon entrée; thinly sliced, it makes a great appetizer. Served at room temperature, it makes an elegant addition to any picnic basket. Leftover bread can be stored in a plastic bag in the refrigerator for two to three days. The cooled bread can be frozen wrapped in foil inside a plastic bag. Defrost it still wrapped.

SERVES 8 TO 10 AS AN APPETIZER; 4 TO 6 AS A LIGHT MEAL

FOR THE DOUGH

1	tablespoon yeast	$^1/_2$	teaspoon basil
3	cups all-purpose flour	$^1/_2$	teaspoon dry mustard
1	teaspoon salt	1	cup warm water
1	tablespoon sugar	$^1/_2$	stick (2 ounces) unsalted butter or
$^1/_2$	teaspoon oregano		margarine

Place all the ingredients in the machine, program for Dough, Basic Dough, or Manual, and press Start. The dough will look sticky but feel oily to the touch.

FOR THE FILLING

1	tablespoon olive oil	1	medium onion, thinly sliced
1	tablespoon unsalted butter or	3	cups (8 ounces) thinly sliced
	margarine		mushrooms

Heat the olive oil and butter over medium-high heat and add the onion slices, cooking for 3 minutes, or until they are slightly translucent. Add the mushrooms and continue cooking for 4 to 5 minutes, or until the onion slices and mushrooms have wilted and the liquid has evaporated. Cool this mixture while you roll out the dough.

TO FINISH THE BREAD

1	tablespoon garlic oil	1	egg beaten with 1 tablespoon
1	cup (4 ounces) thinly sliced		water
	pepperoni	2	tablespoons Parmesan cheese
1	cup (4 ounces) grated mozzarella		
	cheese		

Transfer the dough to a work surface lightly sprayed with nonstick vegetable spray. Let the dough rest for 10 minutes, covered with a clean towel, and then roll it from the center to the edges until you have an 18- to 20-inch circle. Spread the dough with the garlic oil. Distribute the pepperoni slices evenly over the dough, followed by the mushroom and onion mixture and then the mozzarella cheese.

Fold in the sides of the circle to form a 6½-inch square. Cover a baking sheet with foil and grease or spray it lightly with vegetable spray. Lift the square onto the prepared sheet and flatten it to an 8-inch square. Cover it with a clean cloth or plastic wrap and let it rise for 1 hour, or until slightly rounded.

Preheat the oven to 375°F with the rack in the center position. Generously brush the egg glaze over the top of the loaf. Sprinkle with the Parmesan cheese and bake for 30 to 35 minutes, or until it is a deep golden color and crusty on the top. It is better to overbake than underbake it.

Baked Samosas

Traditionally samosas are deep-fried, but for today's conscientious eaters we are providing a baked variation. The potato and green pea filling is brightly accented with coriander, cumin, and black pepper and is enclosed in a very thin flaky crust. Samosas make great picnic fare, a good vegetarian entrée, or an interesting lunch.

The samosas can be frozen, after cooling, tightly wrapped in plastic wrap inside a plastic bag. Defrost them still covered. Defrosted or leftover samosas should be reheated in a medium oven for five to ten minutes.

MAKES EIGHT 5- TO 6-INCH SAMOSAS

FOR THE DOUGH

3	cups all-purpose flour	$1/2$	cup plus 2 tablespoons evaporated milk or more to make a firm ball
$2^1/2$	teaspoons yeast		
$3/4$	teaspoon salt	3	tablespoons unsalted butter or margarine
2	teaspoons sugar		

Place all the ingredients in the machine, program for Dough or Manual, and press Start. The dough will be quite firm but it should be moist enough to hold together. Make the filling while the dough is rising.

FOR THE FILLING

1	medium Idaho potato (about 6 to 8 ounces), cut into $1/2$-inch cubes	2	teaspoons fresh gingerroot, peeled and finely chopped
1	cup fresh or frozen peas	1	teaspoon dried coriander
2	tablespoons vegetable oil	$1/2$	teaspoon ground cumin
1	large all-purpose yellow onion (about 8 ounces), finely chopped	$1/4$	teaspoon freshly ground black pepper
2	garlic cloves, finely chopped	$1/4$	teaspoon salt

Place the potato cubes in a small saucepan and cover with water. Bring to a boil over medium-high heat, lower the heat to medium, and continue cooking for 10 minutes, or until they have slightly softened but are not cooked through. Add the peas to the boiling water for the last minute of cooking. Drain the water from the potato cubes and peas.

Heat the oil in a large frying pan set over medium-high heat and add the onions, garlic, and ginger. Sauté until the onions are translucent. Add the potato cubes, peas, coriander, cumin, pepper, and salt and stir until well mixed. Remove from the heat and cool slightly.

TO FINISH THE SAMOSAS
 1 egg beaten with 1 tablespoon water

Turn the finished dough out on a lightly floured surface and divide it into 8 equal balls. Let the balls rest 10 minutes.

Preheat the oven to 350°F with the rack in the center position. Lightly spray a large baking sheet with vegetable spray. On a lightly oiled work surface, roll each ball of dough to a 7-inch circle, rolling from the middle toward the edge. Distribute the filling evenly among the circles, about 3 heaping tablespoons for each one. Lightly moisten the edge of each circle with water and fold over to form a semicircle. Press the edges together firmly. Fold the pressed edge inward toward the filling and press with your fingertips to seal.

Lift the samosas onto the prepared baking sheet and generously brush the tops with the egg glaze. Bake the samosas for 15 minutes, or until they are a rich golden brown. Serve hot from the oven.

HINTS: *Samosas may also be made in a smaller version (sixteen 3-inch turnovers) as little appetizers.*

Both the large and small versions may also be deep-fried, a few at a time, in 1 cup of vegetable oil.

Broccoli and Cheese Calzone

These calzone are prepared with a small amount of whole wheat flour that adds a slight nutty flavor to an already flavorful combination. Enjoy these hot from the oven or warm or even at room temperature, though they are not nearly as good the next day.

MAKES 6 CALZONE

FOR THE DOUGH

2¼	teaspoons yeast		1½	teaspoons salt
2½	cups all-purpose flour		1	cup plus 2 tablespoons water
½	cup whole wheat flour		2	tablespoons olive oil

Place all the ingredients in the machine, program for Dough, Basic Dough, or Manual, and press Start.

TO FINISH THE CALZONE

1	medium onion, chopped		2	cups grated cheese (mozzarella or
5	tablespoons olive oil			Monterey Jack is just fine)
4	cups (¾ pound) broccoli florets			Olive oil for brushing
	Salt to taste			
	Freshly ground black pepper			
	to taste			

Sauté the onion in the olive oil over medium heat until it is a light golden brown. Add the broccoli and continue cooking until tender. Season with salt and pepper. Let the broccoli mixture cool.

When the dough cycle is completed, transfer the dough to a lightly floured work surface. Cut the dough into 6 even pieces, roll them into balls, and let them rest for 5 minutes. Roll out each piece of dough to a 6-inch circle. Distribute the broccoli filling evenly over the 6 circles and finally top the filling with the grated cheese. Brush the rims of the dough with water and fold the circles in half; they should look like half-moons. Twist the edges together or press them with the tines of a fork so the filling does not spill out during baking. Brush olive oil over the surface of the calzone and, with a sharp knife or scissors, cut a slit in the top of each calzone. Bake the calzone for 20 to 25 minutes, or until the tops are golden brown.

Pepperoni Pizza Roll

And you thought pepperoni pizza was a child of the 1950s! Well, Italian bakers have been preparing this stuffed version of the familiar flatbread favorite for generations. Its traditional horseshoe shape probably evolved from the size of the average cook's pan—this long, skinny loaf must be curved in on itself to fit onto a normal sheet or pizza pan.

SERVES 12 AS AN APPETIZER; 4 AS A MAIN COURSE

FOR THE DOUGH

$1\frac{1}{2}$ teaspoons yeast
$2\frac{1}{2}$ cups all-purpose flour
$1\frac{1}{2}$ teaspoons sugar

$1\frac{1}{2}$ teaspoons salt
1 cup water
$\frac{1}{4}$ cup olive oil

Place all of the ingredients in the machine, program for Manual, Dough, or Basic Dough, and press Start. About 10 minutes before the end of the second knead, check the dough; it should have formed a soft ball.

TO FINISH THE ROLL

8 ounces shredded mozzarella cheese
$\frac{1}{2}$ cup grated Parmesan cheese
1 large egg, lightly beaten

1 teaspoon coarsely ground black pepper
6 ounces pepperoni slices, cut into quarters

When the machine has completed its cycle, remove the dough, punch it down, and roll it out to a 26 × 18-inch rectangle.

In a small bowl, combine the mozzarella, Parmesan, beaten egg, and pepper. Spread this mixture evenly over the surface of the dough. Sprinkle the pepperoni atop the cheese mixture.

Starting with a long edge, roll the dough into a log. Transfer the log, seam side down, to a lightly greased 14-inch round pizza pan, curving it into a horseshoe shape. Tuck the ends under. Tent the dough with lightly greased plastic wrap and set it aside to rise for 1 to $1\frac{1}{2}$ hours, or until doubled in bulk.

Bake the roll in a preheated 350°F oven for 40 minutes, or until it's golden brown. Remove the roll from the oven and transfer it from the pan to a wire rack. Let the roll cool for 20 minutes before slicing.

Chèvre Roll

A goat's milk starter is easy to make and the resulting bread is an aromatic treat. This whole wheat roll wraps around a filling of goat cheese, sun-dried tomatoes, capers, and olive oil. You can serve it warm or at room temperature as a substantial addition to a buffet table or as an accompaniment to a bowl of egg lemon soup. The starter must be made at least twenty-four hours (or as long as one week) ahead.

This recipe makes two rolls. You might wish to freeze one for later. Cool it completely, then wrap it in several layers of plastic wrap. Defrost it still wrapped, then cover it loosely with foil and refresh it in a 300°F oven for fifteen minutes. The rolls can be frozen for three months.

SERVES 16 TO 20

FOR THE STARTER

³/₄ cup fresh goat's milk or 3 tablespoons powdered goat's milk dissolved in ³/₄ cup water	1 teaspoon yeast
	³/₄ cup rye flour

Heat the goat's milk to 90°F and stir in the yeast. When the yeast dissolves, stir in the flour, mixing well. Cover with plastic wrap and keep in a warm place for 12 hours, then refrigerate for 12 hours.

FOR THE DOUGH

2 teaspoons yeast	2 teaspoons fennel seeds
1 cup whole wheat flour	2 teaspoons dill seed
2 cups all-purpose flour, plus up to an additional ¹/₄ cup if needed	1 recipe Starter
1 tablespoon sugar	¹/₄ cup olive oil
2 teaspoons salt	2 extra-large eggs
	²/₃ cup water

Place all the ingredients in the machine, program for Dough or Manual, and press Start. The dough will be very wet and sticky. If after 4 to 5 minutes of kneading it does not form a discrete ball, add additional flour, up to ¹/₄ cup, until the dough no longer sticks to the bottom of the pan. At the end of the final rise, transfer the dough to a lightly oiled bowl, cover it with lightly oiled plastic wrap, and refrigerate it for at least 2 hours. This will make it easier to roll out this very moist dough.

TO FINISH THE ROLL

12	ounces goat cheese (plain or herbed), crumbled		1/4	cup olive oil
			2	tablespoons capers
2/3	cup oil-packed sun-dried tomatoes, cut into 1/2-inch pieces		1	egg beaten with 1 tablespoon water

Mix all the ingredients except the egg glaze in a small bowl and set it aside while you roll out the dough. Roll out the dough on a lightly floured board until it measures 26 × 16 inches, with a long side closest to you. Scatter the filling over the dough, leaving a 2-inch border on all sides. Starting at the far long end, roll the dough into a compact 26-inch cylinder. Tuck the 2 ends underneath and then cut the roll in half to form two 13-inch rolls. Place the rolls, at least 5 inches apart, on a lightly oiled heavy-duty baking sheet, cover with a clean towel, and allow them to rise in a warm place until doubled in bulk.

Preheat the oven to 425°F with the rack in the center position. Brush the tops of the rolls with the egg glaze and bake for 15 minutes at 425°F, then lower the heat to 350°F and continue baking another 30 minutes, or until the rolls are deep golden brown and the undersides are brown as well. If the tops seem to be browning too quickly, cover them loosely with foil. Cool the rolls on the pan for 15 minutes before slicing or placing on a rack to cool completely. Serve warm or at room temperature.

Chèvre, Tomato, and Garlic Braids

This lusty sandwich braid is not for the faint of heart. It features whole cloves of raw garlic, their bite tamed just a bit by thirty minutes in a medium oven. Assertive goat cheese and intensely flavored sun-dried tomatoes round out the filling of this braid, whose golden color comes from the semolina flour in the dough.

SERVES 6 GENEROUSLY

FOR THE DOUGH

2	teaspoons yeast		$1^{1}/_2$	teaspoons salt
2	cups semolina flour		1	cup plus 2 tablespoons
$^3/_4$	cup all-purpose flour			lukewarm water
2	teaspoons sugar		2	tablespoons olive oil

Place all the ingredients in the machine, program for Manual, Dough, or Basic Dough, and press Start. Check the dough 10 minutes before the end of the second kneading cycle; it should have formed a smooth, supple ball. Adjust by adding additional semolina flour or water as necessary.

When the machine has completed its cycle, transfer the dough to a lightly greased work surface.

TO FINISH THE BRAIDS

8	ounces sun-dried tomatoes in olive oil, drained, or dry sun-dried tomatoes, softened in boiling water		8	ounces goat cheese, crumbled
			$^1/_4$	cup olive oil
			2	teaspoons dried basil or $^1/_2$ cup packed fresh basil leaves, shredded
2	ounces whole peeled raw garlic cloves			

Divide the dough in half. Working with one half at a time, roll it into a 15 × 10-inch rectangle. Transfer the rectangle to a lightly greased cookie sheet and brush with olive oil.

Visually divide the rectangle into thirds, each 10 × 5 inches. Working on the middle third of the dough, and leaving 1 inch of space at each end, layer half of the tomatoes, half of the garlic cloves, then half of the goat cheese. Sprinkle with 1 teaspoon of the dried basil or $^1/_4$ cup of the fresh basil.

Using a rolling pizza wheel, a sharp knife, or a pair of scissors, make 6 evenly spaced 5-inch-long cuts in the dough, cutting from the edge of one of the unfilled sides just to where the filling starts. Repeat with the other unfilled side.

Fold the small piece of dough at each end of the filling over the filling. Alternating sides, cross the strips of dough over the filling, tucking them underneath the dough on the opposite side. Repeat the entire process with the other piece of dough.

Tent the braids with lightly greased plastic wrap and set them aside to rise for 1 hour, or until they're noticeably puffy.

Bake the braids in a preheated 350°F oven for 30 minutes, or until they're golden brown and the filling has started to bubble and ooze out. Remove the braids from the oven, transfer them to a wire rack, and allow them to cool for 10 minutes before cutting.

To soften dry sun-dried tomatoes (those not packed in olive oil), place them in a small bowl and cover with boiling water. Let them sit for 2 minutes, then drain. Use them immediately or cover them with olive oil and refrigerate.

Braided Crescia

Crescia, a traditional Italian bread, features two types of cheeses. In Italy, Parmesan and Romano, both grated into the dough, are the cheeses of choice. In this country, grated Parmesan is usually paired with a somewhat milder cheese— Cheddar or Gruyère—which is left in chunks to melt into the bread as it bakes. While most American recipes for crescia call for the cheese to be encased in the dough jelly roll style, here we braid the dough, which we feel makes a more interesting-looking loaf and also acts to better distribute the cheese throughout the bread.

SERVES 16

FOR THE DOUGH

1	tablespoon yeast	½	cup lukewarm buttermilk, fresh or
3	cups all-purpose flour		reconstituted from powder
1	teaspoon salt	¼	cup lukewarm water
1	teaspoon sugar	2	eggs
1	teaspoon coarsely ground black	½	stick (2 ounces) unsalted butter,
	pepper		cut into pieces
1	cup grated Parmesan cheese		

Place all the ingredients in the machine, program for Manual, Dough, or Basic Dough, and press Start.

TO FINISH THE CRESCIA
2   ounces sharp Cheddar cheese,
    cut into ½-inch cubes

When the machine has completed its cycle, transfer the dough to a lightly greased work surface. Divide the dough into 3 pieces and roll each piece into a 24-inch rope.

Braid the ropes together to form a braided loaf about 16 inches long. Transfer the loaf to a lightly greased baking sheet.

Tuck the cheese cubes in between and underneath the strands of the braid; push some of the cubes right into the dough. Cover the braid with a lightly greased sheet of plastic wrap and set it aside to rise till almost doubled in bulk, 1 to 1½ hours.

Bake the braid in a preheated 375°F oven for 30 to 35 minutes, or until the cheese has started to melt and the braid is a deep golden brown. Check the braid after 25 minutes; if it's as brown as you like it, cover it lightly with aluminum foil, shiny side up, till it's completely baked. Remove the crescia from the oven and transfer it to a wire rack to cool. You may serve it hot, warm, or at room temperature.

Why is it important to place the shiny side of aluminum foil up when you're using aluminum foil to prevent bread from overbrowning? Because the dull side actually absorbs heat, browning your bread faster, while the shiny side reflects heat.

Hot Chile Pepper Twists

This hot sandwich is a winner when you're looking for something different and easy to serve. Beans, olives, chiles, and cheese encased in cilantro-spiked cornmeal bread yield a hearty, filling roll that will satisfy vegetarians and meat eaters alike. And, a healthy plus: The complementary combination of beans and wheat flour yields a complete protein, every bit as nutritious as meat but without the fat and cholesterol.

SERVES 6 GENEROUSLY

FOR THE DOUGH

2	teaspoons yeast
1½	teaspoons sugar
2¼	cups all-purpose flour
½	cup yellow cornmeal
1½	teaspoons salt
1	cup plus 2 tablespoons lukewarm water
2	tablespoons vegetable oil, or, for a spicier sandwich, chili oil
⅓	cup lightly packed whole cilantro leaves

Place all the ingredients except the cilantro in the machine, program for Manual, Dough, or Basic Dough, and press Start. Program a kitchen timer to go off 2 minutes before the end of the machine's second kneading cycle and start the timer. Check the dough about 10 minutes before the end of the second kneading cycle; it should have formed a smooth, supple ball. Adjust by adding flour or water as necessary. When the kitchen timer goes off, add the cilantro.

While the dough is rising, ready the filling. When the machine has completed its cycle, transfer it to a lightly greased work surface.

TO FINISH THE TWISTS

1	16-ounce can black beans, pinto beans, refried beans, or "Mexican beans," drained if necessary
1	16-ounce can (1½ cups) small pitted black olives, drained (6 ounces drained weight)
1	4½-ounce can (½ cup) chopped green chiles
4	ounces (½ cup) tomato salsa
8	ounces (2 cups) shredded Monterey Jack cheese

Divide the dough in half. Working with one half at a time, roll it into a 15 × 10-inch rectangle. Transfer the rectangle to a lightly greased cookie sheet.

Visually divide the rectangle into thirds, each 10 × 5 inches. Working on the middle third of the dough, and leaving 1 inch of space at each end, layer on half the beans, half the olives, half the chiles, half the salsa, then half the cheese.

Using a rolling pizza wheel, a sharp knife, or a pair of scissors, make 6 evenly spaced 5-inch-long cuts in the dough, cutting from the edge of one of the unfilled sides just to where the filling starts. Repeat with the other unfilled side.

Fold the small piece of dough at each end of the filling over the filling. Alternating sides, cross the strips of dough over the filling, tucking them underneath the dough on the opposite side. Repeat the entire process with the other piece of dough.

Tent the twists with lightly greased plastic wrap and set them aside to rise for 1 hour, or until they're noticeably puffy.

Bake the twists in a preheated 375°F oven for 30 minutes, or until they're golden brown and the filling has started to bubble. Remove the twists from the oven, transfer them to a wire rack, and allow them to cool for 10 minutes before cutting.

Syrian Garden Ring

This elegant ring of crisp dough is filled with celery, onions, nuts, and raisins. It is large enough to feed a crowd as an appetizer. It also makes a good side dish to serve with stews or roast chicken. You can make it a day ahead, refrigerate it when cool, wrap it in foil, then reheat it in a 300°F oven for about fifteen minutes.

SERVES 15 TO 20 THINLY SLICED AS AN APPETIZER;
8 TO 12 AS A SIDE DISH

FOR THE DOUGH

1	tablespoon yeast	1	teaspoon sugar
3	cups all-purpose flour	1	cup warm water
3	tablespoons nonfat dry milk	¼	stick (1 ounce) unsalted butter
1	teaspoon salt	1	large egg

Place all the ingredients in the machine, program for Dough or Manual, and press Start. The dough will be smooth, moderately firm, and just slightly sticky to the touch. Make the filling while the dough is rising so that it has a chance to cool.

FOR THE FILLING

2	tablespoons olive oil	¼	teaspoon freshly ground black pepper
2	cups finely chopped sweet onions, such as Vidalia or Spanish	⅛	teaspoon cinnamon
1	cup finely chopped celery, stalks and well-rinsed and dried leaves	⅛	teaspoon cloves
¼	cup all-purpose flour	¼	cup pine nuts
1	teaspoon salt	¼	cup golden raisins
¼	teaspoon allspice	¼	cup parsley, finely chopped
		½	cup tahini sauce

Heat the oil in a large skillet over medium-high heat, add the onions and celery, and sauté for 3 to 4 minutes, or until they are translucent but not browned. Remove the skillet from the heat. Mix together the flour, salt, allspice, pepper, cinnamon, and cloves and stir into the celery mixture. Add the pine nuts, raisins, parsley, and tahini and stir until well mixed. Cool to lukewarm.

TO FINISH THE RING

¼	stick (1 ounce) unsalted butter or margarine, melted	1	egg beaten with 1 tablespoon water

Remove the dough to a lightly floured surface, cover it with a clean towel, and let it rest for 10 minutes. Roll the dough to a 27 × 10-inch rectangle and spread with the melted butter. Moisten the outer edges of the dough with water. Spread the filling over the dough, leaving a 1-inch border around the rim. Roll the dough up from a long side like a jelly roll. Seal the seam and the ends carefully, pinching them together so that they will not pull apart during baking.

Grease or spray a baking sheet with nonstick vegetable spray. Using a pastry scraper or wide spatula, lift and slide the filled roll onto the baking sheet, shaping it to form a ring. Moisten the ends of the roll evenly with a little water and join them together by pinching firmly. Using a very sharp knife or scissors, cut 1-inch-deep vents in the top of the ring every 2 inches all around. Be careful to cut only on the top of the ring and not down the sides or the ring may split apart while baking.

Cover the ring with a towel and allow it to rise in a warm place for 1 hour, or until gently puffed but not doubled in bulk.

Preheat the oven to 350°F with the rack in the center position. Generously brush the egg glaze over the ring. Bake for 35 to 40 minutes, or until very dark golden. Cool for 15 minutes before slicing. Serve warm or at room temperature.

Cheddar-Stuffed Taco Logs

These are fun to make with children—and since most kids love these flavors, the logs will disappear fast. Rectangles of whole wheat dough enclose a stick of Cheddar cheese and taco seasoning. After they are rolled up, they are placed next to each other in a baking dish. After rising and baking, the logs are pulled apart to eat.

MAKES 10 LOGS

FOR THE DOUGH

1	tablespoon yeast	1½	teaspoons salt
2	cups White Wheat flour	1	tablespoon sugar
	(page 5)	1⅓	cups water or more to make a
1	cup all-purpose flour		smooth, soft ball

Place all the ingredients in the machine, program for Dough, Basic Dough, or Manual, and press Start.

TO FINISH THE LOGS

2	egg whites beaten with 2	1	package taco seasoning mix
	tablespoons water	1	8-ounce brick Cheddar cheese

At the end of the final cycle, transfer the dough to a lightly oiled work space. Oil a 12 × 7-inch or 13 × 9-inch baking pan. Cut the brick of cheese into 10 sticks each measuring about 6 × ½ × ½ inches.

Roll the dough out to a 20 × 16-inch rectangle. Cut the rectangle in half the long way so you have two 20 × 8-inch rectangles. Cut each of these in 5 equal pieces so you have ten 8 × 4-inch rectangles.

Brush each piece of dough with a thin coat of the egg glaze. Sprinkle each with about ¼ teaspoon of the taco seasoning and then place a stick of cheese in the center. Fold the short ends in over the ends of the cheese, then fold the long ends over the cheese to completely enclose. Moisten the inside flap with a little more egg glaze and pinch the seam to secure.

Place the logs right next to each other on the prepared pan. Cover with a clean towel and allow them to rise in a warm place until doubled in bulk, about 30 to 40 minutes.

Preheat the oven to 400°F with the rack in the center position. Brush the tops of the logs with the remaining egg glaze and bake for 30 minutes, or until the tops are deep brown. Cool them slightly or completely before pulling them apart to eat.

Pesto and Sun-dried Tomato Galette

A galette is a wonderful yeasted tart stuffed with savory fillings. This tart is filled and folded free-form, with the fillings exposed, and baked to a nice golden brown. The galette in this recipe is the result of a refrigerator cleaning. It is just DIVINE.

Pesto and sun-dried tomatoes are best when eaten in their concentrated forms. This savory galette can be cut into wedges and enjoyed as an appetizer or as the main event, served with a salad and a glass of rich red wine.

SERVES 6 TO 8

FOR THE DOUGH

1½	teaspoons yeast	1	large egg
2¼	cups all-purpose flour	5	tablespoons unsalted butter,
¾	teaspoon salt		softened
1	teaspoon sugar	⅓	cup plus 3 tablespoons water

Place all the ingredients in the machine, program for Dough, and press Start.

TO FINISH THE GALETTE

1	cup Pesto (page 30)	Salt
18 to 20	sun-dried tomatoes	Freshly ground black pepper
2	tablespoons olive oil	

Preheat the oven to 400°F. When the dough cycle is finished, transfer the dough to a lightly floured surface. Let the dough rest for 5 minutes. Roll the dough to a 14-inch circle. After the dough has been rolled, transfer it onto a lightly oiled cookie sheet. Spread the pesto out with a spatula, leaving a 2-inch border. Top the pesto with the sun-dried tomatoes.

To fold the tart, slide your hand under an area of the dough and fold it in and over to cover the outer third of the filling, then repeat the folding around the entire galette. (Remember that the filling is exposed during the baking process.) Brush the dough with the olive oil and sprinkle on the salt and pepper around the rim of the dough. Let the galette rest for 5 minutes, then bake it for 30 minutes, or until it is a golden brown.

Roasted Scallion and Fresh Ginger Roulade

This special loaf is rolled around a filling of fragrant flavors often associated with Asian food. Try slicing it to make sandwiches filled with cold roast pork or grilled chicken dotted with hot mustard.

SERVES 8

FOR THE DOUGH

2	teaspoons yeast	1	tablespoon honey
2½	cups all-purpose flour	¼	stick (1 ounce) unsalted butter,
1¼	teaspoons salt		softened
1	cup water	1	teaspoon grated lime zest

Place all the ingredients in the machine, program for Manual, Dough, or Basic Dough, and press Start. The dough will pull away from the sides of the machine; however, it will be slightly sticky. While the dough is rising, prepare the scallions and ginger.

FOR THE SCALLIONS AND GINGER

15	fresh scallions	1	tablespoon freshly grated ginger
	Olive oil for brushing	1	tablespoon peanut oil
	Salt	⅛	teaspoon mild sesame oil
	Freshly ground black pepper		

Preheat the oven to 350°F.
Prepare the scallions by trimming away the dry outer leaves and cutting away the root end. Place the scallions on a baking sheet, lightly oil them, and season them lightly with salt and pepper. Place them in the oven and roast them for 12 to 15 minutes. The scallions should be soft and only slightly browned in some areas. Be careful not to over roast them; don't let the stalks get crisp. Remove the scallions from the oven and let them cool. In a small bowl, mix together the grated ginger and oils. Set aside.

TO FINISH THE ROULADE

Peanut oil for brushing	Freshly ground black pepper
Salt to taste	to taste

Raise the oven to 375°F with the rack in the center position. Lightly grease a 9 × 3-inch loaf pan. Set aside.

When the dough cycle is completed, transfer the dough to a lightly floured work surface, cover it with a clean towel, and let it rest for 5 minutes. Roll the dough into a 9 × 9-inch square. Brush the ginger and oil mixture over the surface of the dough, then lay out the scallions lengthwise across the surface.

Starting with the end closest to you, roll the dough up like a jelly roll. Pinch the seams together. Transfer the roll to the prepared loaf pan, cover with oiled plastic wrap, and let it rise for 25 to 30 minutes until the dough comes up to within 1/2 inch of the top of the pan. Brush the top of the loaf with peanut oil and sprinkle with salt and pepper. Bake for 30 to 35 minutes until golden brown. Remove the loaf from the pan and transfer it to a cooling rack to cool completely before slicing.

Parsley Cheese Buereks

Armenians are masters with bread doughs. Buereks or boeregs, which in Armenian means turnovers, can come in all sizes and shapes with all manner of fillings. Here a traditional combination of Muenster cheese, eggs, and parsley is wrapped in a light, thin, crisp dough. You can make a tiny version to use as appetizers, although it takes a lot of patience, and I've included variations for ten-inch and four-inch Buereks.

The Buereks can be assembled early in the day, refrigerated, and baked when needed. The baked Buereks can be refrigerated for two to three days or frozen, tightly wrapped inside a plastic bag. Defrost them still wrapped and refresh them by placing them on a baking sheet in a 350°F oven for fifteen minutes.

MAKES THIRTY-SIX 2-INCH TURNOVERS; TWELVE 4-INCH TURNOVERS;
THREE 10-INCH TURNOVERS

FOR THE DOUGH

2	teaspoons yeast	$1/2$	stick (2 ounces) unsalted butter or
$2^1/2$	cups all-purpose flour		margarine, cut into small pieces
1	teaspoon salt	2	large eggs
2	teaspoons sugar	$1/4$	cup water
2	tablespoons nonfat dry milk		

Place all the ingredients in the machine, program for Dough, Basic Dough, or Manual, and press Start. The dough will be smooth and not sticky after several minutes of kneading.

FOR THE FILLING

$1/2$	pound Muenster cheese	$1/4$	teaspoon salt
$2/3$	cup finely chopped parsley	$1/4$	teaspoon white pepper
1	large egg, beaten		

Keep the Muenster cheese refrigerated until you're ready to grate it or else it will be too soft; you can put it in the freezer for 10 minutes if necessary. Grate the cheese, either by hand or in a food processor, put it in a large bowl, and mix in the parsley, egg, salt, and pepper. Set the mixture aside.

TO FINISH THE BUEREKS

1	egg beaten with 1 tablespoon water	2	tablespoons sesame seeds

D ivide the dough into thirds. Roll each piece to a 12-inch circle.
For 2-inch Buereks: Cut twelve 3-inch circles from each larger circle, re-working the dough as necessary. Place a level teaspoon of filling in the center of each circle and fold the dough in half over the filling to form a half-moon shape. Pinch or use a fork to crimp the edge to seal the seam.

For 4-inch Buereks: Cut each 12-inch circle into quarters to create "triangle" shapes with a rounded bottom. Place 1 heaping tablespoon of filling in the center of each. Bring the straight sides of the triangle together over the filling and pinch the edges together to seal. Pinch the rounded edges to seal as well. Roll these pinched edges inward toward the filling about ½ inch. Crimp the folded edges like a pie crust by pinching them between your thumb and forefinger.

For 10-inch Buereks: Divide the filling among the three 12-inch circles. Fold each circle in half and pinch the edge to seal. Fold the pinched edge inward ½ inch toward the center. Crimp the folded edge like a pie crust by pinching it between your thumb and forefinger.

Preheat the oven to 350°F with the rack in the center position. Rise the Buereks while the oven preheats. Brush the egg glaze over the Buereks and sprinkle them with the sesame seeds. Bake the 2-inch Buereks for 10 to 12 minutes, the 4-inch Buereks for 15 to 18 minutes, and the 10-inch Buereks for 20 minutes, or until they are deep golden brown. Cool them for 10 minutes on the baking sheet and then remove them to wire racks to cool.

HINT: *Any leftover filling is great melted on bagels in a toaster oven.*

Herb and Cheese–Filled Kolache

Kolache, a sweet pastry native to eastern Europe, take a savory turn in this recipe, the traditional apricot or raisin filling giving way to a delightful home-made herbed cream cheese. While these may be served as a tasty accompaniment with before-dinner drinks, they're also substantial enough to qualify for the main-meal bread basket.

SERVES 12

FOR THE DOUGH

2	teaspoons yeast		1	egg
2	teaspoons sugar		$1/2$	stick (2 ounces) unsalted butter
1	teaspoon salt		$3/4$	cup buttermilk or yogurt
$2^1/2$	cups all-purpose flour		$1/4$	cup water

Place all the ingredients in the machine, program for Manual, Dough, or Basic Dough, and press Start. Check the dough 10 minutes before the end of the second kneading cycle; it should be smooth and supple. Adjust the consistency with flour or water as necessary.

FOR THE FILLING

1	egg		$1/2$	teaspoon parsley
8	ounces cream cheese		$1/4$	teaspoon thyme
2	large garlic cloves, minced		$1/4$	teaspoon freshly ground black
2	teaspoons minced chives			pepper
$3/4$	teaspoon chervil		$1/8$	teaspoon salt
$3/4$	teaspoon tarragon			

Mix all of the filling ingredients together in a food processor or blender (or by hand) and refrigerate.

TO FINISH THE KOLACHE
$1/4$ stick (1 ounce) unsalted butter, melted

When the machine has completed its cycle, transfer the dough to a lightly oiled work surface, cover it with a piece of lightly greased plastic wrap or a damp towel, and let it rest for 10 minutes or so.

Divide the dough into 2 pieces. Roll each piece to a 12-inch square, then cut each square into nine 4-inch squares; a rolling pizza wheel or pastry cutter works well for this. Put 1 scant tablespoon of filling in the center of each square. Bring all four corners of each square to the center and roll and pinch the dough between your fingers to seal. When all the kolache are filled, transfer them to 2 lightly greased cookie sheets, placing them about 2 inches apart. Let them rest for 10 minutes.

Bake the kolache in a preheated 375°F oven for 25 minutes, or until golden brown. Remove them from the oven and brush them with the melted butter. Place them on a wire rack to cool slightly before serving. Serve warm, or at room temperature.

Kolache aren't the only sweet pastry that get a new life when transformed into something savory. Croissants, Danish, kuchen, shortbread, and other traditionally sweet treats may be given a new twist by leaving all but a couple of teaspoons of sugar out of the dough and using a savory, rather than sweet, filling. When cutting back the sugar in dough, you'll need to cut the flour back as well, or increase the liquid; otherwise the dough will be too stiff.

Brie in Brioche
with Praline

If you are looking to knock the socks off your company, then consider this show stopper. A whole Brie is smothered in caramelized pecans, then wrapped in buttery, tender brioche. Sliced warm, the melted cheese, coated with the sweet pecans, oozes onto the surrounding brioche. Served cold, it makes for a stunning presentation: neat wedges of cheese surrounded by deep brown pecans and a lovely slice of bread. A long refrigerated second rise gives the brioche its characteristic flavor and texture; don't be tempted to rush the process.

While the brioche is a lovely dough to work with, you need to have a cool work place and a cool surface for rolling. Granite or marble is great for this, and even Formica in a cool kitchen. In other words, don't attempt this recipe in midsummer in an unair-conditioned kitchen. On page 180 there is a modified version of this recipe which is not as time-consuming.

The cooled baked Brie can be frozen up to three months, wrapped airtight in plastic wrap and then in foil. Defrost it at room temperature still wrapped, then either serve it at room temperature or place it on a baking sheet and heat it in a 350°F oven for twenty minutes.

SERVES 16 TO 20

FOR THE BRIOCHE DOUGH

1	tablespoon yeast	1	stick (4 ounces) unsalted butter, very soft but not melted
3¼	cups all-purpose flour		
2	tablespoons sugar	3	extra-large eggs
3	tablespoons nonfat dry milk	¼ to ⅓	cup water to make a moist, slightly sticky dough
1½	teaspoons salt		

Place all the ingredients in the machine, program for Dough or Manual, and press Start. The dough will be extremely sticky at first, then slightly less so as the kneading progresses. Some will continue to stick to the bottom of the pan. Don't be tempted to add more flour—this is quite a loose dough. It will firm up when chilled.

At the end of the final knead, transfer the dough to a well-oiled 2-quart bowl, cover it with plastic wrap, and refrigerate it for at least 24 hours or as long as 36 hours.

TO FINISH THE BRIOCHE

1¾ cups (7 ounces) pecans
½ cup dark brown sugar, firmly
    packed
1 tablespoon honey
¼ stick (1 ounce) unsalted butter,
    plus 1 tablespoon for preparing
    the pan

1 egg beaten with 2 tablespoons
  water
1 9-inch wheel ripe Brie

In a small saucepan set over low heat, combine the pecans, brown sugar, honey, and the ¼ stick butter. Stir constantly until the butter and sugar melt and the nuts are completely coated with the mixture. Set aside to cool. Generously butter the bottom and sides of a 12 × 3-inch springform pan and wrap the outside with foil (this is to prevent any leaking praline from spilling on your oven).

Punch down the dough and place it on a cold work surface that has been lightly coated with vegetable oil. Cut off one third of it and roll to a 12-inch circle about ¹⁄₁₆ inch thick. Place the dough in bottom of the prepared pan, pushing it out from the center to touch the sides of the pan. Use a pastry brush dipped in the egg glaze to moisten a 2-inch border around the edge of the dough.

Place the Brie in the center of the dough. Separate the pecans and place them over the surface of the Brie, piling them slightly higher in the center.

Cut one fourth off the remaining dough and reserve it for decoration. Roll the large piece of dough to a 14-inch circle (use the springform as a guide, making the circle 2 inches larger). Center the circle over the Brie and tuck the sides down to meet the bottom circle. Pinch the two pieces of dough together (you might want to loosen the springform to do this). Don't worry if there are spots that don't join—they will once the dough rises and bakes. Brush the sides, but not the top, with the egg glaze.

Roll the remaining piece of dough into 1 very long strip, about 20 × 3 inches. Cut the strip the long way into thirds, leaving them attached at one end. Braid the strips and place the braid in a circle atop the top piece of dough. Brush the top and the braid with egg glaze and place the pan, uncovered, in a warm, draft-free place to rise until doubled in bulk, about 40 minutes.

Preheat the oven to 425°F with the rack in the lower third but not lowest position. Bake the brioche for 15 minutes at 425°F, then lower the oven temperature to 375°F and bake an additional 30 minutes. If the top is turning very brown before the baking time is up, cover it loosely with a piece of foil.

Cool the brioche for at least 15 minutes before serving it hot, or cool it completely to room temperature.

HINT: *Brioche loses its lightness when refrigerated. You can leave this at room temperature for at least 24 hours after it is baked.*

Chicken, Artichoke, and Roasted Garlic Galette

A galette, an open-faced tart, is much like a pizza, but with a more substantial filling. To make this a vegetarian dish, substitute 2 cups cooked beans or lentils for the chicken.

SERVES 6

FOR THE DOUGH

1/2	teaspoon yeast		1	large egg
2 1/4	cups all-purpose flour		5	tablespoons unsalted butter, softened
3/4	teaspoon salt			
1	teaspoon sugar		1/3	cup plus 3 tablespoons water

Place all the ingredients in the machine, program for Dough, Basic Dough, or Manual, and press Start.

TO FINISH THE GALETTE

1	large chicken breast, roasted, chilled, boned, and cubed		1	teaspoon oregano
				Salt to taste
1	6-ounce jar artichoke hearts, juice and all			Freshly ground black pepper to taste
10	garlic cloves, roasted			Olive oil for brushing

In a stainless-steel bowl, toss together all the ingredients except the olive oil and refrigerate until needed. Preheat the oven to 400°F.

When the dough cycle is finished, transfer the dough to a lightly floured surface and let it rest for 5 minutes. Roll the dough out to a 14-inch circle and transfer it to a lightly oiled cookie sheet. Spread the chicken filling over the surface of the dough, leaving a 2-inch border. Then slide your hand under an area of the dough and fold it in and over to cover the outer third of the filling and repeat this folding around the entire galette. (Remember that the filling is exposed during the baking process.) Brush the dough with olive oil and sprinkle on salt and pepper around the rim of the dough.

Let the galette rest for 5 minutes, then bake it for 30 minutes, or until golden brown.

Gooey Cheese Bread

This dough is rich and the cheese is gooey. You'll be ready to dig in as soon as this delectable treat is taken from the oven. Start the dough the night before if you are going to serve it for breakfast, or in the morning if you are going to serve it at dinner.

MAKES 1 LOAF, SERVING 6 TO 8

FOR THE DOUGH

2	teaspoons yeast		1	teaspoon honey
2½	cups all-purpose flour		¼	stick (1 ounce) unsalted butter, softened
1	teaspoon salt			
¾	cup water		2	large eggs

Place all the ingredients in the machine, program for Manual, Dough, or Basic Dough, and press Start. The dough will be slightly sticky. After the kneading cycle, transfer the dough to a lightly oiled bowl, cover it with plastic wrap, and let it rise in the refrigerator overnight, or for as long as 24 hours.

TO FINISH THE BREAD

3   cups grated Swiss cheese

Grease and flour a 9-inch cake pan. Preheat the oven to 375°F with the rack in the center position.

Remove the dough from the refrigerator (at this point the dough will be firm and easy to handle) and place it on a lightly floured work surface. Roll the dough to a 14 × 10-inch rectangle with a long side nearest you. Sprinkle 2 cups of the grated cheese over the surface of the dough. Starting with the edge closest to you, roll the dough up like a jelly roll. Press the edges together and turn it over so the seam is now facing down. With the seam still down, roll the cylinder around itself in a coil and transfer it to the prepared pan. Sprinkle the remaining cheese over the top of the loaf and allow to rise, uncovered, for 20 minutes. Bake for 35 minutes at 375°F, then turn the oven down to 350°F and bake for 10 more minutes. The loaf will be firm and the cheese on top will be lightly browned. If the cheese begins to brown quickly during the first 35 minutes, turn the oven down sooner and continue baking at 350°F.

Sweet Potato Cheese Bread

Lynne Bail, who worked on this book with me, tasted this bread at Agnes's bakery in Kailua, Hawaii. She loved the contrast of the sweet dough, salty cheese topping, and crunchy bacon bits. You may use vegetarian bacon, or if you use the real thing, be sure that it is cooked until it is very crisp and dry. Drain it well on paper towels or it may make the dough greasy and heavy.

The completely cooled bread can be stored in a plastic freezer bag and frozen up to three months, then defrosted wrapped.

SERVES 8

FOR THE DOUGH

1	tablespoon yeast		1	cup warm water
2	cups all-purpose flour		1	egg
1	cup whole wheat flour		¼	stick (1 ounce) unsalted butter
1	teaspoon salt			
⅓	cup sugar			
¾	cup mashed sweet potatoes or 1 9-ounce can sweet potatoes, drained and mashed			

Place all the ingredients in the machine, program for Dough or Manual, and press Start. The dough will look loose and sticky as it starts to mix. It will be smooth and only slightly sticky to the touch at the end of the cycle.

TO FINISH THE BREAD

½	cup freshly grated Parmesan cheese		⅓	cup green onions (about 2 large), finely chopped, 1 tablespoon reserved for topping
1	cup shredded mild Cheddar cheese			
3	tablespoons unsalted butter, melted			
2	tablespoons vegetarian bacon bits or 2 tablespoons well-cooked bacon, drained on paper and crumbled			

Grease or spray a 9-inch springform pan with vegetable spray. Mix together the Parmesan and Cheddar cheeses. Turn the dough out on a work surface that is lightly sprayed with vegetable spray and divide the dough in half. Dip your fingers in the melted butter and form one half of the dough into small walnut-sized balls. Arrange the balls evenly on the bottom of the pan. They will not completely cover it, but will rise to fill in the spaces.

Sprinkle the bacon bits, green onions, and cheese mixture over the balls of dough, reserving 1/4 cup of the cheese mixture and 1 tablespoon of the chopped onion for a topping.

Form the remaining dough into walnut-sized balls, dipping your fingers into the melted butter as needed to coat the balls and keep the dough from sticking. Arrange the balls on top of the cheese mixture. They will rise and spread to fill in all the empty places. Cover the pan loosely with plastic wrap and rise the dough for 1 to 1 1/2 hours in a warm place until it is nicely rounded and has filled in the empty spaces in the pan.

Sprinkle the remaining cheese mixture and green onions over the top of the dough, remelt the butter if necessary, and drizzle over all.

Preheat the oven to 350°F and bake the bread for 35 to 40 minutes, or until it is a deep golden color and feels firm and resists pressure when tapped in the center. Although there may be moist places of melted cheese in among the air pockets of dough, the dough itself should be crisp. It's better to err on the side of overcooking.

Loosen the bread from the sides of the pan by running a knife around the edge of the pan. Remove the sides of the pan and then the bottom and cool the bread on a rack to avoid a soggy bottom. The bread may be served warm or at room temperature.

HINT: *Because of its high fat content, this bread keeps well for two to three days. You may line the bottom of the pan with foil for easy cleanup.*

Pan Bagna

Pan bagna—literally, "bathed bread" in Italian—is a round, crusty sandwich, drizzled with olive oil, stuffed with any manner of vegetables, meats, and cheeses, then wrapped well and weighted down for a few hours. The result is a dense, flavorful sandwich whose filling has started to meld just a bit with the bread, a sandwich really worth sinking your teeth into. The bread needs to be slightly stale to make this sandwich, so make it a day or two ahead.

This version of pan bagna features garlic-scented bread and a lusty filling including sun-dried tomatoes, anchovies, and olives. With no meat or cheese, it's particularly low in cholesterol.

SERVES 8 GENEROUSLY

FOR THE DOUGH

2	teaspoons yeast	1¼	cups lukewarm water
3	cups all-purpose flour	4	tablespoons olive oil
1¼	teaspoons salt	6	medium garlic cloves, minced
2	teaspoons sugar		(about 1 tablespoon)

Place all the ingredients into the machine, program for Manual, Dough, or Basic Dough, and press Start. Check the dough 10 minutes before the end of the second knead cycle; it should be quite soft and pliable, but shouldn't be sticking to the sides of the pan. Adjust the consistency with additional water or flour as needed.

FOR THE BREAD
Olive oil for brushing

Generously oil a 12-inch deep-dish pizza pan (first choice) or other pan large enough to hold the loaf. When the machine has completed its cycle, remove the dough and gently pull it into a rough 12-inch circle. Place the dough in the pan, rub the top of the dough with olive oil, and cover it gently with plastic wrap. Set the dough aside to rise till at least doubled in bulk, 1 to 1½ hours.

Preheat your oven to 425°F. Place the bread in the oven and immediately use a plant mister filled with clean water to spray inside the oven for 5 seconds. Close the oven door. Repeat the water spraying again in 5 minutes. Remove the bread from the oven after 25 minutes; it should be brown and crusty. Transfer the bread to a rack to cool completely.

TO FINISH THE PAN BAGNA

½	cup olive oil	1	cup pimiento-stuffed green olives
1	medium onion (about 5 ounces), sliced paper-thin		(4 ounces drained weight), pitted and coarsely chopped (see the Hints)
1	2-ounce tin anchovies (see the Hints)	1	7-ounce jar roasted red peppers in oil
½	cup sun-dried tomatoes marinated in oil or 3 plum tomatoes, seeded, drained, and sliced paper-thin		Coarsely ground black pepper to taste
1	cup black olives (4 ounces drained weight), pitted and coarsely chopped		

The bread should be slightly stale to make this sandwich. Slice it in half cross-wise—you'll have 2 round, flat disks—and set the pieces on a rack. Cover them loosely with a cloth towel and let them rest overnight. If you're in a hurry, place the pieces in a preheated 350°F oven for about 15 minutes, or until they're crusty.

Drizzle half of the olive oil on the inside of each piece of bread. Place the bottom half on a work surface and layer on the thinly sliced onion, anchovies, tomatoes, olives, and peppers. Season to taste with the coarsely ground black pepper. Lay the top crust on the filling, wrap the sandwich tightly in plastic wrap, and weight it down by placing a pan on top of it (a round, flat pan works well), then placing a 5-pound sack of flour or another heavy object on top of the pan. Let the sandwich rest for 2 to 4 hours.

To serve, unwrap the sandwich and cut it in wedges, like a pizza.

> HINTS: *If you don't care for anchovies, substitute one 6½-ounce can of tuna in oil, drained.*
>
> *You can use any combination of pitted, chopped olives, including Kalamata, Niçoise, etc.*

> *Spraying water into your oven during the first 5 and 10 minutes your bread is baking mimics, to a limited extent, the steam-injected ovens used in commercial bakeries. Steam performs two functions: During the first few minutes, it keeps the crust soft, allowing the bread to rise to its full volume. After that, it "caramelizes" the starch on the outside layer of the dough, giving bread a wonderful crust: crispy-crunchy, with a wonderful golden brown sheen.*

Hot Stuffed Sub

A golden brown, sesame-flecked log is cut open to reveal whorls of cheese, meat, and vegetables—that's a hot stuffed sub. This spectacular sandwich is always met with groans of ecstasy when we serve it. Memories of the sub shop (or hoagie, grinder, or hero place) come back to haunt us; when we were brash and daring teens, it was a badge of honor to order "one Italian with everything, extra-hot peppers."

The filling ingredients suggested here are simply a jumping-off point. Use your favorite cold cuts, add more cheese, change the vegetables—it's all up to you. Just don't forget the hot peppers.

3 LARGE OR 6 SMALL SERVINGS

FOR THE DOUGH

2	teaspoons yeast		1½	teaspoons salt
2½	cups all-purpose flour		2	teaspoons sugar
½	cup semolina flour or yellow cornmeal		1⅓	cups water
			3	tablespoons olive oil

Place all the ingredients in the machine, program for Manual, Dough, or Basic Dough, and press Start. Check the dough 10 minutes before the end of the second kneading cycle; it should have formed a smooth ball, one that yields easily to a finger poke but isn't at all sticky. Adjust with flour or water to obtain the desired consistency.

When the machine has completed its cycle, transfer the dough to a lightly oiled work surface. Cover it with a damp towel and let it rest for 10 minutes.

TO FINISH THE SUB

- ¼ pound Genoa salami, thinly sliced
- ¼ pound provolone, thinly sliced and torn into 1-inch pieces
- ¼ pound mortadella, thinly sliced
- ¼ cup (or to taste) hot cherry peppers, chopped, or ground hot peppers in vinegar or peperoncini, chopped
- 1 medium-sized onion (about 5 ounces), thinly sliced
- ½ medium green bell pepper, cored and thinly sliced
- ¼ cup sun-dried tomatoes packed in oil, undrained
- ½ teaspoon dried basil
- 1 egg white whisked with 1 tablespoon water till well combined
- 2 tablespoons sesame seeds

Roll the dough to an 18 × 12-inch rectangle. Layer the meats, cheese, and vegetables onto the dough in the order given. Sprinkle on the basil. Starting with a long side, roll the dough into a log. Don't roll too tightly, you'll push all of the ingredients out the open end. When you get to the final 2 inches of dough and filling, pull the edge of the dough up and seal it to the log, then turn the log over so the seal is underneath. Pinch the ends shut and tuck them underneath.

Transfer the filled dough to a large cookie sheet, preferably one with sides. Brush the dough with the egg glaze and sprinkle with the sesame seeds. Let it rest for 30 minutes while you preheat the oven to 375°F. Bake the sub for 25 minutes until it's golden brown. Remove it from the oven, transfer it to a wire rack, and cool it 10 minutes before cutting. Serve it hot, warm, or at room temperature.

One caveat when using fresh vegetables in yeast bread: They do tend to give off a lot of juice as they bake, making the interior of the bread soggy. Use fresh vegetables sparingly or, a better solution, sauté them first till they're limp and have given off most of their liquid.

Stromboli

This stuffed Italian sandwich takes its title from a volcano of the same name, located on an island off the coast of Sicily. When you cut it open, it oozes meat, vegetables, sauce, and cheese in lavalike fashion. Served with a simple green salad and a glass of Asti Spumante, it makes a satisfying meal, winter and summer.

SERVES 6 MODERATE OR 4 HEARTY EATERS

FOR THE DOUGH

2 teaspoons instant yeast	1½ teaspoons salt
2½ cups all-purpose flour	1¼ cups plus 2 tablespoons
½ cup semolina flour	lukewarm water
1 tablespoon sugar	¼ cup olive oil

Place all the ingredients in the machine, program for Manual, Dough, or Basic Dough, and press Start. Check the dough about 10 minutes before the end of the second kneading cycle; it should have formed a soft but not sticky ball. Adjust the consistency with additional flour or water as needed.

FOR THE FILLING

¼ pound mushrooms (about 6 medium-to-large), thinly sliced	1 pound ground sweet Italian sausage
¼ stick (1 ounce) unsalted butter or margarine	¼ teaspoon salt or to taste
1 medium onion, chopped	¼ teaspoon coarsely ground black pepper
1 green bell pepper, cored and cut into ½-inch squares	1 14-ounce jar spaghetti sauce
	1 tablespoon sugar

In a large frying pan, sauté the mushrooms in the butter until they begin to exude their juices, about 5 minutes. Add the onion and pepper and sauté slowly until the vegetables are just beginning to brown and the juice has evaporated. This will take an additional 5 minutes, more or less.

Add the sausage and cook, stirring often, until it loses its pink color completely. Drain off any fat, if necessary, and add the salt, pepper, spaghetti sauce, and sugar. Bring the mixture to a boil and simmer slowly for 15 minutes. Remove the pan from the heat and set aside.

TO FINISH THE STROMBOLI

8   ounces (2 cups) shredded
    mozzarella cheese

Roll the dough to an 18 × 15-inch rectangle. Cover it with the sausage mixture, leaving a 1-inch border along the long edges. Sprinkle the cheese on top.

Starting with a long end, gently roll the dough into a log. Don't roll the dough tightly, as this will force all of the filling out the end. When there are 2 inches of dough left to roll, stop rolling and pull the unrolled edge of the dough up over the top of the log. Pinch it closed all along the top of the log as best you can, then transfer the log to a lightly greased baking sheet or pizza pan, seam side down. Pinch the ends closed and tuck them underneath. Bend the log into a horseshoe shape. Cover it with a sheet of lightly greased plastic wrap and let it rise for 30 minutes, or until it's somewhat puffy.

Bake the log in a preheated 375°F oven for 20 to 25 minutes, or until it's golden brown. Serve hot or warm in slices.

Substitute hamburger or turkey sausage for the Italian sausage if you like. You may also leave out or add additional vegetables. One of the most flexible of Italian dishes, stromboli was a way for cooks to use up leftover bits and pieces of vegetables and meat. To make this dish vegetarian, leave out the meat entirely, substituting black beans or kidney beans, or additional cooked mushrooms.

Pastrami on Rye

If you're a city person, you know that one of life's truly sublime pleasures is a top-notch pastrami sandwich. There are heretics who like pastrami on squishy white bread with mayo, or even on an onion roll, but true pastrami aficionados know that this upper-class cousin of chipped beef should be served only on rye bread, with mustard and maybe a couple of slices of Swiss cheese. And, of course, a can of Dr. Brown's Cel-Ray.

SERVES 3 TO 4

FOR THE DOUGH

1	tablespoon yeast		1½	teaspoons salt
¾	cup white flour or medium rye flour		1	tablespoon molasses
			1	cup lukewarm water
2	cups all-purpose flour		2	tablespoons cider vinegar
1	tablespoon caraway seeds		2	tablespoons vegetable oil

Place all the ingredients in the machine, program for Manual, Dough, or Basic Dough, and press Start. The finished dough will be slack and quite tacky; this is normal for rye dough.

TO FINISH THE SANDWICHES

½	pound sliced pastrami		½	pound thinly sliced Swiss cheese
2	tablespoons mustard			

Place the pastrami in an ungreased pan and fry it over medium heat for 10 minutes, or until it's lightly browned and crisp around the edges. Remove the pastrami from the pan and set it aside.

When the machine has completed its cycle, transfer the dough to a lightly oiled work surface and roll it into an 18 × 15-inch rectangle. Spread a thin layer of mustard over the surface, leaving a 1-inch uncoated area around the edges. Visualize the dough divided into thirds lengthwise and place the pastrami evenly over the middle third. Fold one of the outer thirds of dough over the pastrami and lay the Swiss cheese atop the dough. Fold the final third of dough over the Swiss cheese and tuck it underneath. Seal the ends of the roll and tuck them underneath. Cover the roll with lightly greased plastic wrap and let it rest for 45 minutes.

Bake the roll in a preheated 375°F oven for 20 minutes, or until it's golden brown and beginning to exude juices. Remove it from the oven and transfer it to a wire rack to cool for 15 minutes. Cut it into 4- to 6-inch slices and serve it warm.

It's not necessary to cook the pastrami (as long as you purchase cooked pastrami); some people like it soft. It's like gently cooked versus hard-fried bacon: If you like bacon that is still soft and fatty, you'll like plain pastrami. If you're a fan of well-done bacon, dark brown and stiff as a board, you'll probably prefer the crackle and crunch of fried pastrami. (We'd say sautéed, but who ever heard of sautéed pastrami? Get a life!)

Portable Reubens

You know how when you order one of those overstuffed Reuben sandwiches and you take your first bite the sauerkraut slides out one end of the bread and the corned beef and Swiss shoot out the other? Well, this braided sandwich roll, which encases the filling within secure boundaries of braided bread, will solve your slippery Reuben problem forever. Made with a sour rye starter (recipe follows), the bread in this sandwich is a good match for the assertive flavors of sauerkraut and mustard. Slice and eat it warm from the oven, or brown-bag it—it's equally good at room temperature.

SERVES 8

FOR THE SOUR RYE STARTER

2	cups white (or light) rye flour	1	tablespoon yeast
1³/₄	cups hot water (120° to 130°F)	1¹/₂	teaspoons caraway seeds

Place all the ingredients in the machine, program for Manual, Dough, or Basic Dough, and press Start. At the end of the first kneading cycle, cancel the machine. The batter will be very thick, somewhere between a heavy pancake batter and a cohesive piece of dough; while it probably won't be pourable, you also won't be able to hold it in your hands without it oozing between your fingers. Adjust water or flour accordingly to reach this consistency.

Place the batter in a large bowl and cover the bowl tightly with plastic wrap. Let it sit for 12 to 24 hours at room temperature; your sour rye starter will then be ready to use.

FOR THE DOUGH

1¹/₂	teaspoons yeast	1	cup Sour Rye Starter
1¹/₂	teaspoons sugar	¹/₂	cup lukewarm water
2	cups plus 2 tablespoons all-purpose flour	1	tablespoon cider vinegar
		3	tablespoons vegetable oil
1¹/₂	teaspoons salt	1¹/₂	tablespoons caraway seeds

Place all the ingredients in the machine, program for Manual or Dough, and press Start. Check the dough midway through the second kneading cycle; it should have formed a smooth, pliable ball. If it's stiff and gnarled, add more water; if it hasn't formed a discrete ball, add more flour.

TO FINISH THE SANDWICHES

2 tablespoons mustard, your choice
½ pound corned beef, thinly sliced
1 16-ounce can sauerkraut, well drained

½ pound Swiss cheese, thinly sliced

When the machine has completed its cycle, remove the dough and punch it down. Divide the dough in half and roll each half out to a 15 × 12-inch rectangle. Transfer each rectangle to a lightly greased 18 × 12-inch cookie sheet.

Work with one piece of dough at a time. Starting with a short end of the dough, make 7 slits from the edge of the dough toward the center, each 5 inches long and 1½ inches apart. Do the same with the other short end of the dough. You'll now have a solid center piece of dough, 12 × 5 inches, and flanking strips of dough; the effect is somewhat like an insect with eight pairs of legs.

Fill the solid center piece of dough by spreading it with 1 tablespoon of mustard, then layering on half the corned beef, half the sauerkraut, then half the cheese. Crisscross the strips of dough over the filling, anchoring the strips opposite their side of origin. Tuck the two ends of the braid underneath. Repeat the entire process with the remaining piece of dough.

Tent the braids with lightly greased plastic wrap and let them rise for 1 hour. Preheat your oven to 375°F.

Bake the braids for 25 to 30 minutes, or until they're golden brown and the filling is starting to sizzle. Remove the braids from the oven and cool them for 10 minutes before cutting.

Can they be frozen? No, the sauerkraut and cheese don't hold up well.

If your starter has been resting, unused, in the refrigerator for several weeks, it will have developed some dark-colored liquid on the top. This liquid is alcohol and is what gives sourdough its marvelous taste. Stir it back into the starter. Before using the starter in a recipe, remove it from the refrigerator, transfer it to a large bowl, and "feed" it with equal parts light rye flour and water. If the starter is thin, add more flour; it should be the consistency of thick pancake batter. Cover it loosely with plastic wrap and allow it to rest, at room temperature, all day or overnight. Remove what you need for your recipe and refrigerate the rest.

PB and J Rolls

Dear Kids,

Have your parents been hogging the bread machine and never giving you a chance to have any fun with it? Well, I made this recipe just for you. It's a peanut butter and jelly sandwich on fluffy white bread. You make the dough for the bread in the bread machine, cut it into circles, and then stick some peanut butter and jelly between the circles before you bake the rolls in the oven. I guess to keep us both out of trouble you'd better make sure Mom or Dad knows that you are messing around with the machine (and the oven)—you might even want to get one of them to help you measure out the ingredients and use the oven. Watch out that they don't eat up all the PB and J rolls—most grown-ups like to eat like kids every once in a while.

You're going to need one of those muffin pans that make giant (or Texas-size) muffins, or you can use a regular muffin or cupcake pan and make miniature rolls.

MAKES 16 BIG OR 24 SMALLER ROLLS

FOR THE DOUGH

1	tablespoon yeast	1	tablespoon sugar
3	cups all-purpose flour	1¹/₂	teaspoons salt
4	tablespoons nonfat dry milk (that's	¹/₃	cup vegetable oil
	what makes the bread fluffy, and	1	extra-large egg
	healthy too)	³/₄	cup water

Place all the ingredients in the machine, program for Dough or Manual, and press Start.

TO FINISH THE ROLLS

¹/₂ cup peanut butter, either chunky or smooth (I like the natural kind)

8 teaspoons thick jam (runny grape jelly isn't good for this, but fruit spreads are great)

When the machine is finished, take the dough out and put it on a counter that has a little flour sprinkled on it. Rub a little vegetable shortening or butter on either a giant muffin pan or a regular-size one. Have someone help you cut the dough in half, so you have 2 equal pieces.

Use a rolling pin to make 2 flat circles of dough that measure 10 inches across (use a ruler to check). If you have a giant muffin pan, then use a cookie cutter or big glass that is 3 inches across (use the ruler again) and cut 8 circles from each piece of rolled-out dough. If you are using a regular muffin pan, then cut twelve 2-inch circles from each piece of dough.

Put 1 circle of dough in the bottom of each muffin place. Then use a table-spoon measure (and your finger—after you've washed your hands) to put a lump of peanut butter in the middle of each circle.

Spread the leftover circles with 1 teaspoon of jam each and then place the jam circle, jam side down, on the peanut butter. Press the 2 circles together gently—you don't want the stuffing to squish out. Put a big piece of plastic wrap over the top of the pan and put it in a warm place. Check the rolls after 30 minutes to see if they are about twice the size they were before. If not, leave them there for another 20 minutes.

Have someone help you preheat the oven to 375°F and put the rack right in the center of the oven. When you put the rolls in the oven, set a timer for 15 minutes. When the timer goes off, have someone help you check to see if the rolls are deep brown on top and lightly browned on the sides. If they are, have your helper take the pan from the oven and put it on a rack to cool.

Don't taste the rolls until they are cool—you don't want to burn your tongue! Don't forget to tell all your friends at school that you made a yummy lunch yourself in your bread machine!

Fajita Pockets

All your favorite Mexican ingredients are right here, enveloped in a rich sour cream dough. If you prefer beef to chicken, just make the substitution. This recipe was inspired by Nancie Coogan, who created it as she and Cindy were taste-testing the Chouriço Rolls (page 233).

MAKES 6

FOR THE DOUGH

2	teaspoons yeast		1/4	cup sour cream
3	cups all-purpose flour or more (see below)		1/4	stick (1 ounce) unsalted butter, softened
1 1/2	teaspoons salt		1	cup water
2	teaspoons sugar			

Place all the ingredients in the machine, program for Dough, Manual, or Basic Dough, and press Start. The dough will be very soft. Add additional flour if necessary to keep the dough from sticking to the work surface.

FOR THE FILLING

1	small red onion, sliced		2	garlic cloves, minced
1	medium green bell pepper, sliced		3	tablespoons salsa, mild or hot, the choice is yours
4	tablespoons olive oil		1	tablespoon chopped jalapeños (optional, for those who like it hot)
3/4	pound chicken tenders, cut in half			
1	large Italian plum tomato, diced			
2	scallions (both white and green parts), diced			

In a large skillet, sauté the onion and pepper in the olive oil over medium heat until tender. Add the chicken tenders and cook them thoroughly on both sides. Add to the skillet the tomato, scallions, garlic, salsa, and jalapeños. Toss the filling together and cook for an additional 3 minutes. Set the filling aside to cool.

TO FINISH THE FAJITA POCKETS

1 cup grated Monterey Jack cheese
1 small egg beaten with 3
   tablespoons water

When the dough cycle is complete, transfer the dough to a lightly floured work surface and let the dough rest for 5 minutes. Preheat the oven to 400°F. Cut the dough into 6 pieces and roll each piece up into a ball and let them rest for an additional 5 minutes. Roll out each ball of dough to a 6-inch circle.

Spoon some of the filling in the center of each circle and top the filling with some of the grated cheese. Fold the pocket by brushing a little egg glaze around the edge of the circle, then lifting the back of the circle over the filling and pressing it over the front of the circle.

Place the pockets on a lightly floured cookie sheet, brush the egg glaze over the top of each pocket, and with a sharp knife, cut a slit in the top of each pocket. Let the pockets rest for 5 minutes, then bake them for 20 minutes until light golden brown. Serve hot, warm, or at room temperature.

Meshwiya Tunisian Baguettes

The baguettes used in this recipe are slightly moist and chewy on the inside and crisp and crunchy on the outside. They are also wonderful for making subs (short for submarine sandwiches; what people in Boston call grinders) with your favorite fillings. The cooled loaves may be frozen up to three months, wrapped airtight in plastic or foil, then defrosted while still wrapped.

Meshwiya is a confit of finely chopped roasted peppers and tomatoes. It is a classic Tunisian dish which can have many other ingredients such as hard-boiled eggs, olives, anchovies, or chunks of tuna. These ingredients are tossed in a dressing of lemon juice, garlic, cumin, pepper, and olive oil. In this recipe the peppers are cut into strips which look wonderful stuffed in the baguettes. Meshwiya can be made up to two or three days ahead and refrigerated.

MAKES TWO 12-INCH LOAVES OR 4 SMALL LOAVES

FOR THE DOUGH

2	teaspoons yeast		1	tablespoon sugar
3	cups all-purpose flour		1	cup warm water or more to make a
1½	teaspoons salt			soft pliable ball

Place all the ingredients in the machine, program for Dough, Basic Dough, or Manual, and press Start. The dough needs to rise for a total of 3 hours. If your machine has the capability to program long-rising times on the dough setting, then do so, spraying the top of the dough with vegetable spray so it won't dry out during the long rising. Or you can remove the dough to an oiled bowl, cover it with a piece of oiled plastic wrap, and let it rise for 3 hours in a room-temperature, draft-free place.

FOR THE BAGUETTES

2 tablespoons cornmeal

At the end of the rising time, punch down the dough and let it rest for 10 minutes before forming. Sprinkle a heavy-duty baking sheet with 2 tablespoons of cornmeal. Either roll and stretch the dough into 1 long baguette or divide it in half and form each piece into a 12-inch-long baguette. For mini baguettes, divide the dough into 4 sections and form small loaves 4 to 7 inches long. Cover the baguette(s) with a clean towel and allow to rise 5 minutes. Using a very sharp knife, scissors, or a razor blade, cut 3 slashes ½ inch deep in the tops of the baguette(s) and brush the baguette(s) with water.

Add ½ inch of boiling water to an ovenproof pan and set it on the bottom of the oven. Set the oven to 400°F and put in the baking sheet without preheating the oven. Bake for 35 to 40 minutes for 1 long baguette, 25 to 30 minutes for 2 small baguettes, and 20 to 25 minutes for mini baguettes, until the crust is golden.

FOR THE PEPPERS AND TOMATOES

1	yellow bell pepper	2	Italian plum tomatoes
1	long yellow-green bell pepper	2 to 3	tablespoons olive oil
1	green bell pepper		

Rub the peppers and tomatoes with the 2 to 3 tablespoons of olive oil and grill, broil, or roast them until slightly blackened. Place the warm peppers in a plastic freezer bag to cool, to facilitate removing the skins. Peel the peppers, remove the seeds, and cut them into ¼-inch strips. Peel, seed, and coarsely chop the tomatoes.

FOR THE DRESSING

1	small onion, finely chopped (about ⅓ cup)	¼	teaspoon freshly ground black pepper
2	garlic cloves, finely chopped	⅛ to ¼	teaspoon cayenne pepper
⅓	cup extra virgin olive oil	¼	cup sliced black olives (optional)
1	tablespoon lemon juice	2	hard-boiled eggs, chopped (optional)
2 to 3	teaspoons ground cumin		
½	teaspoon salt	8	anchovies, chopped (optional)

Mix together the onion, garlic, olive oil, lemon juice, cumin, salt, black pepper, cayenne pepper, and any of the optional ingredients.

TO FINISH THE BAGUETTES

Toss the roasted peppers and tomatoes with the dressing.
   Slice the baguette(s) lengthwise about two thirds of the way down through the top. Do not cut all the way through. Spread the baguette(s) open slightly and fill with the meshwiya. Serve immediately.

◇

HINT: *If you want these for a picnic, pack the baguettes and the filling separately and assemble just before eating.*

◇

Greek Salad Sandwiches

*A salad you'd be served in Greece is probably very different from the ubiqui-
tous American Greek salad available at every diner, corner pizza shop, and supermarket take-out deli. This country's version features three assertive ingredients:
black olives, red onions, and feta cheese. These same ingredients, teamed with
smooth-tasting artichoke hearts in a braided loaf, make a sublime sandwich.*

SERVES 6 GENEROUSLY

FOR THE DOUGH

1½	teaspoons yeast		1	tablespoon dried oregano
2½	cups all-purpose flour		1	cup lukewarm water
1½	teaspoons salt		¼	cup olive oil
1½	teaspoons sugar			

Place all the ingredients in the machine, program for Manual, Dough, or Basic
Dough, and press Start. Check the dough 10 minutes before the end of the
second kneading cycle; it should have formed a smooth, supple ball. Adjust by
adding flour or water as necessary.

While the dough is rising, ready the filling. When the machine has completed
its cycle, punch down the dough and transfer it to a lightly greased work surface.

FOR THE FILLING

¼	cup plus 2 tablespoons olive oil, divided		10	ounces (drained weight) Greek-style black olives, rinsed and pitted
2	medium red onions, peeled and sliced ¼-inch thick			

Pour the ¼ cup of olive oil into a baking pan large enough to hold the onion
slices in one layer. Add the onion slices to the oil, toss to coat, and bake them
in a preheated 350°F oven for 30 minutes, or until golden brown. Set aside.

Toss the olives in the remaining 2 tablespoons olive oil. Set aside.

TO FINISH THE SANDWICHES

1	14-ounce can (8½ ounces drained weight) artichoke hearts, drained and quartered		4	ounces (1 cup) feta cheese, crumbled

Divide the dough in half. Working with one half at a time, roll it to a 15 × 10-
inch rectangle. Transfer the rectangle to a lightly greased cookie sheet.

Visually divide the rectangle into thirds, each 10 × 5 inches. Working on the middle third of the dough, and leaving 1 inch of space at each end, layer half of the onions, then half of the artichoke hearts and half of the olives. Sprinkle with ¹/₂ cup of the feta cheese.

Using a rolling pizza wheel, a sharp knife, or a pair of scissors, make 6 evenly spaced 5-inch long cuts in the dough, cutting from the edge of one of the unfilled sides just to where the filling starts. Repeat with the other unfilled side.

Fold the small piece of dough at each end of the filling over the filling. Alternating sides, cross the strips of dough over the filling, tucking them underneath the dough on the opposite side. Repeat the entire process with the other piece of dough.

Tent the braids with lightly greased plastic wrap and set them aside to rise for 1 hour, or until they're noticeably puffy.

Bake the braids in a preheated 350°F oven for 30 minutes, or until they're golden brown and the filling has started to bubble. Remove the braids from the oven, transfer them to a wire rack, and allow them to cool for 10 minutes before cutting.

Did you know that marjoram and oregano are very closely related? Substitute one for the other if you find yourself in a pinch.

Filled Croissants

Yes, you can make wonderful, flaky croissants with a bread machine. These filled croissants, fat pillows of buttery dough and filling, can be the centerpiece of a light supper or a good brown-bag lunch.

Though there are a number of steps involved, this recipe isn't at all complicated. The first step, freezing the butter, can be done up to several days ahead of time; and the remainder of the process is also quite flexible time-wise. Read the recipe all the way through first, then decide what time you need to start in order for your croissants to be ready when you are.

There are six fillings at the end of the recipe that run the gamut from traditional to eclectic. Let your imagination be your guide to creating your own filling; you'll need about 3 to 4 tablespoons per croissant of a "loose" filling, such as meat and cheese, and 2 to 3 tablespoons of a more homogeneous filling, such as a creamy cheese and vegetable mix.

SERVES 12

TO PREPARE THE BUTTER

2 sticks (8 ounces) unsalted butter, cold	2 tablespoons all-purpose flour

Cut the butter into ½-inch slices. Place the slices in a large plastic bag. Add the flour, close the bag, and toss the butter in the flour to coat both sides of all the pieces. Place the bag in the freezer for at least 2 hours or as long as several days. When the butter is frozen solid, use your fingers to quickly snap each piece into fourths (do this through the bag). Refreeze until ready to use.

FOR THE SPONGE

1 cup milk	1 cup all-purpose flour
1 tablespoon sugar	2½ teaspoons yeast

Place all the ingredients in the machine, program for Manual, Dough, or Basic Dough, and press Start. Knead for 2 minutes, not counting any preknead cycle. Cancel the machine and allow the sponge to rest for 5 minutes while you assemble the remaining ingredients.

FOR THE DOUGH

1	extra-large egg	2¼	cups plus 1 tablespoon all-purpose
1	large egg yolk		flour
¼	cup nonfat dry milk		Frozen Butter (see above)
¾	teaspoon salt		

Program the machine for Manual, Dough, or Basic Dough and press Start. Add the egg, egg yolk, dry milk, salt, and flour to the sponge in the machine. Allow the dough to knead for 5 minutes, or until a discrete ball forms; the surface will be slightly sticky. With the machine running, add the butter, scattering the pieces on top of the dough. Use a rubber spatula to push the butter into the center of the dough—it will look very messy, but don't worry.

Knead for 3 to 4 minutes, or until about two thirds of the butter is incorporated into the dough. Cancel the machine and turn the dough out on a lightly floured work surface. It will still look messy, with pieces of butter sticking out. Sprinkle about 1 tablespoon of flour onto the dough and use your hands and a dough scraper to quickly knead in the rest of the butter. You don't have to be too thorough; some pieces of butter will still show—that's fine.

TO FINISH THE CROISSANTS

1 recipe Filling

Form the dough into a rough, flat brick and wrap it airtight in plastic wrap. Refrigerate for 20 minutes.

This is the step that distributes the butter between the layers of dough, which gives you the flaky layers that croissants have. For this recipe it is repeated four times, with a 30-minute refrigerated rest between each time.

Place the dough on a lightly floured work surface and use a heavy rolling pin to roll the dough to an 18 × 12-inch rectangle with a short end nearest you. Dust off any visible flour. Fold the bottom third up away from you, dust off any visible flour, then fold the top third down toward you to form a three-layered "book"; this step is like folding a business letter before putting it into an envelope. Wrap the dough and refrigerate it for at least 30 minutes, or as long as overnight. The longer you refrigerate the dough, the more time it has to relax and the easier it will be to roll out. Repeat this process three more times.

Line 2 heavy-duty baking sheets with foil. Spray the foil with nonstick vegetable spray. On a lightly floured work surface, roll the dough to a 24 × 12-inch rectangle. Cut the dough in half lengthwise to form 2 long strips. Cut each strip into 6 pieces, giving you twelve 6 × 4-inch rectangles.

Working with one rectangle at a time, place the filling on one short end of the dough, leaving ½ inch of bare dough around the edges. Fold the other end of the dough over the filled end and pinch the edges to seal. Tuck the edges underneath; you'll have a very nearly square packet of dough. Place the croissant on a prepared baking sheet. Repeat with the remaining dough and filling.

Allow the croissants to rise in a warm, draft-free place, uncovered, until nearly doubled in bulk, 45 minutes to 1 hour. If you don't want to cook the croissants immediately, you can give them this last rise in the refrigerator, which will take 2 to 4 hours.

Preheat the oven to 400°F with the rack in the center position. Bake the croissants for 15 to 20 minutes until they're a warm, golden brown. Serve them hot, warm, or at room temperature.

Smoked Turkey, Cream Cheese, and Chutney Filling

A sweet and smoky treat, these are perfect for a light lunch.

4   ounces cream cheese, cut into 12
       pieces
³/₄   cup chutney
¹/₄ to ¹/₂ pound smoked turkey, thinly
       sliced (the greater amount will
       make a more assertively smoke-
       flavored croissant)

Fill each croissant with a piece of cream cheese, 1 tablespoon of chutney, and some of the smoked turkey. Seal and bake.

Cream Cheese and Lox Filling

Serve these, hot from the oven, as the centerpiece of a Sunday brunch. Back them up with scrambled eggs and home fries.

8   ounces cream cheese, cut into 12
       pieces
6   ounces lox, diced (about ³/₄ cup)

1   small-to-medium onion, finely
       diced (about ³/₄ cup)

Fill each croissant with a piece of the cream cheese and 1 tablespoon each of the lox and onion. Seal and bake.

Blue Cheese, Apple, and Toasted Walnut Filling

A glass of chilled dry white wine is the perfect accompaniment to these interesting croissants.

1/4	stick (1 ounce) unsalted butter	3	ounces blue cheese, crumbled
1	firm apple, such as Granny Smith, cored and cut into 12 slices	3/4	cup (3 ounces) chopped toasted walnuts (see the Hint)
1	tablespoon sugar		
8	ounces cream cheese, divided into 12 pieces		

Melt the butter in a small frying pan and sauté the apple slices for about 10 minutes, turning them once, or till they're just tender and beginning to turn golden. Stir in the sugar and sauté them an additional 2 minutes. Remove the apples from the heat and set aside.

Fill each croissant with a piece of cream cheese and about 1 tablespoon each of blue cheese and walnuts. Lay 1 apple slice on top. Seal and bake.

Ham and Swiss Filling

A classic combination, these are wonderful croissants to pack on a picnic along with the potato salad and chocolate cake.

1/4	cup sweet-hot mustard or mustard of your choice	1/2	pound ham, thinly sliced
		1/4	pound Swiss cheese, thinly sliced

Spread each croissant with 1 teaspoon of mustard, then layer on a slice of ham and cheese. Seal and bake.

Broccoli and Cheddar Filling

3	tablespoons unsalted butter	4	ounces extra-sharp Cheddar cheese, shredded (1 cup)
3	tablespoons all-purpose flour	1	10-ounce package frozen chopped broccoli, thawed and drained
1/8	teaspoon salt		
1	cup milk		

In a small saucepan set over medium heat, melt the butter and stir in the flour and salt. Stir till well combined. Gradually add the milk, stirring as you go; if the mixture is lumpy, don't panic. Just keep stirring and it'll smooth out. Add the cheese and stir till it melts. Stir in the broccoli. Refrigerate the filling till well chilled.

Fill the croissants, be sure to seal them well—the filling gets very thin as it heats, then solidifies again as it cools—and bake.

Honey-Cinnamon, Peanut Butter, and Banana Filling

3/4 cup peanut butter (crunchy or smooth)
6 tablespoons honey

1/2 teaspoon ground cinnamon
3 small-to-medium bananas, cut into 1/2-inch slices

In a small bowl, mix together the peanut butter, honey, and cinnamon. Place 1 heaping tablespoon of the peanut butter mixture on each croissant, then lay 2 slices of banana on top. Seal and bake.

> HINT: *To toast walnuts, place them on a cookie sheet and bake them for 5 to 8 minutes at 350°F, or until they're just beginning to brown and smell toasty.*

Deep-Dish Pies

Deep-Dish Stuffed Pizza

One of the few problems involved in this line of work is that sometimes I can't stop "taste-testing" one of the recipes. After I single-handedly finished off this pizza meant to serve eight famished souls, I looked in the yellow pages for a twelve-step program to help me conquer my powerlessness in the pizza department. I am issuing fair warning: Don't trust yourself alone in the house when this pizza comes out of the oven. The combination of hot herbed crust surrounding melting smoked mozzarella cheese, roasted red peppers, and turkey is too much for one person to resist.

This pizza makes especially good picnic fare. You can omit the turkey to make it a vegetarian pizza.

SERVES 8

FOR THE HERB DOUGH

1	tablespoon yeast	1¼	cups water
3½	cups all-purpose flour	1	teaspoon dried basil
2	teaspoons salt	½	teaspoon dried oregano
4	tablespoons nonfat dry milk	1	teaspoon dried parsley
⅓	cup olive oil		

Place all the ingredients in the machine, program for Dough or Manual, and press Start. The dough should form a smooth, firm ball after the first few minutes of kneading. At the end of the final cycle, remove the dough from the machine to a lightly oiled work surface. Cover it with a clean towel and allow it to rest while you assemble the filling.

TO FINISH THE PIZZA

8	ounces thinly sliced turkey breast (smoked turkey breast is also delicious)	½	teaspoon dried basil
		½	teaspoon dried oregano
8	ounces roasted red peppers, split open so they lie flat	1	teaspoon freshly ground black pepper
8	ounces smoked mozzarella cheese, cut into ½-inch slices		Olive oil for brushing

This pizza goes into a cold oven, so there is no preheating step. Oil or spray a 12-inch springform pan or a deep-dish pizza pan with nonstick vegetable spray. Divide the dough into 2 pieces and roll 1 out to a 14-inch circle. Lay it in the bottom of the prepared pan. It will shrink slightly, so push the dough out from the center to the edges so that the edges touch the pan as much as possible.

Leaving a 1-inch border around the edge, lay the turkey over the dough, then the red peppers, and finally the cheese. Sprinkle with the dried herbs and the pepper. The cheese and turkey are salty, so additional salt is not necessary. Moisten the edge of the dough with a little water and then roll out the second piece of dough to a 14-inch circle. Lay the second circle over the filling, pushing the edge of the dough down firmly to seal the 2 layers. Brush the top with olive oil and place the pizza on the center shelf of a cold oven. Set the oven to 450°F and bake the pizza for 30 minutes, or until the top is a deep golden brown.

Allow the pizza to cool for 10 minutes in the pan before releasing the springform or cutting. Enjoy it hot, warm, or at room temperature.

Sloppy Joe Pie

This pie has a cobblestone top which is made by placing diamond-shaped pieces of dough over the filling. They resemble a cobblestone street after they rise and bake. This is a family-size pie that is hearty enough to make a meal when accompanied by salad or vegetable. It makes a great potluck supper dish. It is made simple by using packaged sloppy joe seasoning mix, which you can find in your supermarket in the dry mix department.

The dough for the crust can be started in the morning and programmed to be ready at the end of the day. The assembled pie needs only one hour to rise before baking. To freeze it, cool the pie in the refrigerator, then wrap it in plastic wrap. Defrost it still covered in the refrigerator and reheat it, covered loosely with foil, in a 300°F oven for twenty to thirty minutes, or until a cake tester or knife stuck in the center comes out hot. Do not overcook if reheating it in a microwave or the bread crust topping will become rubbery.

SERVES 8 TO 10

FOR THE DOUGH

1	tablespoon yeast	1¼	cups milk, heated to 120°F and cooled to lukewarm
3	cups all-purpose flour		
1	tablespoon sugar	2	tablespoons margarine
1½	teaspoons salt	2	tablespoons vegetable shortening
¼	teaspoon white pepper	1	tablespoon Dijon mustard

Place all the ingredients in the machine, program for Dough, Basic Dough, or Manual, and press start. The dough will be very sticky and look like biscuit dough at first. It will become firmer and smoother as it finishes kneading.

FOR THE FILLING

2	teaspoons olive oil	1	envelope (1½ ounces) Durkee Sloppy Joe Mix
2	all-purpose yellow onions, finely chopped (about 1 cup)		
1½	pounds diet or extra-lean hamburger	1	6-ounce can tomato paste
		1¼	cups water

Heat the olive oil in a large skillet over medium-high heat. Sauté the onions for 2 to 3 minutes, or until they are translucent, adding a few drops of water if necessary to keep them from sticking. Add the hamburger and cook, breaking up any large pieces, until there is no more pink meat. Drain any fat carefully. Sprinkle the Sloppy Joe mix over the hamburger. Add the tomato paste and water gradually to avoid splattering and stir until mixed. Bring to a boil and simmer, uncovered, for 10 minutes until the liquid is reduced, stirring occasionally.

TO FINISH THE PIE

Grease or spray a 13 × 9-inch baking dish with nonstick vegetable spray and spread the hamburger mixture over the bottom of the dish.

Transfer the dough to a generously floured work surface and roll it to a 14 × 10-inch rectangle. Cut the rectangle diagonally in 2-inch strips and then cut it diagonally in the opposite direction to form diamond shapes. Lift the diamonds onto the top of the hamburger mixture in the same order they were on the counter, overlapping each diagonal row slightly.

Allow the dough to rise for 1 hour. Preheat the oven to 350°F with the rack in the center position and bake the pie for 30 to 35 minutes or until golden brown. Serve hot from the oven.

HINT: *To keep hamburger dishes from being overly greasy, use a nonstick pan for browning so that you do not have to add any additional oil or fat. When onions or other vegetables are cooked along with the hamburger, use a minimum amount of oil to start them cooking and then add a few drops of water instead of more oil.*

Shaker Onion Pie

*This rich, hearty supper pie was only one of the dishes found on farmhouse ta-
bles for supper after a hard day of work in the fields. With today's less rigorous
work and lighter-eating styles it can serve as the main dish. A rich herb-flavored
crust is filled with caramelized onions and bacon and then smothered with an
egg and sour cream mixture. You can use a slow cooker to caramelize the onions
or cook them a day ahead (see page 22). The baked pie can be frozen tightly
wrapped.*

SERVES 8 TO 12 AS AN APPETIZER; 6 AS A MAIN COURSE

FOR THE DOUGH

1	tablespoon yeast	6	tablespoons (3 ounces) unsalted
2½	cups all-purpose flour		butter or margarine
1	teaspoon salt	½	cup sour cream
1½	teaspoons sugar	½	teaspoon dried basil
½	cup water	¼	teaspoon dried oregano

Place all the ingredients in the machine, program for Dough or Manual, and
press Start. The dough will be soft and sticky at first but will become smooth
and elastic by the end of the final kneading cycle.

When the dough has finished, turn it out on a work surface and roll it out to a
12-inch circle. The dough should not stick but roll out easily because of the high
fat content. You might need to flour the rolling pin very lightly. Grease or spray a
10½-inch pie plate with nonstick vegetable spray. Fold the rolled-out dough in
half and carefully lift it into the pie plate. Pat it gently to the shape of the pie
plate, letting the dough come right to the edge. Cover with a clean towel and let
the dough rise in a warm place for about 1 hour, or until slightly puffed. Meanwhile, prepare the filling.

FOR THE FILLING

6 slices bacon, fried until crisp, with the drippings reserved, or (vegetarian option) 1 tablespoon margarine plus 1 tablespoon olive oil

1½ pounds (4 cups) sweet onions, such as Spanish or Vidalia, thinly sliced

1 cup sour cream or nonfat sour cream

4 eggs or 1 cup egg substitute

¼ teaspoon white pepper

½ teaspoon salt if you are not using bacon

½ cup fresh parsley with thick stems removed, finely chopped

¼ cup scallions, finely chopped

Heat 2 tablespoons of the bacon drippings or 1 tablespoon margarine and 1 tablespoon olive oil in a large heavy-bottomed skillet over medium-high heat. Add the onion slices and sauté for 10 minutes until they just start to caramelize and turn brown. Spread the onion slices evenly over the dough in the pie plate. Sprinkle with the bacon if desired.

Beat together the sour cream and eggs. Add the white pepper and salt if you are not using the bacon. Add the parsley and scallions and stir with a fork until well mixed. Pour this sour cream mixture evenly over the onions and bacon.

TO FINISH THE PIE

Preheat the oven to 350°F with the rack in the center position. Pour the filling into the pie plate. Bake the pie for 45 minutes to 1 hour, or until a knife inserted in the center comes out clean and the crust around the edge is browned. You can cover the edge with strips of aluminum foil if it starts to darken too much. Serve warm, cut into wedges.

HINT: *The vegetarian version of this recipe works well with shiitaki mushrooms. Soak 2 ounces dried mushrooms in 3 cups warm water for 30 minutes. Weight the mushrooms down with a small plate to keep them submerged. Drain the mushrooms thoroughly. Remove the stems and discard, for they are tough to chew. Thinly slice the caps and add to the filling with the parsley and scallions.*

Old-fashioned Chicken Pie

A version of this recipe originally came from Mrs. Leavitt, my neighbor's mother. Those of you on a low-fat diet will probably shudder at the amount of fat, but let me tell you, this is one of those great "down-home" recipes; you should at least try this once. You can eat little portions. The creamy sauce, tender chicken pieces, and light, airy bread topping are heavenly. Read through this entire recipe and note the order and timing of the various stages.

This dish can be assembled early in the day and baked at serving time. I prefer not to freeze it as the topping may get soggy. You can reheat leftovers in a microwave but do not overheat.

SERVES 6 TO 8

FOR THE DOUGH

1	tablespoon yeast	$^1/_2$	teaspoon dried tarragon
$3^1/_2$	cups all-purpose flour	$^1/_4$	stick (1 ounce) unsalted butter
$1^1/_2$	teaspoons salt	2	tablespoons vegetable shortening
$^1/_4$	teaspoon white pepper	$1^1/_4$	cups whole milk, heated to 120°F
1	tablespoon sugar		and cooled to lukewarm

Place all the ingredients in the machine, program for Dough or Manual, and press Start. The dough will be very sticky at first, like biscuit dough. It will become firmer and smooth by the end of the kneading. While the dough is kneading, prepare the filling.

FOR THE FILLING

$2^1/_2$	pounds split chicken breasts with bones, skin, and fat intact	3	tablespoons chicken fat reserved after cooking the chicken
1	celery stalk, coarsely chopped	3	tablespoons unsalted butter
1	yellow all-purpose onion, coarsely chopped	$^1/_3$	cup all-purpose flour
4	cups water	$1^1/_2$	cups heavy cream or light cream if you prefer
$1^3/_4$	teaspoons salt	$^1/_4$	teaspoon white pepper
$2^1/_2$	cups chicken broth reserved from cooking the chicken		

Place the chicken, celery, onion, water and 1 teaspoon of the salt in a large pot and cook, uncovered, over medium-high heat for 15 to 20 minutes, or until the chicken is just barely cooked through. Remove the chicken from the pot, and as soon as you can handle it, remove the meat from the bones. Cut the meat into

1- to 2-inch pieces and refrigerate. Defat the chicken broth left in the pot (see the Hint). Strain the broth into a separate container and discard the vegetables.

Melt the chicken fat and the butter in the pot and slowly whisk in the flour. Gradually whisk in the reserved chicken broth, whisking after each addition, until smooth. Whisk in the cream, pepper, and the ¾ teaspoon of salt. Remove from the heat and stir in the chicken.

TO FINISH THE PIE
    1   egg, beaten

Lightly spray a 13 × 9-inch baking dish with nonstick vegetable spray. Place the chicken mixture in the baking dish. Transfer the dough to a generously floured work surface, cover it with a clean towel, and let it rest for 5 minutes. Flour a rolling pin and roll the dough to a 14 × 10-inch rectangle. Cut the rectangle diagonally every 2 inches with a large, sharp knife. Then cut it diagonally every 2 inches in the opposite direction, making diamond shapes.

Lift the diamond-shaped pieces of dough onto the top of the chicken mixture in the baking dish. Keep them in the same order they were on the work surface and overlap each diagonal row slightly. This will give the dough topping a cobblestone appearance as it rises and bakes.

Generously brush the top of the dough with the beaten egg. Preheat the oven to 350°F with the rack in the center position. The dough rises slightly while the oven is heating and more while it bakes. Bake the pie for 30 to 45 minutes, or until it is a rich golden color. Serve hot from the oven.

HINT: *You may want to cook the chicken a day ahead to make defatting the broth easier. Chill the broth overnight in the refrigerator and the fat will solidify on top, which makes it easy to remove with a slotted spoon. Otherwise, skim the fat from the hot broth with a large spoon and reserve it.*

Mushroom Stroganoff Lattice Pie

This beautiful dish is a great vegetarian entrée and makes a hearty side dish as well. The woven lattice topping is light, airy, and not too thick. The filling is a flavorful mixture of thinly sliced, sautéed onions and mushrooms in a sour cream and parsley sauce.

The baked and cooled pie can be frozen, tightly wrapped in several layers of plastic wrap. Defrost it at room temperature and reheat it in a 300°F oven for about fifteen to twenty minutes. The pie reheats well in a microwave, but do not overcook it or the bread topping will get tough and rubbery.

SERVES 6 TO 8 AS A SIDE DISH; 4 AS A MAIN DISH

FOR THE DOUGH

1	tablespoon yeast		2	tablespoons solid vegetable shortening
3	cups all-purpose flour			
1	teaspoon salt		$1/4$	stick (1 ounce) unsalted butter or margarine
2	teaspoons sugar			
$3/4$	cup water		$1/2$	teaspoon dried thyme

Place all the ingredients in the machine, program for Dough or Manual, and press Start. The dough will be firm and not sticky to the touch.

FOR THE FILLING

1	tablespoon unsalted butter or margarine		10	ounces fresh mushrooms (about 5 cups), thinly sliced
1	tablespoon olive oil		$1/2$	teaspoon salt
2	large garlic cloves, minced		$1/4$	teaspoon white pepper
3	medium yellow all-purpose onions (about 1 pound or 2 cups), thinly sliced		1	cup sour cream or nonfat sour cream
			$1/4$	cup fresh parsley, finely chopped

Heat the butter and oil in a large skillet placed over medium-high heat. Add the garlic and onions and sauté for 2 to 3 minutes, or until the onions are soft. Add the mushrooms and sauté until there is no more liquid, about 10 to 15 minutes. Scrape the bottom of the skillet more frequently as the liquid is reduced. Remove the skillet from the heat and cool for 5 minutes. Add the salt, white pepper, sour cream, and parsley and mix in gently.

TO FINISH THE PIE

1   egg beaten with 1 tablespoon
    water

Spray a 12-inch round quiche, pie, or baking dish with nonstick vegetable spray. Spread the filling over the bottom of the dish. Transfer the dough to a lightly floured work surface and roll it to a 14-inch circle. With a fluted pastry wheel, pizza cutter, or large, sharp knife dipped in flour, cut the circle into 1-inch strips.

Lay half of the strips across the filling, using the longer strips across the center and the shorter ones for the sides and leaving about ½ inch between the strips. Fold back every other strip halfway.

To begin the weaving, lay one of the remaining long strips perpendicular to the first strips across the middle of the pie. Now take each of the strips you had folded back and unfold them over this perpendicular strip and you should see the beginning of the weaving of the lattice top.

To weave in the next strip, lift every other strip of dough to form an over/under pattern opposite to the first perpendicular strip and ½ inch away from it. Continue weaving the remaining strips. Trim the ends of the strips to about ½ inch longer than the dish and tuck these ends down inside the edge of the dish.

Preheat the oven to 350°F with the rack in the center position. Generously brush the egg glaze over the woven strips. Let the dough rise for a few minutes while the oven is heating. Bake the pie for 20 to 30 minutes, or until the lattice top is a rich golden color. Serve it warm.

HINT: *With a pie such as this with no bottom crust and a soft, warm filling, use a large serving spoon for serving.*

Jalapeño Beef and Bean Bonanza

Why bonanza? Because this buxom wheel of bread, airy and high-rising, is topped with a spicy mélange of beef, beans, and barbecue sauce, then smothered in cheese. And besides, this is the kind of thing Little Joe and Hoss would have eaten, had Pa ever learned to bake.

SERVES 8

FOR THE DOUGH

1	tablespoon yeast	1	small can chopped green chiles, thoroughly drained
2½	cups all-purpose flour		
½	cup cornmeal	¾	cup lukewarm water
1	tablespoon sugar	2	teaspoons Tabasco sauce
1½	teaspoons salt	2	tablespoons vegetable oil

Place all the ingredients in the machine, program for Manual, Dough, or Basic Dough, and press Start. The dough will be soft yet will form a nice ball as it kneads; adjust the consistency with additional flour or water as needed.

FOR THE FILLING

½	pound ground beef	¼	cup barbecue sauce
¼	teaspoon salt		
1	16-ounce can Mexican beans in sauce (see the Hint)		

In a medium frying pan over medium heat, fry the ground beef for 5 to 8 minutes, or until all the red is gone. Drain the fat, if necessary, and stir in the salt, beans, and barbecue sauce. Set the filling aside.

TO FINISH THE BONANZA

8 ounces (2 cups) grated longhorn cheese or yellow Cheddar cheese

When the machine has completed its cycle, transfer the dough to a lightly oiled work surface. Pat or roll the dough to a 12-inch circle and place it in a 12-inch deep-dish pizza pan or on a cookie sheet.

Spoon the ground beef filling atop the dough. Use the end of a spatula to crosshatch the dough 8 to 10 times, cutting almost to the bottom; this will allow the beef filling to sink into the dough a bit as it rises rather than sit on top, where it's more likely to fall off as the bread bakes. Sprinkle the cheese atop the beef filling. Cover with lightly greased plastic wrap and let the dough rise for 45 minutes.

Bake the bonanza in a preheated 375°F oven for 20 to 25 minutes, or until it's deep brown, the cheese is bubbling, and the bottom of the crust is golden. Remove it from the oven and serve it warm, right from the pan.

HINT: *Kidney beans, black beans, or most any firm canned beans (not baked beans) work well here if you can't find Mexican beans.*

The amount of Tabasco called for here seems like a lot, but flavors tend to get lost in bread dough (as opposed to in salad dressing or a stir-fry). This amount of Tabasco will produce a bread that is noticeably hot, though certainly not sweaty-brow hot.

Country-Style
Skillet Pork Pie

Hearty, homey, and custom-made to warm you on a cold winter night, this unpretentious dish is the prefect après-ski meal. I like to make it in a cast-iron skillet. Before you can prepare the dough, you must first cook the pork, since the juices rendered from the pork are used for the liquid in the dough.

SERVES 8

FOR THE PORK FILLING

1½	cups chopped onions		2¼	teaspoons salt
4	tablespoons olive oil		2	teaspoons freshly ground black pepper
3	garlic cloves, minced			
2	tablespoons red wine		3	tablespoons seasoned bread crumbs
2	pounds freshly ground pork			
½	pound freshly ground beef		1	teaspoon dried sage
3	cups water		2	large eggs, slightly beaten

In a large skillet over medium heat, cook the onions in the olive oil until they are tender. Stir in the minced garlic and red wine and continue cooking for 2 minutes over medium heat. Add the pork, beef, water, salt, and pepper, stirring the mixture constantly with a fork to ensure that the meat breaks up. When the meat is browned and cooked, strain 1¼ cups plus 2 tablespoons of the juices from the pan for the dough. Transfer the remaining juice and meat into a large clean mixing bowl. Stir in the bread crumbs, sage, and eggs, cover the filling, and refrigerate until you are ready to assemble the pie.

FOR THE DOUGH

1¼	cups plus 2 tablespoons pork cooking juices		3	cups all-purpose flour
			1½	teaspoons salt
2	teaspoons yeast			

Place all the ingredients in the machine, program for Dough or Basic Dough, and press Start. When the dough cycle is finished, transfer the dough to a floured work surface and let it rest for 5 minutes.

TO FINISH THE PIE

Grease and flour a 10-inch cast-iron skillet and set it aside. Preheat the oven to 350°F with the rack in the center position. Divide the dough in half. Roll out the bottom crust a little larger than the top crust. Line the skillet with the larger piece of dough; there will be only about 1/4 inch of dough over the lip of the pan. Fill the skillet with the pork filling. Place the smaller piece of dough over the surface of the pork and crimp the top and bottom pieces together. With a small knife, make three 1-inch vents in the top crust before baking.

Bake the pie for 25 minutes at 350°F, then lower the oven to 300°F and continue baking for an additional 10 minutes. Serve hot from the oven.

Easter Pie

Easter pie, a two-crusted "pizza" filled with ham, eggs, and cheese, can be found on many an Italian table at Easter, and in many incarnations. Some cooks add sausage, some pepperoni, some even mushrooms or peppers. This version, converted from a family recipe that began "Take 3 dozen eggs . . ." is perfect in its simplicity. The mellow filling, with just the tiniest "bite" of sharp Parmesan, is set off nicely by the sweet-glazed crust.

Serve this pie warm or at room temperature; in most households it appears at all three meals on Easter Sunday, as sure a harbinger of spring as the holiday itself.

SERVES 12

FOR THE DOUGH

1½	teaspoons yeast
1½	teaspoons sugar
2/2	cups plus 2 tablespoons all-purpose flour
1½	teaspoons salt
1	cup plus 2 tablespoons lukewarm water
2	tablespoons olive oil

Place all the ingredients in the machine, program for Manual, Dough, or Basic Dough, and press Start. Check the dough 10 minutes before the end of the second kneading cycle; it should have formed a smooth ball. Adjust the consistency by adding more flour or water as necessary.

FOR THE FILLING

½	pound ham: boiled, baked, hock, or "ham ends"
3	hard-boiled eggs
3	uncooked eggs
½	cup (2 ounces) ricotta cheese
3	tablespoons Parmesan cheese
1	tablespoon dried parsley
1½	teaspoons coarsely ground black pepper
¼ to ½	teaspoon salt

Cut the ham into chunks and place it in a food processor. Process it, in pulses, until the ham is coarsely chopped. Add the hard-boiled eggs and process again until the eggs are chopped and the mixture is of uniform consistency. It should be crumbly, not so finely chopped that it's pasty.

Transfer the ham mixture to a bowl and stir in the uncooked eggs, cheeses, parsley, and pepper. Taste the mixture and add salt if necessary. (The amount of salt needed, if any, depends on what kind of ham you used, ham ends or hocks being saltier than baked or boiled ham.)

TO FINISH THE PIE
1 egg yolk beaten with 1
tablespoon sugar

When the machine has completed its cycle, transfer the dough to a lightly oiled work surface. Divide the dough in half and roll half into a thin 12-inch circle. Transfer the circle to a 12- or 14-inch round pizza pan. Spread the filling evenly over the surface of the dough, leaving a ½-inch border around the edge. Roll the remaining piece of dough into a 12-inch circle and place it over the filling, stretching it gently to cover, and using your thumb and fingers to seal it around the edges, just as you'd seal a pie.

Cut a hole about the size of a quarter in the middle of the top crust; this is most easily accomplished by pinching a piece of dough and snipping it off with a pair of scissors. Brush the egg glaze all over the dough, including the edges. Set the pie aside to rest for 30 minutes and preheat the oven to 325°F.

Bake the pie for 50 minutes to 1 hour, or until it's golden brown. Remove the pie from the oven and cool it completely on a wire rack. Serve warm, cold, or at room temperature; refrigerate till ready to serve.

The egg yolk and sugar glaze on this pie is a hallmark of many Italian pastries, giving them a sweet, golden brown, shiny crust. For a neutral-flavored, shiny crust that's less brown, use 1 whole egg beaten with 1 tablespoon of water. For a shiny crust only as brown as the bread dough beneath it, use 1 egg white beaten with 1 tablespoon of water.

Coulibiac

This classic Russian dish is an extravaganza of poached salmon, rice, fresh dill, and hard-boiled eggs encased in a picture-perfect buttery, rich brioche. The whole coulibiac is presented in all its beauty before being sliced into jewellike servings and served with (hold on to your hats) melted butter or sour cream. No wonder those Cossacks had to dance the kazatski.

While this dish is time-consuming to make, it can be done in stages. The brioche dough can be made up to three days ahead (it must be made at least twenty-four hours ahead) and kept in the refrigerator in an oiled bowl covered airtight with plastic wrap. The filling can be made the day before. If you wish, you can even substitute canned salmon for fresh salmon. The coulibiac can be assembled four to five hours ahead of time and left to rise in the refrigerator, or you can assemble and bake it ahead, chill it, and serve it cold. The easiest way to "make" fish stock is to dissolve ½ cube Knorr's fish bouillon in 1 cup boiling water. Take care when adding additional salt to your recipe since bouillon cubes are very salty.

The very easiest way to cook and present this is on a long oven-to-table platter so you don't have to move the coulibiac from a baking dish to a serving dish and risk breaking the pastry crust.

SERVES 10

FOR THE DOUGH

1	tablespoon yeast	1	stick (4 ounces) unsalted butter, melted and slightly cooled
3¼	cups all-purpose flour		
1½	tablespoons sugar	3	extra-large eggs
3	tablespoons nonfat dry milk	¼ to ⅓	cup water, to make a very soft, sticky dough
1½	teaspoons salt		

Place all the ingredients in the machine, program for Dough or Manual, and press Start. The dough will be extremely sticky at first, then slightly less so as the kneading progresses. Some will continue to stick to the bottom of the pan. Don't be tempted to add more flour—this is quite a loose dough. It will firm up when chilled.

At the end of the final knead, place the dough in a well-oiled 2-quart bowl, cover with plastic wrap, and refrigerate for at least 24 hours or as long as 36 hours.

½   stick (2 ounces) unsalted butter
1   large onion, chopped (about
    1½ cups)
½   pound mushrooms, cleaned and
    sliced
⅓   cup chopped fresh dill
4   cups cooked white long grain rice
3   hard-boiled eggs, finely chopped
2   pounds skinless salmon fillets,
    poached in 1 cup dry white wine
    or 1 cup fish stock, cooking liquid
    reserved, or 2 16-ounce cans plus
    1 8-ounce can salmon, well
    drained, skin and bones removed,
    plus ½ cup dry white wine or fish
    stock

Salt to taste
Freshly ground black pepper
to taste

Melt the butter in a large skillet placed over medium heat. Sauté the onion, stirring occasionally, until it is translucent. Add the mushrooms and cook for just 3 minutes. Place the onion and mushrooms and their cooking juices in a large bowl and add the dill, rice, and chopped eggs. Break the salmon into bite-sized pieces and add it as well as ½ cup cooking liquid, wine, or fish stock. Mix gently but thoroughly, then add salt and pepper to taste.

TO FINISH THE COULIBIAC

¼   stick (1 ounce) unsalted butter, for
    greasing the baking dish
1   egg slightly beaten with 2
    tablespoons milk

Melted butter or sour cream, for
garnish

Select an oven-to-table baking dish at least 17 inches long and 10 inches wide. Generously coat it with butter. Remove the dough from the refrigerator, punch it down, and place it on a cold surface that has been lightly coated with vegetable oil. Divide the dough into 2 pieces, one slightly larger than the other, and roll the smaller piece to a 16 × 8-inch rectangle. Use a knife and ruler to trim the dough so that the sides are straight, then roll the dough around the rolling pin and unroll it on the prepared baking dish.

Mound the filling down the center of the dough (in a meat loaf shape), leaving at least a 1-inch border of dough on all four sides. Roll out the remaining dough to a 20 × 12-inch rectangle, trimming it as above. Roll the dough up on the rolling pin and then unroll it over the filling. Seal the edges of the 2 pieces of dough together by pressing them firmly with a fork. Carefully cut out a 1-inch hole from the center of the top piece of dough for a steam hole. You can use the leftover scraps of dough to make decorations for the top.

Use a pastry brush to paint the entire surface of the dough with the egg glaze. Allow the coulibiac to rise, uncovered, in a warm place for 30 minutes, then place it in a cold oven. Immediately turn the oven on to 425°F with the rack in the lower third but not lowest position. When the oven comes up to temperature, bake for 15 minutes, then reduce the heat to 375°F and cook an additional 45 minutes. If the top is browning too quickly, cover it loosely with foil.

To serve, present the coulibiac and then remove it to the kitchen to slice, with a very sharp serrated knife, placing the slices on dinner plates. Pass melted butter or sour cream separately.

Spinach and Onion Pie

Spinach and onions accented with Dijon mustard make this hearty winter dish. A hands-down winner, it's even great the next day—reheated or eaten cold.

SERVES 6

FOR THE DOUGH

2	teaspoons yeast		1	tablespoon sugar
3	cups all-purpose flour		1	cup water
1	teaspoon salt		1	large egg

Place all the ingredients in the machine, program for Dough or Basic Dough, and press Start.

FOR THE FILLING

1	pound fresh spinach leaves		2	garlic cloves, minced
	Salt for the spinach		5	eggs, beaten
1	large onion, sliced in 1/4-inch rings		1/4	teaspoon freshly ground black
6	tablespoons olive oil			pepper to taste
2	tablespoons Dijon mustard			Salt to taste

To prepare the spinach, remove any large stems and place the spinach in a large bowl. Heavily salt the leaves. This salting helps to extract any excess water that is contained in the spinach. Let the spinach sit for a few minutes. Rinse the spinach thoroughly under cold water and let the water drain off, or if you have a lettuce spinner, spin the spinach dry. Transfer the spinach to a clean large bowl and set aside. Sauté the onion slices in the olive oil until tender. Remove the onion slices from the heat and stir in the mustard and garlic. Stir the onion slices into the spinach, followed by the eggs, salt, and pepper. Toss all the ingredients together so they are well distributed. Preheat the oven to 400°F and lightly grease a 9-inch pie pan.

TO FINISH THE PIE

1	egg beaten with 2 tablespoons water

When dough cycle is finished, transfer the dough to a lightly floured work surface, cut the dough into 2 pieces, and let it rest for 5 minutes. Roll out each piece to a 10-inch circle. Line the pie pan with 1 circle of dough, then add the filling. Top the pie with the second piece of dough. Tuck the top piece under the bottom piece and crimp the edges. Brush the egg glaze over the surface of the dough, and with a pair of scissors, cut 3 slits in the top. Bake the pie for 25 minutes, or until golden brown. Serve hot or warm.

Quitza Lorraine

What do you get when you cross pizza and quiche? Quitza, of course. This substantial and abundantly tasty dish makes a classy first course, a satisfying main course, as well as a snack for a crowd. It makes for great leftovers too. This herb crust is filled with a traditional bacon, cheese, and egg combination. Two nontraditional versions follow.

There are two tricks for success here: allowing the dough to rise before the filling is added so you won't have a dense, soggy bottom crust, and using the right kind of pan. You need a heavy-duty, shallow springform pan. The one I like best is a conical springform pan made by Kaiser Bakeware. It's got a nonstick finish that makes removing the sides of the pan a breeze. You can serve the quitza right on the springform bottom, or slide it off onto a cutting board or serving tray.

SERVES 12 AS A FIRST COURSE; 8 AS A MAIN COURSE;
UP TO 20 AS A SNACK

FOR THE DOUGH CRUST

1	tablespoon yeast	1/2	teaspoon dried sage
3	cups all-purpose flour	1/2	teaspoon ground rosemary
1	teaspoon salt	1	cup water
3	tablespoons nonfat dry milk	3	tablespoons olive oil
1/2	teaspoon dried tarragon		

Place all the ingredients in the machine, program for Dough or Manual, and press Start. At the end of the final cycle, transfer the dough to a lightly oiled work surface and roll it to a 15-inch circle. Lightly oil a 12- or 13-inch springform pan with 2-inch-high sides. Lay the dough in the bottom and up the sides of the pan, forming a fluted edge on the crust by pinching the dough together with your fingers. Allow the dough to rise, uncovered, in a warm place for 30 to 40 minutes, or until puffy.

TO FINISH THE QUITZA

1	pound lean bacon, thickly sliced, cooked until crisp, and crumbled into 1-inch pieces	6	eggs
		2	cups heavy cream
1/3	pound (4 ounces) Gruyère cheese, cut into 1/2-inch cubes	1/2	teaspoon salt
		1	teaspoon freshly ground black pepper

Preheat the oven to 425°F with the rack in the center position. Place the pan containing the crust on a baking sheet (this makes it easier to lift). Prick the bottom of the crust all over with a fork. Sprinkle the bacon over the bottom of the crust. Top this with the cheese. In a mixing bowl, whisk together the eggs, cream, salt, and pepper. Pour the mixture over the bacon and cheese.

Bake the quitza for 15 minutes and then reduce the oven temperature to 375°F and bake for another 30 minutes, or until the custard is set. Wait 10 minutes before removing the springform sides. Serve hot, at room temperature, or cold.

Pizza Rustica

This masterpiece makes a magnificently hearty meal. All you need to complete it is a nice salad and a glass of red wine. This tall pizza is layered with salami, ricotta, basil, and provolone.

SERVES 8

FOR THE DOUGH

2	teaspoons yeast		2	tablespoons olive oil
3	cups all-purpose flour		1	tablespoon fresh rosemary,
1	tablespoon sugar			chopped, or 2 teaspoons dried
2	teaspoons salt			rosemary
1¼	cups plus 2 tablespoons milk			

Place all the ingredients in the machine, program for Manual, Dough, or Basic Dough, and press Start. The dough will be firm and pull away from the side of the machine. While the dough is rising, you can prepare the filling.

FOR THE RICOTTA CHEESE FILLING

1	pound container ricotta cheese		½	teaspoon salt
2	large eggs		¼	teaspoon freshly ground black
½	cup grated Romano cheese			pepper
1	tablespoon chopped parsley			

In a mixing bowl, whisk together all the ingredients and refrigerate until you are ready to assemble the pizza.

TO FINISH THE PIZZA

15	slices Genoa salami, thinly sliced		12	slices provolone cheese, thinly
	Ricotta Cheese Filling			sliced
20 to 25	fresh basil leaves, coarsely			Olive oil for brushing
	chopped			Salt to taste
1	16-ounce jar roasted red peppers,			Freshly ground black pepper
	drained			to taste

Preheat the oven to 400°F with the rack in the center position. Grease a 9-inch springform pan with 3-inch-high sides. When the dough cycle is completed, transfer the dough to a lightly floured work surface, cover it with a clean towel, and let it rest for 5 minutes. Cut the dough in 2 pieces; one piece should be one third of the dough and the other piece should be two thirds. Roll out the larger piece to a 14-inch circle. Line the springform pan with the circle. A small amount of dough (1 inch) should overlap the top of the pan. Now you are ready to assemble the pizza. Arrange 5 slices of salami on the bottom. Spread a third of the ricotta filling over the salami, then sprinkle on a third of the basil. Lay out a third of the peppers (if they are still whole, simply open them up so they will lie flat). Lay out 4 slices of provolone. Repeat this pattern for the next 2 layers. Roll out the small piece of dough to a 9-inch circle. Brush water around the rim of the dough already in the pan, then fit the 9-inch circle on top. Trim away about ½ inch of the overlapping dough from the bottom circle. Crimp together the top and bottom edges. Brush the top of the dough with olive oil and salt and pepper. With a pair of scissors, cut a vent in the top crust about 1 inch in diameter.

Bake for 15 minutes at 400°F, then at 350°F for 15 minutes. The crust will be a rich golden brown. Remove the pizza from the oven and immediately remove the sides of the springform. Cool the pizza completely before slicing it to serve; cooling allows the layers to set.

Spinach Tahini Pie

This vegetable-filled bread is great for a light supper with soup and a salad. The spinach-tahini combination, a common Armenian filling, here is sandwiched between layers of flaky dough. The cooled pie can be frozen up to 6 months, wrapped tightly in plastic wrap. Defrost it still wrapped and reheat it in a 300°F oven for fifteen to twenty minutes.

SERVES 12 AS AN APPETIZER; 4 TO 6 AS MAIN COURSE

FOR THE DOUGH

1	tablespoon yeast	1	teaspoon salt
3½	cups all-purpose flour	½	cup warm water
2	tablespoons nonfat dry milk	2	eggs
2	teaspoons sugar	⅓	cup sour cream
3	tablespoons margarine		

Place all the ingredients in the machine, program for Dough, Basic Dough, or Manual, and press Start. Make the filling while the dough is mixing so that it will have time to cool.

FOR THE FILLING

1	tablespoon unsalted butter or margarine	½	teaspoon salt
1	tablespoon olive oil	¼ to ½	teaspoon freshly ground black pepper
1	large Spanish onion (12 ounces), finely chopped (about 2 cups)	¼	cup tahini
1	pound fresh spinach, washed, large stems removed, and coarsely chopped, or 2 10-ounce packages frozen chopped spinach, thawed and the water pressed out	¼	cup bread crumbs

Heat the butter and olive oil in a large frying pan. Add the onion and sauté over medium-high heat for 3 to 4 minutes until translucent. If you are using fresh spinach, add it now and lower the heat to medium. Cook for 7 to 10 minutes, or until the spinach is well wilted. If you are using frozen spinach, add it to the cooked onion and stir until well mixed. Drain this mixture in a fine strainer and press gently to remove additional liquid. Return the spinach and onion to the frying pan and, off the heat, add the salt, pepper, tahini, and bread crumbs, stirring until well mixed. Set aside to cool.

TO FINISH THE PIE

| 3 | tablespoons melted butter or margarine | 1 | tablespoon sesame seeds |

Remove the finished dough to a very lightly floured work surface. Divide the dough in half and cover one half with a clean towel. Roll the dough from the center toward the edges, turning and stretching it until you have an 18 × 11-inch rectangle.

Brush the dough with the melted butter or margarine. Visually dividing the dough in thirds and taking a short end, fold a third of it over and brush with butter. Then fold the other short end over to form a three-layered "book" and brush with butter. Fold the dough in half to make a 5½ × 6-inch square and put the folded dough in the freezer. Roll, butter, and fold the second piece of dough and put it in the freezer, removing the first piece of dough.

Lightly spray an 8-inch square baking dish with vegetable oil. Roll the chilled folded dough to a 9-inch square (it will shrink a little in handling) and lay it in the bottom of the prepared baking dish. Spread the filling over the dough. Remove the second piece of folded dough from the freezer and roll it to a 9-inch square. Place it on top of the filling. Use your fingertips to poke the dough down slightly around the edges of the baking dish.

Brush the top crust with melted butter and sprinkle with the sesame seeds. Let the dough rise, uncovered, in a warm place until doubled in bulk and gently rounded over the edges of the baking dish.

Preheat the oven to 375°F with the rack in the center position. Bake for 40 to 45 minutes, or until the top is well rounded and a deep golden brown. Remove the pie from the baking dish immediately by loosening the edges with a knife and slipping a large pancake turner under the pie and lifting it out. Serve it warm or at room temperature. If necessary, cool it on a wire rack.

HINT: *This dough works very well with other savory or fruit fillings.*

Zucchini and Onion
Two-Crust Pizza

Vidalia onions are sweet enough to eat raw. They are shipped from the South during the spring months. If you have a hankering for this bountiful garden pizza, but cannot get Vidalias, use Spanish onions instead.

SERVES 4 AS A MAIN COURSE

FOR THE DOUGH

2½	teaspoons yeast	1½	teaspoons salt
3	cups all-purpose flour	1½	cups water
1	teaspoon sugar	1	tablespoon olive oil

Place all the ingredients in the machine, program for Dough, Basic Dough, or Manual, and press Start. The dough will be slightly sticky. While the dough is rising, prepare the filling.

FOR THE FILLING

1	pound zucchini, scrubbed and thinly sliced	2	garlic cloves, minced
1	pound summer squash, scrubbed and thinly sliced		Salt to taste Freshly ground black pepper to taste
8	tablespoons corn oil		
1	pound Vidalia onions, peeled and thinly sliced		

In a large pan, cook the squash in 4 tablespoons of the oil until tender. In a separate pan, cook the onions in the remaining 4 tablespoons of oil until tender. Combine the cooked squash and onions, toss in the garlic, and season with salt and pepper. Strain the mixture, reserving the liquid.

TO FINISH THE PIZZA

2	medium tomatoes, cut into 1-inch slices

Preheat the oven to 400°F with the rack in the center position. Lightly flour a baking sheet and set it aside. When the dough cycle is completed, transfer the dough to a lightly floured work surface, cover it with a clean towel, and let it rest for 5 minutes. Divide the dough in half and roll out each half to a 12-inch circle. Transfer 1 circle to the prepared baking sheet, spoon on and spread out the squash mixture, leaving a 1-inch border, then lay out the tomato slices over the squash. Brush some of the reserved liquid around the perimeter of the dough, which will help the top dough adhere to it. Lay the second piece of dough on top of the filling and press the top and bottom seams together. Brush more of the reserved liquid over the surface of the dough. Cut three 1-inch vents with a pair of scissors in the top. Bake for 25 minutes. The finished pizza will be a rich golden brown.

Cut it into wedges and serve it hot, warm, or at room temperature.

Royal Crown Brie

An herb-scented braided brioche wreath cradles a whole Brie. This is seriously glamorous (yet fairly easy to execute) party fare. It makes a marvelous fancy picnic dish as well as a gorgeous centerpiece for a buffet table. It is served by slicing the brioche and the Brie and layering the two for a delectable open-faced mini-sandwich.

The braid is formed around a layer cake pan which is slipped out after the bread is baked, leaving the perfect space for a wheel of Brie.

The braid can be frozen for three months after it has been baked and completely cooled, wrapped in several layers of plastic wrap. Defrost it at room temperature still wrapped. Add the Brie after the braid has completely defrosted.

SERVES 20

FOR THE DOUGH
1   recipe Brioche Dough (page 122)
1   tablespoon herbs de Provence or
$\frac{1}{2}$ teaspoon of each of the
following: dried tarragon, dried
rosemary, dried chervil, dried
thyme, dried sage

Place all the ingredients in the machine, program for Dough or Manual, and press Start. The dough will be extremely sticky at first, then slightly less so as the kneading progresses. Some will continue to stick to the bottom of the pan. Don't be tempted to add more flour—this is quite a loose dough. It will firm up when chilled.

At the end of the final knead, place the dough in a well-oiled 2-quart bowl, cover it with plastic wrap, and refrigerate it for at least 24 hours or as long as 36 hours.

TO FINISH THE BRIOCHE BRAID
$\frac{1}{4}$ stick (1 ounce) unsalted butter for
greasing the pans
1   egg slightly beaten with 2
tablespoons water

2   tablespoons sesame seeds
1   9-inch wheel ripe Brie

Select a 9 × 2-inch layer cake pan and a 14- or 15-inch round pizza pan. Coat the outside rim of the cake pan generously with butter and place it right side up, centered, on the pizza pan. Butter the rim of the pizza pan that extends beyond the cake pan.

Remove the dough from the refrigerator to a cold work surface that has been lightly coated with vegetable oil. Cut the dough into 3 equal pieces and roll each one into a 25-inch rope. Join the 3 ropes securely at one end, braid them, and secure the other end. Gently stretch the braid until it is long enough to fit around the outside of the cake pan with a small overlap (31 inches). Lay the braid around the pan and pinch the ends together securely to form a wreath. Tuck any ends underneath. Brush the braid with the egg glaze. Place the braid, uncovered, in a warm, draft-free place to rise until doubled in bulk.

Preheat the oven to 425°F with the rack in the center position. Very gently brush the braid one more time with the egg glaze and sprinkle with the sesame seeds. Bake for 15 minutes at 425°F, then lower the oven to 375°F and bake an additional 30 minutes. If the braid appears to be browning too much, cover it loosely with a piece of foil.

Cool the braid on a wire rack for 15 minutes before removing the cake pan, then cool completely before attempting to lift it off the pizza pan. Just before serving, place the Brie in the center of the braid, trimming the brioche slightly if necessary to allow the Brie to lie flat.

HINTS: *You can heat the brioche with the Brie in place just before serving by covering the whole thing loosely with foil and placing it in a 300°F oven for 20 minutes. The Brie will be runny, which will make serving it a tad messy, but the taste of warm brioche and warm cheese is heavenly.*

It's best not to refrigerate brioche, as it will lose its lovely light texture. If it's uncut and wrapped in plastic, you can store it at room temperature for 24 hours.

Baduni

Creating this recipe was a milestone event for Cindy. For the last five years her aunt Nancy has been trying to re-create and perfect a dish that her aunt Nancy made as a long-standing tradition for the family on New Year's Eve. Sicilian in origin, it is a twice-cooked (panfried and then baked) turnover, filled with chicory, anchovies, and fresh plum tomatoes. The Salvato family christened it "baduni."

Armed with dough and chicory, Cindy arrived at her aunt's house eager to learn how this family favorite was assembled. They discussed everything from the best types of dough to how to wash the chicory to whether or not it should be fried or baked. They made it the way that Cindy's aunt remembers how her aunt made it. She says she is sure you'll be as thrilled with the results of her research as she is.

P.S. The Salvato family always drinks a cup of strong coffee with the baduni—no one knows exactly why.

SERVES 4

FOR THE DOUGH

2	teaspoons yeast	2	teaspoons sugar
3	cups all-purpose flour	1¼	cup water
2	teaspoons salt	2	tablespoons olive oil

Place all the ingredients in the machine, program for Manual, Dough, or Basic Dough, and press Start. The dough will be firm and pull away from the machine while kneading. While the dough is rising, prepare the filling.

FOR THE FILLING

1¼	pounds fresh chicory	1	2-ounce can flat anchovies, with
3	medium plum tomatoes		the oil reserved

Trim the chicory and discard any old leaves. Wash the leaves thoroughly in cold water and spin them dry in a salad spinner. Lay out the leaves on paper towels and roll them up to absorb any excess water. Cut the tomatoes into ½-inch slices and set them aside. Drain the anchovies, reserve the oil, and set them aside.

TO FINISH THE BADUNI

Freshly ground black pepper	2	tablespoons olive oil for frying

You are going to assemble this dish in a pie pan, fry it, then bake it. Preheat the oven to 400°F with the rack in the center position. Lightly flour a 9-inch metal pie pan. Have ready a 12-inch nonstick frying pan and a large platter or dinner plate for turning the baduni over.

When the dough cycle is completed, transfer the dough to a lightly floured work surface, cover it with a clean towel and let it rest for 5 minutes. Cut the dough in half and roll out each half to a 14-inch circle. Line the pie pan with 1 circle of dough and pile the chicory leaves on it, building a mound. (Do not panic; it looks like a lot, but remember the leaves will wilt.) The mound will be about 6 inches high. Grind black pepper over the top of the leaves. Place the anchovies around the top and then sprinkle on the anchovy oil. Place the sliced tomatoes over the surface of the chicory. With a pastry brush, brush a small amount of water around the perimeter of the dough and then lay the second circle of dough over the top. Crimp the bottom and top together to seal very well.

You are now ready to fry. Place the olive oil in the frying pan and heat it over medium heat. Transfer the baduni carefully into the pan and cook it for 3 to 4 minutes. Turn it over by placing a dinner plate over the top, and with one swift movement, holding the plate firmly, invert the baduni onto the plate, transfer it back into the pan, and cook the other side for 3 minutes.

To bake, place the pie pan over the top of the baduni while it is still in the frying pan, and again invert it into the pie pan. The baduni itself will be large and will slightly hang over the sides of the pan. Bake it for 15 minutes until it is a rich golden brown. To serve, slice it in wedges and enjoy it hot or warm.

Flatbreads, Crackers, and Breadsticks

Sesame Seed Flatbread

You will amaze your family and guests with these gently puffed square loaves. When sliced, they reveal many thin layers with airy spaces in between which are created by the particular way in which the dough is layered and folded during shaping. I like to make one bread filled (see the Hint) and the other plain. The cooled bread can be stored in a plastic bag and refrigerated for one to two days, or frozen up to a month if tightly wrapped in plastic wrap inside a plastic bag; then defrost it still wrapped.

MAKES 2 LOAVES, EACH SERVING 6 TO 8

FOR THE DOUGH

1	tablespoon yeast		1	large egg
2³/₄	cups all-purpose flour		2	tablespoons dark Karo syrup
1	teaspoon salt		¹/₄	teaspoon nutmeg
²/₃	cup evaporated milk			
1	stick (4 ounces) unsalted butter or margarine			

Place all the ingredients in the machine, program for Dough, Basic Dough, or Manual, and press Start. The dough looks light and sticky but is not sticky to the touch.

TO FINISH THE FLATBREAD

12	tablespoons (1¹/₈ cups) all-purpose flour		1	egg beaten with 1 tablespoon water
¹/₂	stick (2 ounces) unsalted butter, melted		2	tablespoons sesame seeds

Remove the dough from the machine to a work surface lightly sprayed with nonstick vegetable spray. Divide the dough into 12 equal balls, cover them with plastic wrap, and let them rest for 10 minutes.

Roll a ball of dough to a 4- to 5-inch circle, rolling from the center out. Sprinkle the circle with 1 tablespoon of flour and spread it around with your fingers. Roll the next ball in the same way and place it on top of the first floured circle. Sprinkle this second circle with another tablespoon of flour and continue with the remaining circles, stacking them in 2 piles of 6 circles.

Roll each stack of circles to a large 24-inch circle, rolling from the center out.

This should roll out very easily; if it resists you, let it rest 5 minutes and try again. Spread the top of each large circle with 2 tablespoons of melted butter or a filling.

Fold each 24-inch circle inward to a 6-inch square. Lift the circles to a baking sheet lightly sprayed with nonstick vegetable spray. Flatten each to an 8-inch square. Rise for 1 to 1½ hours, or until slightly puffed. The squares will puff much more in the oven.

Preheat the oven to 350°F with the rack in the center position.

Generously brush the egg glaze over the squares and sprinkle with sesame seeds.

Bake for 20 minutes until they are puffed and golden, then cool them on a wire rack. The loaves will sink as they cool.

HINT: *You can spread the 24-inch circles of dough with a thin layer of savory filling such as chopped olives, mushrooms, roasted peppers, or cheese before folding. Many prepared dips, spreads, and sauces such as pesto, hummus, caponata, etc., work as well.*

Rye Flatbrod

This is a very typical example of a Scandinavian flatbrod, *an extremely thin, crisp cracker that can be served at any time of the day—with plain sweet butter in the morning, with a salad at lunch, or with a meat-and-cheese spread in the evening. Rye is a staple grain in the far north because of its hardiness in withstanding and even thriving in cold, gray, damp weather, just like the Scandinavian people.*

MAKES 16 FLATBRODS

FOR THE DOUGH

1 cup pumpernickel flour	1½ teaspoons salt
1 cup white rye flour (light rye, cream rye, medium rye, or dark rye, whatever you're able to get, may be substituted)	2 tablespoons sugar
	½ stick (2 ounces) unsalted butter, melted
1 cup all-purpose flour	1 cup hot water

Place all the ingredients in the machine, program for Manual, Dough, or Basic Dough, and press Start. Leave the lid of the machine open. Check the dough after 5 minutes; it should be quite stiff and very sticky (it won't form a ball).

TO FINISH THE FLATBROD

Preheat your oven to 425°F and have several lightly greased baking sheets ready.

Transfer the dough to a well-floured work surface and divide it into 16 pieces. Working with 1 piece at a time, roll the dough to a thin 7- to 8-inch circle about ¹⁄₁₆ inch thick. (Be sure to keep both your work surface and your rolling pin well floured; this dough tends to be sticky, but with judicious use of flour will roll out very nicely.) Set the circle on a prepared baking sheet. Repeat with the remaining pieces of dough.

Bake the flatbrods for about 7 to 9 minutes, or until they're crisp and just beginning to brown (you'll have to do this in shifts). Remove the flatbrods from the pan and cool them completely on a wire rack. Store them in an airtight container.

> HINT: *Don't make flatbrods on a very damp or humid day; they won't become crisp enough as they cool.*

Rye terminology can be confusing. Look at it this way: White rye flour (or cream, light, medium, or dark rye flour) is to the rye berry what all-purpose flour is to the wheat berry— it's flour milled from the endosperm of the berry and doesn't include the germ or bran. Pumpernickel flour (or rye meal) is the equivalent of whole wheat flour—it's made by milling the entire rye berry, endosperm, germ, bran, and all. Where, then, do the light, white, cream, medium, and dark come in? White rye comes from the very center of the rye berry, just outside the germ. The farther out toward the bran layer the miller goes, the darker the flour becomes. Thus we go from white ("light") to cream to dark; medium rye is a combination of all of these.

Ksra

This flat, round, hearty Moroccan bread gets its leavening from sourdough. Many cultures discovered long ago how to make sourdough by capturing the wild airborne yeast released by fairly liquid doughs that had been left uncovered in a warm place for a few days. A recipe for sourdough starter can be found on page 20. You can go the easy route by borrowing some starter from a friend or mail-ordering it (page 301). The cooled bread can be frozen for up to one month, tightly wrapped in plastic wrap inside a plastic bag.

SERVES 6 TO 8

FOR THE DOUGH

2	cups sourdough starter		2	teaspoons sugar
1	cup whole wheat flour		$1/4$	stick (1 ounce) unsalted butter
1	cup barley flour		$1/2$	cup milk
1	teaspoon salt		1	teaspoon caraway seeds

Place all the ingredients in the machine, program for Dough or Manual, and press Start. The dough will be light and sticky.

TO FINISH THE KSRA

3 tablespoons cornmeal

Using 2 tablespoons of cornmeal, sprinkle a 10-inch circle on a heavy baking sheet. Remove the dough from the machine and put it on top of the cornmeal. Sprinkle it with the remaining 1 tablespoon of cornmeal and press the dough to a 10-inch circle. Use the tines of a fork to prick a star design on the top of the dough. Cover the dough loosely with plastic wrap and let it rise in a warm place for 1 hour. Preheat the oven to 375°F with the rack in the center position. Bake the bread for 30 minutes, or until it sounds hollow when tapped.

Finnish Flatbread

This is a slightly sweet, airy flatbread with a crunchy crust. Eat it warm from the oven cut into narrow wedges and slathered with butter. In Finland it is common to serve this for breakfast or as a homey dessert, spread with butter and sprinkled with sugar. It is not too sweet for a dinner or appetizer bread, and it is particularly good with a thick coating of blue cheese. You can freeze it when it's completely cooled, wrapped in foil and placed in a plastic bag; then defrost it still wrapped.

MAKES ONE 10-INCH LOAF

FOR THE DOUGH

1	tablespoon yeast		1½	teaspoons salt
1½	cups all-purpose flour		¾	cup plus 1 tablespoon water
1½	cups rye flour		3	tablespoons unsalted butter or
3	tablespoons light brown sugar			margarine

Place all the ingredients in the machine, program for Dough, Basic Dough, or Manual, and press Start. The dough will hold a ball shape while kneading and will be tacky but not sticky.

TO FINISH THE FLATBREAD
1   tablespoon cornmeal

Sprinkle a baking sheet with the tablespoon of cornmeal. Remove the dough from the machine and flatten it between your palms to a 6-inch disk. Place the disk on top of the cornmeal on the baking sheet and flatten it further to a 9½-inch circle. Take care to make it as round and as flat as possible. Use the side of your hand to make a sharp edge.

Cover the circle lightly with plastic wrap and let it rise in a warm place for 1½ to 2 hours, or until it is almost doubled in height and the edges have puffed and rounded. Preheat the oven to 425°F. Bake the loaf for 15 to 20 minutes, or until browned but not black—lift a corner of it to check that the bottom is not getting too dark. The loaf should sound hollow when tapped.

HINT: *You must cover the dough as it rests and rises so that it will not form an unpleasant dried-out layer that will crack when the bread bakes. Plastic wrap works well, but be sure to wrap it loosely so that the plastic does not keep the dough from rising fully. In the case of this bread, the oily surface of a baking sheet is apt to form a tight seal with the plastic wrap, trapping the dough as it tries to rise. An alternative to plastic wrap is a clean tea towel.*

Trail Mix Flatbread

Take these durable snacks along next time you hit the trail (or need something to nibble on during a ball game or plane ride). They make great picnic fare as well. Choose your favorite trail mix from the hundreds available in your local health food store. These keep for a long time when you store them in an airtight tin at room temperature.

MAKES 24 WEDGES

FOR THE DOUGH

2	cups all-purpose flour	1/4	cup honey
1	cup whole wheat flour	1	cup water, plus an additional 2 to
1	teaspoon salt		3 tablespoons if necessary to form
1	teaspoon baking powder		a smooth ball of dough
1/4	cup molasses	1 1/4	cups trail mix

Preheat the oven to 350°F with the rack in the center position. Line 2 baking sheets with parchment. Use a chopstick to stir together the flours, salt, and baking powder in the bread machine. Add the molasses and honey and water (reserving the additional water). Press Start (since you are only kneading briefly, the setting doesn't matter) and allow the dough to knead into a smooth ball. Add more water if necessary after the first 3 minutes of kneading. Add the trail mix and continue to knead until well incorporated.

TO FINISH THE FLATBREAD

Divide the dough in 2. Roll each half to a 10-inch circle. Cut each circle into 12 wedges. Transfer the wedges to the baking sheets, placing them 1/2 inch apart. Bake for 12 to 14 minutes, or until dry and slightly browned. Cool on racks until cool.

Norwegian Flatbread

These crispy rounds, which are cooked in a pan on the stove top, are just the thing to serve alongside pâté or cheese spreads. Look for barley flour in your health food store or send for it by mail order (page 301).

MAKES TEN 10-INCH ROUNDS

FOR THE DOUGH

½   teaspoon salt
1½ cups barley flour

1½ cups whole wheat flour
1   cup water

Place all the ingredients in the machine, program for Dough or Manual, and press Start. After the dough has come together and formed a ball, about 2 to 3 minutes, cancel the machine, transfer the dough to a lightly floured work surface, cover it with a clean towel, and allow it to rest for 5 minutes.

TO FINISH THE FLATBREAD

Use your hands to roll the dough out to a rope 20 inches long. Use a knife or pair of scissors to cut the rope into ten 2-inch pieces. Using plenty of flour, roll out each piece to a paper-thin free-form 10-inch circle.

Heat a 10- to 12-inch heavy frying pan; cast-iron works beautifully. Over medium-low heat, slowly cook each round about 5 minutes on each side. The finished flatbreads should be crispy. Cool them completely on racks before storing them in an airtight container until you are ready to serve them. This flatbread will keep several months.

Lefse

This wonderful flatbread was inspired by James Beard and is adapted from his book Beard on Bread. *The word* lefse *means "leaf," which is the perfect name to describe its thinness and crispiness.*

MAKES 12 FLATBREADS

FOR THE DOUGH
3½ cups all-purpose flour
⅛ teaspoon salt
¼ cup sugar
½ teaspoon baking soda

¼ teaspoon cardamom
3 tablespoons buttermilk
6 tablespoons corn syrup
1 cup water

Place all the ingredients in the machine, program for Dough or Basic Dough, and press Start. Mix the dough for approximately 3 minutes, or until it forms a ball. Cancel the machine and transfer the dough to a lightly floured work surface and let it rest for 5 minutes.

TO FINISH THE LEFSE
Flour for rolling

Using plenty of flour, roll out the dough to ¼ inch thick. Using a round 4-inch cookie cutter, cut out 8 circles. Gather the leftover dough and roll it together, let it rest for 5 minutes, then roll it again and cut out the last 4 circles. On plenty of flour, roll out each circle to a 7-inch circle and set them aside. Heat a 9-inch cast-iron skillet sprinkled with a little flour. Place 1 lefse at a time in the skillet and cook each side on low heat for approximately 5 minutes. The lefses will be lightly browned when finished.

We tried to find some newfangled way to enjoy this yummy bread, but there is something to be said for tradition. Enjoy it as is nice and warm from the skillet with a creamy cheese like Havarti or with your favorite fruit preserve.

Skillet Bread

The dough for this simple fried bread is removed from the machine, rolled or patted into 9-inch circles, and panfried. An electric frying pan makes it easier to control the heat. Hot out of the pan, the bread may be sprinkled with sugar or cinnamon and sugar, or fresh herbs or grated cheese. The dough can be made a day ahead and stored in a plastic bag in the refrigerator until you fry it. Fried doughs are best eaten warm.

MAKES FOUR 9-INCH FLATBREADS

FOR THE DOUGH

1   teaspoon yeast
1   teaspoon baking powder
2½   cups all-purpose flour
1   teaspoon salt

1   cup milk, heated to 120°F
¼   stick (1 ounce) unsalted butter
     or margarine

Place all the ingredients in the machine, program for Dough, Basic Dough, or Manual, and press Start. The dough will look and feel slightly sticky.

TO FINISH THE FLATBREADS
About ¼ cup vegetable oil

At the end of the final cycle, transfer the dough to a floured work surface and divide it into fourths. Pat or roll each piece of dough to a 9-inch circle, using as much flour as necessary to keep the dough from sticking.

Heat an electric frying pan to 360°F or set a skillet over medium heat and add about 3 tablespoons of oil. When the oil spatters when a drop of water hits it, fry the circles of dough, 1 at a time, until they are a deep golden brown. This will take about 2 to 2½ minutes per side. Add additional oil as needed. Drain the bread on paper towels. While it's hot, sprinkle it with either a sweet or savory topping, and serve it warm.

◇

HINT: *Be sure that your oil is hot enough before you start frying or the dough will absorb too much oil and become soggy. Fry the circles one at a time because cooking more than one at a time will cool the oil too much and the bread will steam.*

◇

Vera's Tahini Bread

When Lynne was researching Armenian breads for this book, her friend Vera shared this recipe, a favorite Armenian Lenten recipe, which Lynne adapted for the bread machine. There are many versions of this sweet, crisp flatbread; in this version it is rolled and coiled with a layer of tahini, cinnamon, and sugar. Tahini (sesame paste) can be found in supermarkets near the peanut butter.

The finished flatbreads, after cooling, can be stored in a tightly covered container at room temperature for several days. To freeze them, wrap them tightly with plastic and store them in a rigid container with a tight-fitting lid. The rigid container will keep the flatbreads from breaking.

MAKES SIX 7-INCH FLATBREADS

FOR THE DOUGH

1	stick (4 ounces) unsalted butter		1	teaspoon salt
$^1/_2$	cup milk		$^1/_2$	teaspoon sugar
$1^1/_2$	teaspoons yeast		2	large eggs
$3^1/_2$	cups all-purpose flour			

Melt the butter in the milk and cool to lukewarm. Place all the ingredients in the machine, program for Dough or Manual, and press Start. The dough will look sticky at first but should be medium-firm toward the end of the kneading.

TO FINISH THE FLATBREADS

4	tablespoons tahini		2	tablespoons cinnamon
4	tablespoons plus 3 optional teaspoons sugar		1	egg

Remove the dough from the machine to a work surface. Using a little flour if necessary, knead the dough by hand a few times until it is smooth, then divide it into 6 equal balls. Let the balls rest for 10 minutes, covered with a clean towel, so that they will be easier to roll out.

Preheat the oven to 350°F with the rack in the center position. Lightly spray a heavy baking sheet with nonstick vegetable spray and set aside.

Roll each ball to a 10-inch circle, rolling from the center out. Spread each circle with 2 teaspoons of tahini. Mix together the 4 tablespoons sugar and the cinnamon and sprinkle 1 slightly rounded tablespoon of the mixture over the tahini on each circle.

Take a circle and roll it up jelly roll fashion until you have a long rope. Twist the rope 4 or 5 times but stop if the dough starts to tear. If it starts to tear, you can gently squeeze and stretch the rope. Hold 1 end of the rope up about an inch, making a little tail, and coil the rest of the rope around it. Tuck the last part of the opposite end under the coil. Set the coil aside and cover with plastic wrap or a towel. Repeat with the remaining circles of dough.

When you finish the last coil, take the first coil you made and roll it to a 7-inch very flat circle by rolling from the center out. If the coils don't roll out easily, let them rest a little longer. Using a pastry scraper or large spatula, place the circles on the prepared baking sheet.

Beat the egg with a fork until foamy and generously brush it on the tops of the circles. Sprinkle them with the 3 teaspoons sugar if desired. Bake for 15 to 25 minutes, depending on how crisp and firm you like flatbread. I've had it so crisp that it breaks apart like a cracker, but I like it a little softer.

HINT: *If your tahini has liquid on the top when you open it, get a butter knife and stir up the hard layer from the bottom, mixing it until it is smooth. This may take some elbow grease.*

MoJo's Cheese Melts

This recipe is inspired from a tiny take-out stand called MoJo's off Commer-cial Street in Provincetown on the very end of Cape Cod. Flat circles of bread are topped with layers of cream cheese, sautéed mushrooms, tomatoes, cheese, and sprouts. Once you taste this, you'll understand why there is always a long line at MoJo's. Have your napkins ready—these must be eaten hot from the oven.

MAKES 6

FOR THE DOUGH

1	tablespoon yeast		2	teaspoons sugar
2½	cups all-purpose flour		1¼	cups warm water
1	cup whole wheat flour		2	tablespoons olive oil
1	teaspoon salt		¼	teaspoon cayenne pepper

Place all the ingredients in the machine, program for Dough or Manual, and press Start. The dough will be firm and stiff.

FOR THE BREAD

Preheat the oven to 450°F with the rack in the lowest position. Preheat a baking stone or ungreased heavy baking sheet for 15 minutes.

Transfer the dough to a lightly oiled work surface. Divide it evenly into 6 balls and let them rest, uncovered, for 10 minutes. Roll each ball to a 6-inch circle. Us-ing a wide metal spatula or small cookie sheet, slide the circles onto the baking stone or baking sheet and bake for 5 minutes until they are light golden brown on the bottoms. Cool them, covered with a towel, and place them in unsealed plastic bags as soon as they are cool enough to handle. Seal the bags when they are com-pletely cooled.

TO FINISH THE MELTS

1	tablespoon olive oil		6	tablespoons plain or herb cream cheese
10	ounces white mushrooms, thinly sliced (about 20 medium-size mushrooms, or 10 to 12 large)		2	small tomatoes, chopped
			1	cup grated Cheddar cheese, firmly packed
1	cup thinly sliced Spanish onion		1	cup alfalfa sprouts, tightly packed
1	garlic clove, minced			

Heat the oil over medium-high heat in a large heavy skillet. Add the mush-rooms, onion, and garlic and sauté until they have turned a rich golden color and the liquid is evaporated. This should take about 15 to 20 minutes, and watch them carefully toward the end so that they don't scorch.

While the mushroom mixture is cooking, spread each of the baked breads with 1 tablespoon cream cheese. Preheat the boiler to high with the pan 4 inches from the heating element. Distribute the mushroom mixture evenly over the breads. Sprinkle with the tomato and top with the grated cheese. Broil for 3 minutes, or until the cheese is melted and starting to brown. Remove from the heat and distribute the sprouts evenly over the cheese.

HINT: *When you are in a hurry, use store-bought pitas for the bread.*

Vicki Caparulo's Parchment Bread

New Jersey cooking teacher, journalist, and baker extraordinaire Vicki Caparulo brought me a basket of these wafer-thin cracker breads. I ate them all, down to the last crumb, and looked around for more. It's a good thing they are nonfat—doesn't that mean I can eat as many as I want?

Serve these to your guests with drinks, or include them in a bread basket for a change of pace from traditional fare. They are just about perfect as they are, or you can gild the lily by offering softened goat cheese to spread on top. You have the option of making the breads plain or varying the flavors by adding dried herbs or seeds or cheese.

Semolina flour is available in specialty food shops and Italian markets and by mail order (page 301).

For this recipe, you must preheat the oven before you make the dough.

MAKES 16 PIECES

FOR THE DOUGH

2 cups all-purpose flour
1 cup semolina flour

2 teaspoons salt
1 cup water

At least 15 minutes before making the dough, preheat the oven to 450°F with the rack or a pizza stone in the center position. Place all the ingredients in the machine, program for Dough, Basic Dough, or Manual, and press Start. At the end of the first knead you should have a thick, stiff dough.

TO FINISH THE BREAD

Approximately 16 teaspoons of the following seasonings, either individually or in combination: dried dill, dried basil, dried oregano, dried thyme, toasted sesame seeds, toasted fennel seeds, poppy seeds, freshly ground black pepper, grated Parmesan or Romano cheese, dried minced onion, dried minced garlic, caraway seeds

Remove the dough to a lightly floured work surface and divide it in half. Cover one half with plastic wrap and divide the remaining half into 8 pieces (kitchen scissors are good to use for this).

Working with 1 piece of dough at a time, flour both sides and use a rolling pin to roll it as thin as possible. Flip the dough over, dust with flour, and roll again.

Continue rolling, flouring, and flipping until the dough is irregular in shape and thin enough to see your hand through, about $1/16$ inch or less for plain bread.

To season the bread with seeds, roll the dough to $1/8$ inch. Sprinkle 1 teaspoon of seeds on top, sprinkle with a dusting of flour, then using heavy pressure on the rolling pin, continue rolling the seasoning into the dough, making the dough as thin as possible.

If you choose to add dried herbs to the dough, moisten it with 1 tablespoon of water and sprinkle it generously with the herbs, working them into the dough in a kneading motion.

If you are not using a pizza stone, line a baking sheet with parchment paper and place the pieces of dough on the baking sheet (they can be right next to each other but should not overlap). If you are using a pizza stone, arrange them as above, but slide the paper onto the stone, removing the baking sheet. Bake for 3 to 4 minutes, or until the bread is bubbled and beginning to brown (the color will be uneven). Use tongs to turn the bread and continue baking for an additional 2 to 3 minutes more. Remove the bread to a rack to cool and continue to bake the rest. These are best served the next day as they will become crisper. Store in a covered container at room temperature for up to one month.

Potato Flatbread with Sour Cream, Chives, and Bacon

If you love a baked potato with all the fixin's, this one's for you!

MAKES ONE 12-INCH FLATBREAD

FOR THE DOUGH

1	teaspoon yeast
2	cups all-purpose flour
$1/2$	teaspoon salt
$1/4$	teaspoon freshly ground black pepper

$1/2$	cup whole milk or $1/2$ cup water plus 3 tablespoons nonfat dry milk
$1/2$	cup mashed potatoes (you can use your leftovers or instant)

Place all the ingredients in the machine, program for Manual, Dough, or Basic Dough, and press Start. The dough will be firm and pull away from the sides of the machine.

TO FINISH THE FLATBREAD

$2/3$	cup sour cream
2	tablespoons dried chives
3	strips of bacon, cooked and crumbled, bacon fat reserved

Salt to taste
Freshly ground black pepper to taste

In a stainless-steel bowl, blend together these ingredients.
Preheat the oven to 400°F with the rack in the center position. Lightly flour a cookie sheet and set it aside. When the cycle is finished, transfer the dough to a lightly floured work surface, cover it with a clean towel, and let it rest 5 minutes. Roll out the dough to a 12-inch circle and brush on some of the reserved bacon fat. Spread the sour cream mixture over the surface of the dough, leaving a $1/2$-inch border all around. Bake the bread for 25 minutes until well browned. Enjoy it hot, warm, or at room temperature.

Lavosh

Lavosh is the popular Middle Eastern cracker bread that is great as a snack or served with soups and salads. It is very easy to make and since you are going to use your machine as a mixer only, it should take you approximately thirty minutes to prepare from beginning to end.

MAKES 3 TO 4 DOZEN PIECES

FOR THE DOUGH

¹/₄	teaspoon yeast	¹/₂	teaspoon salt
1¹/₂	cups all-purpose flour	1	tablespoon unsalted butter, melted
¹/₂	cup whole wheat flour	³/₄	cup plus 2 tablespoons water
1	teaspoon sugar		

Place all the ingredients in the machine, program for Dough or Basic Dough, and press Start. As soon as the dough has come together in a nice smooth ball, approximately 5 minutes, cancel the machine and transfer the dough to a lightly floured work surface. Divide the dough in half and let it rest for 10 minutes. You may be wondering about the yeast! The purpose of the yeast in this recipe is not for leavening, since this is a flatbread. The yeast gives the lavosh its characteristic air pockets.

TO FINISH THE LAVOSH

2 to 3	tablespoons water	2	tablespoons sesame seeds

Preheat the oven to 400°F and lightly flour 2 cookie sheets. Using plenty of flour, and rolling slowly, roll out one half of the dough to the length of a cookie sheet. Transfer the dough onto the sheet and repeat this procedure with the second half of dough. Brush each bread lightly with water and sprinkle with sesame seeds. Bake the breads 10 to 15 minutes; they will be browned in some areas and just crispy in others. Cool the breads and break them up into manageable pieces.

Macadamia Nut Lavosh

This recipe is dedicated to Lynn Lee, the gracious and multitalented dynamo who orchestrates and runs Hawaii's Liberty House's culinary programs. An hour with Lynn is like a trip to a spa; imagine how great I felt after two whole days of classes in Hawaii. She regaled me with fragrant leis, fed me the finest in Pacific Rim cuisine, rounded up the biggest audience I've ever seen at a cooking class, and kept me smiling with her delightful charm. If macadamia nuts are one of Hawaii's natural treasures, Lynn Lee has to be another one.

These buttery, crisp, sweet crackers will keep for several weeks in an airtight container or plastic bag.

MAKES ABOUT 5 DOZEN PIECES

FOR THE DOUGH

1   cup whole wheat flour
2   cups all-purpose flour
1   teaspoon salt
1   cup raw (turbinado) sugar (available in health food and specialty food stores) or 1 cup dark brown sugar, firmly packed
8   ounces macadamia nut butter (available in health food and specialty food stores or made by processing 8 ounces toasted macadamia nuts in a food processor until smooth)
3/4   cup water
4   ounces (2/3 cup) macadamia nuts, finely chopped (if you cannot find unsalted macadamia nuts, shake them in a wide-mesh strainer to remove as much salt as possible before chopping)

Place all the ingredients except the macadamia nuts in the machine, program for Dough, Basic Dough, or Manual, and press Start. When a ball forms, add the macadamia nuts and knead for another 3 to 4 minutes, or until the macadamia nuts are incorporated.

TO FINISH THE LAVOSH

Preheat the oven to 450°F with the rack in the center position. Line 3 baking sheets with parchment paper.

Remove the dough to a floured work surface and cut it into 4 pieces. A metal dough scraper is good for this job as well as for cutting and moving the lavosh to the baking sheet. Dust 1 piece of dough liberally with flour and roll it out as thin as possible, sprinkling with additional flour as needed to keep the dough from sticking to the surface and the rolling pin. You'll know you've rolled it too thin when it starts to tear. Cut the dough into $2\frac{1}{2} \times \frac{1}{2}$-inch strips. Lay the strips right next to each other on a prepared baking sheet. Repeat with the remaining dough.

Bake the lavosh for 18 to 20 minutes, or until they start to turn deep brown. Loosen them from the parchment paper and allow them to cool on the baking sheet before storing them in plastic bags.

Hazelnut Lavosh

This is a cross between a cookie and a cracker. If you love the rich buttery taste of hazelnuts but aren't crazy about supersweet cookies, then this should please you. The trick here is to get the dough as thin as possible and remove it from the oven as soon as the lavosh is browned but not burned. This recipe calls for rolling out the dough and baking it on the underside of an oiled jelly roll or sheet pan. Since you cook these at a very high temperature, make sure that there are no burned-on foods stuck to the bottom of your oven—they will smoke and make the lavosh taste unpleasant.

Toasted filbert butter is available in health food stores (look in the peanut butter section) as is raw (or Turbinado) sugar. If you cannot find it, substitute a like amount of dark brown sugar. You can make your own hazelnut butter by processing 8 ounces toasted, skinned hazelnuts in a food processor until smooth.

MAKES ABOUT 7 DOZEN PIECES

FOR THE DOUGH

1	cup whole wheat flour		1/4	stick (1 ounce) unsalted butter, very soft
2	cups all-purpose flour			
1 1/2	teaspoons salt		1	cup water
1/2	cup raw sugar or 1/2 cup dark brown sugar, firmly packed		1	8-ounce jar toasted filbert butter (including the oil at the top)

Place all the ingredients in the machine, program for Dough or Manual, and press Start.

TO FINISH THE LAVOSH

Preheat the oven to 500°F with the rack in the center position. Spray the undersides of 2 jelly roll or sheet pans with nonstick vegetable spray.

When the dough is well mixed and has formed a soft, smooth ball, remove it from the machine and divide it into 4 pieces. Roll 1 section of dough directly on a pan. Roll carefully away from the center where the dough is the thickest, out to the edges, trying to achieve as even a layer as possible. The dough should be paper-thin. You don't have to rush—it's better to take your time because the thinner you get the dough in the center, the crispier all the pieces will be. If you find that the pan is sliding around on the counter, try placing a wet dish towel or couple of damp sponges underneath it to keep it in place.

Using a knife or pizza cutter, cut the dough into 4 strips lengthwise, and then cut each strip into 5 to 6 strips crosswise. Place the pan in the oven and bake for 8 to 10 minutes, or until the pieces on the edges are browned. While the first pan is baking, roll out another section of dough on the second pan. Remove the first pan from the oven and use a metal spatula to lift off the browned pieces. Return the pan to the oven and continue baking until all the pieces are brown. Repeat with the second pan.

Allow the lavosh to cool on racks and cool the pans before proceeding with the remaining dough. It isn't necessary to respray the pans.

Sourdough Rye Cracklebread

I was so excited when I nailed down this recipe that I threw some in a basket and went from house to house in my neighborhood to show them off. Fortunately my neighbors are used to my loco behavior to recipe triumphs. They patted me on the head and thanked me for sharing. After one bite they all asked for the recipe!

If you take the time (not a lot) to roll these as thin as possible and bake them to a lovely deep golden brown, you will achieve a taste and texture sensation that will make every store-bought cracker pale in comparison. This recipe calls for a few things that not every home cook might have lurking in the refrigerator or on the pantry shelf. Sourdough starter can be made from the recipe on page 20, borrowed from a friend, made from a dry mix, or mail-ordered (page 301). Black caraway seeds can be found in most spice stores and are also available by mail order. You can substitute regular caraway seeds if you can't find black (also called Russian) caraway seeds, but the search is worth the extraordinary difference in taste. These are cooked on the underside of a baking sheet.

MAKES ABOUT 7 DOZEN PIECES

FOR THE DOUGH

1	cup sourdough starter		2	tablespoons black caraway seeds
2	cups rye flour		½	cup dark beer plus an additional 1
1	cup all-purpose flour			to 2 tablespoons if necessary to
2	teaspoons salt			form a smooth, elastic, slightly
1	teaspoon freshly ground black			sticky dough
	pepper			

Place all the ingredients in the machine, program for Dough or Manual, and press Start. The dough will be dry and crumbly at first but should smooth out after a few minutes of kneading. At the end of the first knead cycle, cancel the machine, transfer the dough to a lightly oiled work surface, and cover it with plastic wrap while you prepare the pans.

TO FINISH THE CRACKLEBREAD

Preheat the oven to 500°F with the rack in the center position. Spray the undersides of 3 heavy-duty jelly roll or sheet pans with nonstick vegetable spray. Cut the dough into 3 pieces and roll each piece right on a prepared pan. Roll carefully away from the center where the dough is the thickest, out to the edges, trying to achieve as even a layer as possible. The dough should be paper-thin. You don't have to rush—it's better to take your time because the thinner you get the dough in the center, the crispier all the pieces will be. If you find that the pan is sliding around on the counter, try placing a wet dish towel or couple of damp sponges underneath it to keep it in place.

Using a knife or pizza cutter, cut the dough into 4 strips lengthwise, and then cut each strip into 5 to 6 strips crosswise. Place the pan in the oven and bake for 8 to 10 minutes, or until the cracklebread turns a deep golden brown. The pieces on the edges will color first, so use a long-handled metal spatula to remove them and allow the center pieces to continue cooking until they too are brown. Remove the cracklebread to a rack to cool compeltely. Repeat with the other pans.

When the cracklebread has cooled completely, it can be stored up to 1 month in a sealed container.

Pesto Crackers

A little crunch, a bit of cheese—here's something novel to serve with drinks or as a snack. These quick-to-make tidbits will satisfy you pesto lovers out there—and perhaps even win a few converts.

MAKES ABOUT 5 DOZEN PIECES

FOR THE DOUGH

$1/2$ cup cornmeal	$3/4$ cup (6 ounces) pesto
1 cup whole wheat flour or White Wheat flour (page 5)	1 cup water plus an additional 1 to 2 tablespoons to make a smooth ball after the first few minutes of kneading
2 cups all-purpose flour	
1 teaspoon salt	
$1/2$ teaspoon freshly ground black pepper	

Preheat the oven to 450°F with the rack in the center position. Place all the ingredients in the machine, program for Dough, Basic Dough, or Manual, and press Start. Add additional water if necessary to form the dough into a smooth ball. Knead for 5 to 6 minutes. Line 2 baking sheets with parchment or spray them with nonstick vegetable spray.

TO FINISH THE CRACKERS

$1/2$ cup freshly grated Parmesan cheese

Remove the dough to a floured work surface and cut it in 4 pieces. A metal dough scraper is good for this job as well as for cutting and moving the dough to the pan. Dust 1 piece of dough with flour and roll it out as thin as possible, sprinkling a small amount of additional flour as needed to keep the dough from sticking to the surface and the rolling pin. Cut the dough into $2^{1}/_{2} \times {}^{1}/_{2}$-inch strips. Lay the strips right next to each other on the prepared pan. Repeat with the remaining dough. Sprinkle the strips with cheese and bake for 13 to 15 minutes, or until the tops are browned. Cool the crackers on the baking sheet, then store them in an airtight container at room temperature.

Spicy Beer Cheese Crackers

These crisp munchies will warm your whistle. The combination of red pepper flakes, Tabasco sauce, and beer makes a mighty hot combination. You can tone down the heat by reducing the amount of pepper, or just make sure there's lots of cold beer on hand.

These will keep for several weeks when stored (after they are cool) in an airtight container at room temperature.

MAKES ABOUT 7 DOZEN CRACKERS

FOR THE DOUGH

3$^{1}/_{3}$	cups all-purpose flour		8 to 10	drops Tabasco sauce
$^{1}/_{3}$	cup cornmeal		3	tablespoons tomato paste
2	teaspoons seasoned salt		3	tablespoons olive oil
1 to 2	teaspoons red pepper flakes		$^{1}/_{2}$	cup grated Cheddar cheese
1$^{1}/_{3}$	cups beer			

Preheat the oven to 475°F with the rack in the center position. Line 3 baking sheets with parchment paper.

Place all the ingredients in the machine, program for Dough or Manual, and press Start. The dough will form a smooth, soft ball after the first 5 to 6 minutes of kneading.

TO FINISH THE CRACKERS

Remove the dough to a lightly floured work surface and divide it into 4 pieces. Working with 1 piece at a time, roll it out as thin as possible, then use a sharp knife or metal dough scraper to cut it into 1$^{1}/_{2}$-inch squares. Place the squares right next to each other on a prepared pan. Repeat with the remaining dough.

Bake for 15 to 17 minutes, or until the crackers are browned. Loosen them from the parchment paper and allow them to cool on the pans before storing them in an airtight container.

Carta da Musica

This bread is found around the island of Sardinia off Italy. This dough is rolled out very thin so that it resembles paper, hence the name "Music Sheet." Its cracker quality made it ideal for the shepherds who would spend days away from home; they would either eat it in its cracker form or rehydrate the sheets in a little water. Music sheets are great as part of an antipasto table or as a snack. Another wonderful way to use this dough is to roll it out and grill it for a pizza shell.

Since this is a nonyeasted bread, you will be using your bread machine only to mix the dough.

MAKES 3 TO 5 DOZEN PIECES, OR 4 PIZZA CRUSTS

FOR THE DOUGH

2	cups all-purpose flour	1¼	teaspoons salt
1	cup semolina flour	1¼	cups water

Preheat the oven to 400°F. Place all the ingredients in the machine, program for Dough, Basic Dough, or Manual, and press Start.

Mix the ingredients for 3 minutes, or until they come together to make a dough. Cancel the machine and transfer the dough to a lightly floured surface.

TO FINISH THE BREAD

Let the dough rest for 10 minutes. Cut the dough into 4 pieces. On a floured work surface, roll out the dough slowly; believe it or not, the dough will roll out into a 16 × 12-inch rectangle. Transfer the sheet of dough onto lightly floured cookie sheet. Bake the bread 15 to 20 minutes until golden brown. Cool the bread and break it up into manageable pieces.

◇

> *To grill the dough for individual pizzas, cut the dough into 4 pieces and roll out each piece to a 6-inch circle. The grill should be hot and lightly oiled, which will prevent the dough from sticking. Grill the circles on each side for 3 or 4 minutes, being careful not to burn them; they should have grill marks on them. Then top them with your favorite pizza toppings and bake them in a 400°F oven for 10 to 15 minutes.*

◇

Sesame Wheat Crisps

Yes, these crackers include a lot of sugar; but fear not, they're still crackers, not cookies. The sugar just works to point up the naturally sweet flavor of whole wheat, and it's a nice counterpoint to the nutty snap of the sesame seeds.

MAKES 8 DOZEN CRACKERS

FOR THE DOUGH

1	cup pastry flour or cake flour	1/2	teaspoon salt
1	cup whole wheat flour	1/4	stick (1 ounce) unsalted butter, cut
1/4	cup sesame seeds		into 6 pieces
1/2	cup sugar	1/3	to a scant 1/2 cup milk

Place the flours, sesame seeds, sugar, and salt in the machine, program for Manual, Basic Dough, or Dough, and press Start. Leave the lid of the machine open. Let the ingredients mix for 1 minute, then add the butter. Let the mixture mix for 5 minutes; it should be the consistency of coarse crumbs. If there are still lumps of butter in the dough, let it knead an additional 1 or 2 minutes.

Add the 1/3 cup of milk, and mix 15 to 20 seconds more, until the dough starts to clump up. Gather a handful of the dough and squeeze; if it holds together easily, cancel the machine and remove the dough. If it's too dry to hold together well, knead an additional 15 seconds. Transfer the dough to a lightly floured work surface, gather and gently squeeze it into a ball, and divide it into 3 pieces.

TO FINISH THE CRISPS

Working with 1 piece at a time, roll the dough to a rough rectangle 1/16 inch thick. Using a rolling pizza wheel, a pastry wheel, or a sharp knife, cut the dough into 2 × 1-inch rectangles. Transfer the rectangles to lightly greased baking sheets. Repeat with the remaining pieces of dough.

Bake in a preheated 325°F oven for 20 to 25 minutes, or until the crackers are a light golden brown.

> *These are typical nonleavened crackers: very thin, very crisp. Be sure to keep the work surface and rolling pin well floured as you roll; the secret of success is a very thin sheet of dough. Thick dough will produce a cracker that is hard and leaden rather than crisp.*

Rye Squares

These rye crackers, ultra-thin and crisp, are the perfect vehicle for cheese, pâté, or herring in sour cream, all classic elements of a smorgasbord. Rye flour is, after all, a staple in Scandinavia, and the Scandinavians know how to get the most out of this assertively flavored grain.

MAKES 7 DOZEN CRACKERS

FOR THE DOUGH

1	cup white, light, or medium rye flour	1	tablespoon unsweetened cocoa powder
1	cup all-purpose flour	1/4	cup shortening
1	teaspoon salt	1	tablespoon molasses
3	tablespoons caraway seeds	5	tablespoons water

Place the flours, salt, caraway seeds, and cocoa powder in the machine, program for Manual, Basic Dough, or Dough, and press Start. Leave the lid of the machine open. Let the ingredients mix for 1 minute, then add the shortening. Let the mixture mix for 3 to 4 minutes; it should be the consistency of coarse crumbs. If there are still large lumps of shortening in the dough, let it knead an additional 1 to 2 minutes.

Add the molasses and water and mix 15 to 20 seconds more, until the dough starts to clump up. Transfer the dough to a lightly floured work surface, gather and gently squeeze it into a ball, and divide it into 3 pieces.

TO FINISH THE SQUARES

Working with 1 piece at a time, roll the dough into a rough rectangle 1/16 inch thick. Be sure to keep your work surface sufficiently floured, lifting the dough with the edge of a spatula and sprinkling flour underneath as necessary; rye dough tends to be quite sticky. Using a rolling pizza wheel, a pastry wheel, or a sharp knife, cut the dough into 2-inch squares. Transfer the squares to a lightly greased baking sheet. Repeat with the remaining dough.

Bake in a preheated 325°F oven for 20 to 25 minutes, or until the crackers begin to brown and smell toasty.

Hey, accept it. Rye dough is sticky; it just is. Avoid the temptation to add more and more flour—the dough will practically fall apart, leaden with flour, before the stickiness disappears. A thin but even sprinkling of flour underneath as you roll, a thin sprinkling on top (or a rolling pin with a flour-imbued muslin cover)—that's the way to roll out rye dough.

Golden Cheese Crackers

These deep orange crackers feature a mellow cheese flavor and either faint or strong taste of Tabasco, depending on your preference. Since they have an assertive taste on their own, serve them with a mild cheese or spread, rather than with anything heavy.

MAKES 6 DOZEN CRACKERS

FOR THE DOUGH

2	cups all-purpose flour	$^1/_4$	cup sun-dried tomato tapenade
1	teaspoon salt		(see the Hint)
1	cup grated Parmesan cheese	1	egg
1	teaspoon baking powder	$^1/_4$	cup plus 2 tablespoons water
$^1/_2$ to 1	teaspoon Tabasco sauce to taste		

Place the flour, salt, cheese, baking powder, Tabasco, tapenade, and egg in the machine, program for Manual, Dough, or Basic Dough, and press Start. Let the ingredients mix until they're evenly combined; they'll look crumbly. Add the water, 1 tablespoon at a time, just until the dough holds together; you may need a bit more or a bit less water. Cancel the machine and transfer the dough to a lightly floured surface.

TO FINISH THE CRACKERS

Divide the dough in half and work with half at a time. Roll the dough, quickly and gently, to $^1/_8$ inch thick on the lightly floured surface. Using a rolling pizza wheel, bench knife, or other sharp knife, cut the dough into 2-inch squares. Transfer the squares to 2 lightly greased baking sheets. Bake in a preheated 350°F oven for 15 to 20 minutes, or until the crackers are just beginning to brown around the edges.

HINT: *A mixture of minced sun-dried tomatoes, garlic, and olive oil, tomato tapenade is available in the specialty foods section of some markets. You may also make your own tapenade or substitute tomato paste.*

There are two basic kinds of crackers: dense/crisp and puffy/crisp. The difference? Baking powder or baking soda (or sometimes even yeast), which causes crackers to rise as they bake. Dense crackers can be made light by the addition of 1 teaspoon baking powder for each 3 cups flour in the recipe. Likewise, an ultra-thin, crisp cracker can be made from a "puffy" recipe simply by leaving out the leavening. Keep in mind what you're going to be serving with crackers: A thin, dense cracker is a better choice for very stiff spreads and heavy toppings.

Onion–Poppy Seed Crackers

These light-textured crackers aren't soggy at all, despite the fresh onion. Serve them with a bowl of tomato soup, use them as a base for a mild cheese or dip, or eat them plain; they're yummy as is.

MAKES ABOUT 7 DOZEN CRACKERS

FOR THE DOUGH

1	cup plus 2 tablespoons all-purpose flour
1	cup unbleached pastry flour or cake flour
1¼	teaspoons salt
2	teaspoons sugar
3	tablespoons poppy seeds

2	teaspoons baking powder
1	small-to-medium onion, finely diced (a heaping ¾ cup)
1	stick (5 ounces) plus 2 tablespoons unsalted butter, cold
1	egg

Place the flours, salt, sugar, poppy seeds, and baking powder in the machine, program for Manual, Dough, or Basic Dough, and press Start. Leave the lid of the machine open. Let the ingredients mix for 1 minute. Add the onion and butter and allow to knead for 5 minutes, or until the mixture is uniformly crumbly. Add the egg and knead 1 additional minute, or until the dough has formed a sticky, coherent mass. Cancel the machine and transfer the dough to a floured surface.

TO FINISH THE CRACKERS

Divide the dough in half and work with half at a time. Roll the dough, quickly and gently, to ⅛ inch thick on the floured surface; you'll need to use quite a bit of flour at first. Using a rolling pizza wheel, pastry wheel, bench knife, or other sharp knife, cut the dough into 2-inch squares. Transfer the squares to 2 lightly greased baking sheets.

Bake in a preheated 350°F oven for 20 to 25 minutes, or until the crackers are golden brown.

It's sometimes possible to substitute those very convenient minced, dried onions for the fresh variety, but don't try it in this recipe; the dried onions will burn, giving your crackers a nasty, scorched taste.

Cheddar Crisps

Remember cheese straws, that ubiquitous favorite of the 1960s appetizer tray? These light-textured crackers snap with sharp Cheddar flavor, with just a hint of mustard adding its own special piquancy.

MAKES ABOUT 14 DOZEN CRACKERS

FOR THE DOUGH

2	cups all-purpose flour	$^1/_2$	teaspoon dry mustard
$^3/_4$	teaspoon salt	8	ounces (2 cups) extra-sharp
2	teaspoons sugar		Cheddar cheese, shredded
$^1/_2$	teaspoon baking soda	$^3/_4$	cup buttermilk

Place the flour, salt, sugar, baking soda, and dry mustard in the machine, program for Manual, Dough, or Basic Dough, and press Start. Leave the lid of the machine open. After 1 minute of kneading, add the cheese. Knead for an additional 1 minute, or until the cheese is well incorporated. Add the buttermilk and knead 1 minute more, or until the mixture has formed a smooth dough. Cancel the machine and transfer the dough to a lightly oiled work surface.

TO FINISH THE CRISPS

Divide the dough into 2 pieces. Working with 1 piece at a time, roll the dough to $^1/_8$ inch thick. Using a rolling pizza wheel, pastry cutter, or other sharp instrument, cut the dough into 2-inch squares, then cut each square in half to make 2 triangles. Transfer the triangles to a lightly greased baking sheet and repeat with the remaining dough.

Bake in a preheated 325°F oven for 30 minutes, or until the crackers are golden brown. Remove them from the oven and transfer them to a wire rack to cool. When they're completely cool, store them in an airtight container.

For a different flavor, substitute Monterey Jack cheese with peppers, Swiss cheese, or even goat cheese. For variety, sprinkle the top of the dough with coarsely ground black pepper or dust it with cayenne pepper before cutting it into squares.

Sourdough Snap Sticks

I was looking for the perfect quick-fix to serve with a before-dinner glass of wine and came up with these dramatic, crisp, light as air, flat "breadsticks" which have moved from cocktail hour to the breakfast table. They are fun to make, have a long shelf life, and can be made with a variety of seeds. Sourdough starters are available by mail order (page 301) or they can be made with a packaged mix from the recipe on page 20. These crackers are rolled and baked on the undersides of the baking sheets or jelly roll pans.

MAKES ABOUT 5 DOZEN STICKS

FOR THE DOUGH

1	cup rye flour	1 cup sourdough starter
1	cup whole wheat flour	1½ teaspoons salt
1	cup all-purpose flour	⅓ to ½ cup dark beer

Preheat the oven to 500°F with the rack in the center position. Place all the ingredients in the machine, program for Dough, Basic Dough, or Manual, and press Start. Allow the dough to knead for 3 to 4 minutes, adding just enough beer to form a soft, pliable dough.

TO FINISH THE STICKS

4 tablespoons assorted seeds, such as poppy seeds, caraway seeds, sesame seeds, fennel seeds, or black caraway seeds	1 tablespoon coarse salt
	2 teaspoons freshly ground coarse black pepper

Spray the undersides of three 17 × 11-inch jelly roll pans or baking sheets with nonstick vegetable spray. Divide the dough into 3 equal pieces and cover 2 with plastic wrap. Using a lightly floured rolling pin, roll 1 piece of dough onto the back of a prepared pan. Sprinkle with a third of the seeds, salt, and pepper. Continue rolling, pressing the seeds and seasonings into the dough until the dough is as thin as possible. Take care to roll from the center toward the edges to create as uniform a layer as possible.

Using a sharp knife or pizza wheel, cut the dough the short way into seventeen 1-inch strips. Do not move or disturb the strips. Place the sheet in the oven and bake for 5 to 7 minutes, or until the strips on the edges of the pan are quite brown (the thinner and browner, the crisper they will be). Use a metal spatula to slide the browned strips onto a cooling rack. Continue baking until the rest of the strips are done. Repeat with the other pieces of dough. Cool the strips completely and store them in a closed tin.

HINT: *If you make these in humid weather, they will become soft. You can crisp them by placing them on a baking sheet in 1 layer in a 300°F oven for 5 to 10 minutes.*

Blue Corn–Rye Fat Sticks

These homey morsels are great either hot from the oven or at room tempera-ture, and they freeze beautifully as well. They have a delicate lightness, thanks to the blue cornmeal, and when cool, a satisfyingly crunchy crust. They can be a snack or a wholesome addition to a meal. You have a choice of topping them with either toasted pine nuts or poppy seeds, and you can substitute chili oil for regular vegetable oil for a warm afterglow.

Bread Machine Boost®, finely ground blue cornmeal, and chili oil are avail-able by mail order (page 301), and directions for toasting pine nuts can be found on page 267.

MAKES 16 FAT STICKS

FOR THE DOUGH

1	tablespoon yeast	1⅓	cups all-purpose flour
3	teaspoons Bread Machine Boost® (optional for fatter sticks)	2	tablespoons honey
		1	tablespoon molasses
2	teaspoons salt	⅓	cup vegetable oil or ⅓ cup chili oil
1	cup finely ground blue cornmeal	¾	cup water
1	cup rye flour		

Place all the ingredients in the machine, program for Manual or Dough, and press Start. The dough will be soft but should not be tacky. Add just enough flour so that the dough forms a discrete ball and none is left on the bottom of the pan.

TO FINISH THE STICKS

1	egg white beaten with 1 tablespoon water	⅔	cup toasted pine nuts (page 267) or 2 tablespoons poppy seeds

At the end of the final knead, remove the dough from the machine, dust it lightly with flour while you form it into a ball, place it on a lightly floured work space, and cover it with a clean cloth. Allow it to rest for 20 minutes. Cut the dough into quarters, then cut each quarter into 4 pieces. Roll each piece into a 5-inch-long rope and place the ropes 2 inches apart on 2 lightly oiled baking sheets. Press the ropes slightly to flatten the tops and then brush them with the egg glaze. Sprinkle with pine nuts (pressing them down with your fingers to make them stick to the top) or sprinkle liberally with poppy seeds.

Cover the baking sheets with a cloth and place them in a warm place for the dough to rise for 30 minutes.

Place the oven racks close to the center and preheat the oven to 375°F. Bake the sticks for 22 to 24 minutes, or until the tops are lightly browned.

To freeze the sticks, cool them completely and store them in a heavy-duty plastic freezer bag. Defrost them while still in the bag, then refresh them in a single layer on a baking sheet in a 300°F oven for 10 minutes.

Dipsticks

These tiny sesame seed–covered breadsticks are just the right size to serve with a bowlful of your favorite dip. They are short enough that guests won't be tempted to redip.

Dipsticks keep well for several weeks at room temperature in a tightly covered container.

MAKES ABOUT 18 DOZEN STICKS

FOR THE DOUGH

1	tablespoon yeast	½	stick (2 ounces) unsalted butter
4	cups all-purpose flour		or margarine
¼	cup sugar	¼	cup vegetable shortening
1	teaspoon salt	1	large egg
1	cup milk, heated to 120°F and		
	cooled to lukewarm		

Place all the ingredients in the machine, program for Dough, Basic Dough, or Manual, and press Start. The dough will look firm and feel oily to the touch.

TO FINISH THE STICKS

1	egg beaten with 1 tablespoon	¼	cup sesame seeds
	water		

Transfer the dough from the machine to a lightly oiled work surface and divide it in half. Roll one half to an 18 × 9-inch rectangle. Cut the rectangle lengthwise into thirds. Cut these 3 pieces crosswise into ½-inch strips. You will notice that the width of the strips shrinks as you make the cuts; that's fine since they don't need to be ½ inch thick in the end. Grease or spray several baking sheets with nonstick vegetable oil. Arrange the strips ¼ inch apart in rows on the baking sheets. This spacing will also make it easier to brush on the egg glaze before baking. Repeat with the remaining half of the dough. Cover the strips with plastic wrap and let them rise in a warm place for about 1 hour until they are nicely puffed and almost doubled in height.

Preheat the oven to 350°F with the racks in the centermost positions. Brush the egg glaze over the dipsticks and sprinkle them evenly with the sesame seeds. Bake for 15 to 20 minutes, or until the dipsticks are light golden brown. Rotate the baking sheets as necessary to bake the dipsticks evenly. When they are completely cooled, store them in an airtight container.

Scandinavian Oatcakes

A touch of cardamom gives these hearty crackers their distinctive Scandinavian flavor. The sweetness of the oats, reinforced with a bit more sugar than you'll find in your usual cracker, allows these treats to fall somewhere in between a cookie and cracker, ideal for spreading with cream cheese and jam. Or, if you're really into traditional tastes, try them with Norway's famous gjetost cheese, a firm, golden brown cheese with its own unique texture and flavor.

MAKES ABOUT 5 DOZEN CRACKERS

FOR THE DOUGH

1¹/₂ cups all-purpose flour
³/₄ cup old-fashioned rolled oats
³/₄ teaspoon salt
¹/₂ teaspoon baking soda
¹/₂ teaspoon cardamom

6 tablespoons unsalted butter, cut into 12 pieces
4 teaspoons sugar
¹/₂ cup sour cream

Place all the ingredients except the sour cream in the machine, program for Manual, Dough, or Basic Dough, and press Start. Leave the lid of the machine open. After 5 or 6 minutes of kneading, or when the mixture resembles coarse crumbs, add the sour cream. Knead for an additional 1 to 2 minutes, or until the dough has come together in a shaggy mass.

TO FINISH THE OATCAKES

Transfer the dough to a lightly floured work surface and divide it into 2 pieces. Working with 1 piece at a time, roll the dough to ¹/₈ inch thick. Using a rolling pizza wheel, pastry cutter, or knife, cut the dough into 2-inch squares. Transfer the squares to a lightly greased cookie sheet. Repeat with the remaining dough.

Bake in a preheated 375°F oven for 15 minutes, or until the crackers are a uniform golden brown. Remove them from the oven and transfer them from the pan to a wire rack to cool completely.

This recipe is based on Sweden's traditional Knäckebröd *—"hardtack"—which is served either as a cookie or cracker, depending on the occasion. For a more cookielike final product, increase the sugar to 3 tablespoons.*

Cheese and Caraway Beer Sticks

These long, skinny breadsticks feature the winning combination of cheese and caraway. Though beer is used as the liquid in this recipe, its alcohol evaporates, leaving only a faint, yeasty tang. Serve these in a tall flower vase or an extra-large beer stein.

SERVES 8

FOR THE DOUGH

2	teaspoons yeast	³/₄	cup grated Parmesan cheese
2³/₄	cups all-purpose flour	2	tablespoons caraway seeds
1¹/₂	teaspoons salt	¹/₄	cup olive oil
2	teaspoons sugar	1	cup (8 ounces) beer

Place all the ingredients in the machine, program for Manual, Dough, or Basic Dough, and press Start. Check the dough 10 minutes before the end of the second kneading cycle; it should have formed a nice ball, just barely tacky to the touch. Adjust the consistency with additional flour or beer as necessary.

TO FINISH THE STICKS

When the machine has completed its cycle, transfer the dough to a lightly oiled work surface and divide it into 2 pieces. Working with 1 piece at a time, roll the dough to a 15 × 8-inch rectangle about ¹/₄ inch thick. Using a rolling pizza wheel or pastry cutter, cut the dough lengthwise into 16 strips, each ¹/₂ inch wide. Transfer the strips to a lightly oiled baking sheet. Repeat with the remaining dough. Cover the baking sheets with lightly greased plastic wrap and set aside to rise for 40 minutes, or until lightly puffed.

Bake in a preheated 300°F oven for 25 to 30 minutes, or until the sticks are a rich golden brown. Remove them from the oven, transfer them to a wire rack, and cool them completely. For better flavor and texture, let the sticks sit overnight, uncovered, before serving.

◇

You'll notice these breadsticks brown very quickly once they get to a certain point in baking. This is due to the fat (limited though it is) and milk solids in the Parmesan cheese. Check the breadsticks often toward the end of their time in the oven; they can go quickly from brown to burned.

◇

Piñole Bread Staffs

Bigger than your average breadstick. So big, in fact, that I think Teddy Roosevelt would have been proud to carry one around while he talked softly. Made from a pesto-enhanced dough and punctuated with toasted pine nuts (also called pignolis), these mega sticks make a smashing presentation and will delight friends and family. You'll be pleased when you see how simple they are to make.

While they taste best the day they are made, they are also pretty swell the next day—if they are not refrigerated. Store them, uncovered, at room temperature.

MAKES TEN 17-INCH STICKS; TWENTY 8$^1/_2$-INCH STICKS

FOR THE DOUGH

1	tablespoon yeast
3	cups all-purpose flour
$^1/_3$	cup cornmeal
2	teaspoons salt
$^1/_3$	cup garlic oil or $^1/_3$ cup olive oil

	plus 1 large garlic clove, peeled and finely minced
1	cup water or more to make a smooth ball

Place all the ingredients in the machine, program for Dough, Basic Dough, or Manual, and press Start. At the end of the final cycle, remove the dough to a work surface and allow it to rest 10 minutes, uncovered (this is a very oily dough that doesn't required covering), while you prepare the pans.

TO FINISH THE STAFFS

1	cup toasted pine nuts
$^1/_3$	cup freshly grated Parmesan cheese

Select two 17 × 11-inch baking sheets and sprinkle them with cornmeal. Roll the dough out on the work surface to a 16 × 10-inch rectangle. Use a pizza wheel or knife to trim the sides to make them straight. Sprinkle half the pine nuts over the surface of the dough and go over the dough with a rolling pin to gently press them in. Flip the dough over (some of the nuts will fall out; don't worry, you can stick them in the other side) and repeat with the rest of the nuts and the grated cheese.

Using the pizza wheel or knife, cut the dough into ten 1-inch strips. If you want to make more strips, cut these in half the short way so you end up with twenty 16$^1/_2$ × 1-inch strips. Place half the strips, at least 1$^1/_2$ inches apart, on each of the prepared sheets and allow them to rise, uncovered, until almost doubled in size.

Preheat the oven to 450°F with the rack in the center position. Bake the sticks for 12 to 15 minutes, or until golden brown. Cool them on a rack before serving.

Soft Wheat Pretzels

I was fortunate enough to teach at the Oceans Reef Culinary Arts Center in Key Largo, Florida, where I met Marcia Welsh, whose family business is Bachman's Pretzels. I'm not sure if it was the delicious taste of those pretzels mingling with the salt air or the impressive Bachman boat (Pretz-sail) that inspired me to run home to see if I could whip up pretzels in my bread machine. I don't think the Bachman family needs to worry about the competition volume-wise; taste-wise these are right on the mark.

This recipe calls for King Arthur's White Wheat Flour (page 5). While you can substitute regular whole wheat flour, you won't get quite the same texture and taste. Commercially made pretzels are boiled in a bath made of very diluted lye. This isn't easy to do at home, so this recipe accomplishes almost the same thing with a baking soda bath.

MAKES 12 LARGE OR 18 SMALLER PRETZELS

FOR THE DOUGH

1	tablespoon yeast	1	tablespoon sugar
2	cups White Wheat flour	1⅓	to 1½ cups water to make a
1	cup all-purpose flour		smooth ball after 5 to 10 minutes
1½	teaspoons salt		of kneading

Place all the ingredients in the machine, program for Dough, Basic Dough, or Manual, and press Start. At the end of the final cycle, remove the dough to a lightly floured work space. Knead the dough briefly, adding up to ½ cup additional flour so that the dough is no longer sticky. Form the dough into a ball and cover it with a clean towel and allow it to rest for 10 minutes. Oil a heavy-duty baking sheet.

TO FINISH THE PRETZELS

6	cups water	Coarse salt
2	tablespoons baking soda	Caraway seeds (optional)
1	egg white beaten with	
	1 tablespoon water	

Divide the dough into 12 or 18 equal pieces and shape each one into a rope 12 or 9 inches long. You may have to allow the ropes to relax for several minutes during this process before they will stretch completely. Form each rope into a loose pretzel-shaped knot. Place the pretzels on the prepared baking sheet, cover with a clean towel, and allow to rise in a warm place for 30 minutes, or until almost doubled in bulk. At the end of the rising time, preheat the oven to 400°F with the rack in the center position and prepare the baking soda bath.

Place the water in a large skillet or frying pan set over high heat, bring it to a boil, and add the baking soda. Use a metal spatula to carefully lift the pretzels, one at a time, from the baking sheet and lower them into the water. Cook, at a low simmer, about 15 seconds, or until the pretzels are puffed up. Remove the pretzels with a slotted spoon (gently tapping the spoon to drain excess water) and place them back on the baking sheet ½ inch apart.

Brush the tops of the pretzels with the egg glaze, then sprinkle with the salt and caraway seeds if desired. Bake for 20 minutes, or until they are a deep golden brown.

Rolls,
Muffins,
Scones, and
Pancakes

Sesame Pillows

These tender, flaky square rolls make a wonderful addition to an assorted bread basket. You can make them ahead and freeze them when cooled in a plastic bag. Then you defrost the pillows still wrapped and refresh them in a 350°F oven for 10 to 15 minutes.

MAKES 32 ROLLS

FOR THE DOUGH

1	tablespoon yeast	1	tablespoon sesame oil
4	cups all-purpose flour	3	tablespoons unsalted butter or
¼	cup sugar		margarine
1	teaspoon salt	¼	cup vegetable shortening
1	cup milk, heated to 120°F and	1	large egg
	cooled, or 1 cup warm water and 3		
	tablespoons nonfat dry milk		

Place all the ingredients in the machine, program for Dough, Basic Dough, or Manual, and press Start.

TO FINISH THE ROLLS

1	egg beaten with 1 tablespoon	¼	cup sesame seeds
	water		

At the end of the final cycle, transfer the dough to a lightly oiled work surface and divide it in half. Roll one half to a 10 × 5-inch rectangle and cut it in half the long way, making two 10 × 2½-inch rectangles. Cut each long strip into 8 equal pieces for a total of 16 pieces. Repeat with the remaining half.

Grease or spray 2 baking sheets with vegetable oil. Beat together the egg and water in a small bowl. Pour the sesame seeds in another small bowl. Dip each piece of dough first in the egg mixture and then in the sesame seeds. Arrange the coated pieces on the prepared baking sheets leaving about ½ inch between each. Cover lightly with plastic wrap and let them rise in a warm place for ½ hour, or until slightly puffed. The rolls will rise more while baking. Meanwhile, preheat the oven to 350°F with the rack in the center position.

Bake the rolls for 20 minutes, or until well puffed and golden brown. Serve hot or at room temperature.

Chouriço Rolls

While researching material for this book, Cindy was drawn to southern New England, specifically Fall River. There she found wonderful Portuguese bakeries with a special ethnic twist. Her tour guide, Neil Fernandes, who grew up in Fall River, gave her the grand tour of these bakeries, most of which are located below ground. This recipe is dedicated to those men who are basement-bound.

The cooled rolls can be stored in the refrigerator in plastic bags for two days or can be frozen up to two months.

MAKES 6 ROLLS

FOR THE DOUGH

2 teaspoons yeast	3 tablespoons vegetable shortening
3 cups all-purpose flour	1¼ to 1⅓ cups water to make a soft,
1 teaspoon sugar	moist dough
1½ teaspoons salt	

Place all the ingredients in the machine, program for Dough, Basic Dough, or Manual, and press Start. The dough will be soft and quite moist.

TO FINISH THE ROLLS

1 large onion, sliced	1 pound chouriço, sliced into
2 to 3 tablespoons olive oil or	¼-inch-thick rounds (see the
vegetable oil	Hint)

In a large skillet, sauté the onion slices in the oil until they are tender. Remove them from the pan and in the same pan cook the chouriço until browned. Remove the sausage from the pan, leaving the fat behind, and mix it with the onion.

When the dough cycle is completed, preheat the oven to 375°F and transfer the dough to a lightly floured surface and let it rest for 5 minutes. Divide the dough into 6 pieces. On the floured surface, roll the dough out into 6-inch circles. Put about ⅓ cup of the sausage mixture in the center of each circle. Fold the 4 "sides" of the circle so they overlap in the center and gently roll the dough so you have a 6-inch roll. Place each roll on a lightly floured cookie sheet with the seam side down. Brush each roll with oil and with a sharp knife make a slit in each roll.

Bake the rolls for 15 minutes, or until the tops are golden brown. Cool them on a rack for 15 minutes before serving or serve them warm.

 HINT: *Chouriço is a wonderful Portuguese sausage. If this is not available in your neck of the woods, you can use Italian sausage or kielbasa.*

Cheoregs

Cheoreg rolls are an important part of every festive Armenian meal or banquet. When the women's groups from the various churches get together in Watertown, Massachusetts, there are as many recipe versions as there are women. There are serious disagreements as they get together to cook massive amounts of these rich buttery rolls, but in the end they all hug and set aside their differences.

They can be frozen for up to one month or refrigerated for two days if tightly wrapped in plastic wrap inside a plastic bag. Cool them completely after baking.

MAKES 12 ROLLS

FOR THE DOUGH

³/₄ teaspoon mahleb (found in Middle
    Eastern grocery stores) or ¹/₄
    teaspoon ground nutmeg
¹/₂ cup water
1 tablespoon yeast
3 cups all-purpose flour
2 tablespoons powdered milk

1 teaspoon baking powder
¹/₃ cup sugar
1 teaspoon salt
1 stick (4 ounces) unsalted butter,
    melted and slightly cooled
2 large eggs

Soak the mahleb in the water for 10 minutes. Then place this mixture along with all the other ingredients in the machine, program for Dough, Basic Dough, or Manual, and press Start. The dough will be medium-firm and not sticky. At the end of the final cycle, let the dough rise 1 additional hour in the machine. You don't need to program anything fancy, just let it sit there.

TO FINISH THE CHEOREGS

1 egg beaten with 1 tablespoon
    water

¹/₄ cup sesame seeds

Lightly spray a baking sheet with nonstick vegetable spray. Transfer the dough to a lightly floured work surface, divide it into 6 pieces, cover it with a clean towel, and let it rest for 10 minutes. Roll each piece of dough to a long pencil-thin rope and cut it into six 8-inch pieces. Rework any leftover dough with a new piece of dough.

Take 3 of the 8-inch pieces at a time and pinch them together at one end. Braid the pieces together and pinch at the other end to seal. Lay the cheoregs ³/₄ inch apart on the prepared baking sheet. Cover with plastic wrap and let rise until doubled in bulk, 1 to 1¹/₂ hours.

Preheat the oven to 350°F with the rack in the center position.

Generously brush the egg glaze over the cheoregs and generously sprinkle with sesame seeds. Bake the cheoregs for 15 minutes, or until puffed and slightly golden around the edges. Cool them on a wire rack.

Pepper Knots

Fennel seeds and a copious amount of coarsely ground black pepper give these Italian bowknots a flavor as assertive as the strong-willed grandmother I know who used to make them. Don't be tempted to cut back on either the pepper or fennel; if you can't stand the heat, make something else. Hot from the oven, served with plain, sweet butter, these crunchy rolls give your taste buds a wonderful jolt.

MAKES 16 ROLLS

FOR THE DOUGH

2	teaspoons yeast	$^1/_4$	cup shortening
2$^1/_2$	cups all-purpose flour	1	tablespoon coarsely ground black
1	tablespoon sugar		pepper
1$^1/_2$	teaspoons salt	1	tablespoon fennel seeds
1	cup lukewarm water		

Place all the ingredients in the machine, program for Manual, Dough, or Basic Dough, and press Start. Check the dough 10 minutes before the end of the second kneading cycle; it should be soft and tacky but should hold its shape.

TO FINISH THE KNOTS

When the machine has completed its cycle, remove the dough and cut it into 16 pieces. Cover the dough with a damp dish towel and let it rest for 10 minutes.

Roll each piece of dough into an 8-inch rope. Twist each rope into a knot, tucking the loose ends underneath. Place the rolls on 2 lightly greased cookie sheets and cover them loosely with lightly greased plastic wrap. Set the rolls aside to rise till doubled in bulk, about 45 minutes.

Bake the rolls in a preheated 425°F oven for 20 minutes, or until golden brown. Remove them from the oven and cool them completely on a wire rack.

◇

Why do recipes call for you to let your dough rest before shaping it? The gluten in yeast dough—the protein that gives the dough its strength and structure—tends to tighten up each time it's handled. Giving the dough a short rest allows the gluten to relax, making the dough softer, more pliable, and easier to work with.

◇

Soft Onion Rolls

You know those onion rolls you get that are just crying for a couple of slabs of liverwurst and some sweet-hot mustard? The ones that are shaped like a rectangle and feature not only browned onions on the top but a layer of soft onions inside? Well, get your liverwurst ready—these are the rolls you've been looking for.

MAKES 6 LARGE ROLLS

FOR THE DOUGH

1	tablespoon yeast
2¹/₂	cups all-purpose flour
1¹/₂	teaspoons salt
2	tablespoons sugar

1	cup lukewarm milk
6	tablespoons (3 ounces) unsalted butter, cut into ¹/₄-inch slices

Place all the ingredients in the machine, program for Manual, Dough, or Basic Dough, and press Start. Ten minutes before the end of the second kneading cycle, check the consistency of the dough; it should be soft but should hold its shape fairly well. Adjust the consistency with additional flour or milk as needed.

FOR THE FILLING

6	tablespoons unsalted butter
³/₄	pound sweet onions (Vidalia or Spanish), cut into ¹/₄-inch dice (a scant 1¹/₂ cups)

1¹/₂	teaspoons sugar

Melt the butter over medium-low heat in a large frying pan and add the onions. Sauté the onions slowly, stirring occasionally, until they're just beginning to brown; this should take 25 to 30 minutes. Add the sugar and sauté an additional 5 minutes. Turn the heat off and let the onions cool in the pan.

TO FINISH THE ROLLS

1	egg white beaten with 1 tablespoon water

1	small sweet onion (about 3 ounces), diced (¹/₂ cup)

When the machine has completed its cycle, transfer the dough to a lightly oiled work surface and divide it into 3 pieces. Working with 1 piece at a time, roll it into a 12 × 9-inch rectangle. Divide the dough in half the short way; you now have two 9 × 6-inch rectangles.

Mentally divide each rectangle into three 6 × 3-inch sections. Spread one sixth of the sautéed onions over the middle section. Fold one of the side sections over the onions and seal. Fold the other side over the first side and seal again. Pinch the edges of the roll closed and tuck them under. Repeat with the remaining dough. Place the rolls on a couple of lightly greased baking sheets.

Brush the rolls with the egg glaze, then top them with a heaping tablespoon of the diced onion. Cover the rolls with a lightly greased piece of plastic wrap and set them aside to rise till puffy but not doubled in bulk, 30 to 45 minutes.

Bake the rolls in a preheated 375°F oven for 25 to 30 minutes, or until they're golden brown. Remove them from the oven and transfer them to a wire rack to cool.

Za'tar Rounds

Za'tar is a Middle Eastern blend of spices, available in stores that specialize in Middle Eastern foods. In this recipe, soft, flat rounds of bread dough are covered with a paste of za'tar and oil. The edges are pinched in intervals around the edge and the rounds are baked. This is a common breakfast food served with coffee and is eaten sprinkled with lemon juice and topped with chopped tomatoes. The rounds can be rolled around fresh leafy greens.

These rounds are delicious eaten warm from the oven. They may also be frozen and thawed to room temperature before eating. Add the lemon juice, tomatoes, and greens after thawing.

SERVES 4

FOR THE DOUGH

2½	teaspoons yeast	1	cup plus 2 tablespoons warm water
3¼	cups all-purpose flour		
2	teaspoons sugar	2	tablespoons olive oil
1	teaspoon salt		

Place all the ingredients in the machine, program for Dough or Manual, and press Start. At the end of the final cycle, remove the dough to a floured surface and divide it into 3 balls. Cover the balls with a slightly damp cloth and let them rest for 10 minutes.

FOR THE ZA'TAR

6	tablespoons za'tar	3	tablespoons olive oil

Mix together the za'tar and oil, making a thick paste, and set it aside.

TO FINISH THE ROUNDS

	Juice of 1 lemon	4	leaves of salad greens of your choice
1	cup chopped vine-ripe tomatoes or plum tomatoes		
		4	sprigs of fresh mint (optional)

Preheat the oven to 425°F with the rack in the center position. Grease a baking pan or cookie sheet. Roll each ball of dough to an 8-inch round and spread the rounds with the za'tar paste to within ½ inch of the edge. Pinch the edges of the rounds every inch or so all the way around. Bake the rounds for 10 minutes, or until lightly browned but still floppy.

Dribble the lemon juice evenly over the warm rounds, using more or less according to taste. Distribute the chopped tomatoes. Add the greens and mint across the center of the rounds and fold the rounds around them. Enjoy.

Avery Island Pirogues

A pirogue is a sturdy, flat-bottomed skiff that Louisiana fishermen use to gather the bounty of the bayou, notably the succulent crayfish. These boats, so much a part of Avery Island, home of Tabasco Brand Hot Sauce, inspired the name and shape of these rolls while Tabasco sauce gives them their zing and zest. Try using an Avery Island pirogue to scoop up a mess of boiled crayfish.

While the pirogues are best eaten the day they are made, they can be frozen up to 6 months after they are completely cooled.

MAKES EIGHT 5-INCH ROLLS

FOR THE DOUGH

1	tablespoon yeast	³/₄	cup water, plus up to an additional
3	cups bread flour		¹/₄ cup to make a smooth, firm
¹/₃	cup yellow cornmeal		dough after 5 minutes of kneading
¹/₃	cup chili oil	1	teaspoon salt
1	extra-large egg	1	teaspoon crushed red pepper
¹/₂	cup chopped onion		flakes
¹/₄	cup minced fresh coriander	6 to 10	drops Tabasco sauce

Place all the ingredients in the machine, program for Manual or Dough, and press Start. At the end of the final knead cycle, transfer the dough to a lightly floured work space.

TO FINISH THE PIROGUES

1 tablespoon olive oil
2 teaspoons coarse jalapeño salt
   (see the Hint)

Divide the dough into 2 pieces and roll each piece into an 8-inch rope. Cut each rope into 4 pieces. Roll each piece into a 5-inch "cigar," placing them 2 inches apart on a baking sheet dusted with cornmeal. Use your fingers to gently flatten each cigar, applying the most pressure in the middle and tapering the ends so that you have a long oval. Cover the pirogues with a clean dish towel and allow them to rise for 30 minutes, or about doubled in bulk.

Preheat the oven to 450°F with the rack in the center position. Brush the top of each pirogue with the oil and sprinkle with the salt. Bake for 15 to 17 minutes, or until the tops turn a golden brown. Serve hot, warm, or at room temperature.

HINT: *For the coarse jalapeño salt, combine 1 tablespoon coarse salt with 8 to 10 drops Tabasco Brand Jalapeño Sauce.*

You can make 16 miniature pirogues by cutting each 8-inch rope of dough into 8 pieces, then forming each piece into a 3 × 2^1/$_2$-inch roll, following the directions above. Bake the smaller size for 10 to 12 minutes.

Irish Muffins

These hearty muffins are skillet-baked and then toasted like English muffins. Or if you prefer, you can bake them in the oven with an egg glaze to get puffy little breads with crispy crusts. The whole wheat dough is flavored with allspice, molasses, and sherry-soaked raisins and currants. They are fabulous slathered with butter.

Skillet-baked muffins will keep for several days, stored after cooling in a plastic bag in the refrigerator. To freeze them, keep them tightly wrapped in a plastic bag.

Oven-baked muffins will keep for two days, tightly wrapped in plastic. They may be frozen, tightly wrapped. Reheat them in a toaster oven to retain the crispy crusts; do not microwave them.

MAKES 22 MUFFINS

FOR THE DOUGH

½	cup (3 ounces) currants		½	teaspoon ground allspice
½	cup (3 ounces) raisins		1¼	teaspoons salt
¼	cup sweet sherry		1½	cups water
2	cups all-purpose flour		¼	cup molasses
1½	cups whole wheat flour		3	tablespoons unsalted butter or
1	teaspoon baking soda			margarine
2	tablespoons powdered buttermilk			

Soak the currants and raisins in the sherry overnight or see the Hint.

Place all the ingredients except the currants, raisins, and sherry in the machine, program for Dough, Basic Dough, or Manual, and press Start. The dough will be sticky during the first part of the kneading cycle. At the end of the final cycle, add the raisins, restart the machine, and allow it to knead just until the fruit is mixed in.

TO FINISH THE MUFFINS

3   tablespoons cornmeal

Roll the dough out on a floured surface to a thickness of ½ inch. Flour the rolling pin as necessary to keep the dough from sticking. Cut rounds with a 3-inch floured cutter. You can use a tuna fish can as a cutter if you cut off both ends. Sprinkle a baking sheet with the cornmeal and arrange the cut muffins 1½ inches apart on the baking sheet.

TO BAKE IN A SKILLET

Cover the muffins with plastic wrap and let them rise in a warm place for 1 hour. Preheat an electric skillet to 250°F and oil it or spray it lightly with non-stick vegetable spray. Place the muffins in the skillet with the cornmeal side down. You can probably cook 4 to 8 at a time depending on the size of your skillet. Leave room for them to be turned easily.

Cook the muffins for 10 minutes, or until they are deep golden brown on the bottom. Turn the muffins and continue baking for another 10 minutes. Cool the muffins on wire racks. Split them and toast them like English muffins.

TO BAKE IN THE OVEN

1	egg beaten with 1 tablespoon water	1	tablespoon sugar (optional)

Form the muffins as above, but only allow them to rise while the oven preheats to 350°F with the rack in the center position. They do not need longer than a 10 to 15 minute rising time for they will rise in the oven. Generously brush the egg glaze over the muffins. Sprinkle with the sugar and bake for 15 to 20 minutes or until slightly browned.

> HINT: *If you haven't planned ahead and soaked the raisins and currants overnight, you can microwave them with the sherry. Add the raisins and currants to a microwavable container and pour the sherry over them. Tightly cover the container with plastic wrap and microwave for about 2 minutes, or until well heated. The liquid should be absorbed by the time your machine signals to add the raisins and currants. This is a great trick unless you've gotten to a forgetful age of life and leave them in the microwave until your muffins are all baked. I set the container out by the bread machine to remind myself to add them.*

Sourdough English Muffins

These light and puffy English muffins with a slight sourdough flavor are sure to become a breakfast favorite. Use a fork to split them to expose the nooks and crannies, then smear them with butter and your favorite jam.

The cooled muffins can be frozen, tightly wrapped in plastic bags. They will keep refrigerated for several days stored in a plastic bag.

A recipe for sourdough starter is on page 20, or it is available by mail order (page 301).

MAKES 12 MUFFINS

FOR THE DOUGH

1	tablespoon yeast	1	tablespoon sugar
2½	cups all-purpose flour	1	teaspoon salt
½	teaspoon baking soda	1	cup warm water
3	tablespoons buttermilk powder	1	cup sourdough starter

Place all the ingredients in the machine, program for Manual, Dough, or Basic Dough, and press Start. The dough will look sticky and loose but will hold somewhat of a shape as it kneads. (The dough will rise a little over the rim of the machine baking pan in a large machine.)

TO FINISH THE MUFFINS
3 tablespoons white or yellow
cornmeal

Remove the dough to a generously floured work surface and roll it to ½ inch thick. Using a 3- to 4-inch floured biscuit cutter, cut 12 muffins, reworking any leftover pieces of dough as necessary. Grease or spray a baking sheet with vegetable spray and sprinkle with the cornmeal. Lift the muffins to the prepared sheet and allow them to rise in a warm place for 30 to 45 minutes, or until almost doubled in bulk.

Heat an electric frying pan or griddle to 250°F and lightly spray it with nonstick vegetable spray. Using a pastry scraper or spatula, carefully lift the muffins and slide them into the pan or griddle. Leave room for turning them. It is best to cook only 4 to 6 at a time depending on the size of your pan or griddle. Cook them for 5 minutes on each side, or until they are a rich golden color on the bottom. Turn them and cook them for 5 minutes on the opposite side. Remove them to wire racks to cool.

Split them with a fork and serve them warm.

HINTS: *You can make a buttermilk alternative by mixing 1 tablespoon lemon juice to 1 cup of milk.*

A pastry scraper is an indispensable tool for lifting dough that is sticky or has risen which you don't want to deflate with rough handling.

Bialys

No New Yorkers in their right mind would make bialys in a bread machine. They'd buy them from the corner deli. This recipe is dedicated to all those displaced souls who, having fled the Big Apple for places where a bialy is as foreign as an egg cream, would go to any length to savor the taste of what one baker calls "an unbaked onion-filled Jewish/English muffin." Flatter than a bagel, homelier than your basic rye, able to sustain a mound of cream cheese only after it's toasted: the humble bialy, worth its every bite.

If you've never tasted a bialy, here's what to expect according to George Greenstein, author of Secrets of a Jewish Baker: "Real bialys are dense, blistered, and chewy, with a toasted flourlike taste. They taste best when slathered with cream cheese." He goes on to note that "bialys have a short shelf life and should be frozen unless consumed the day they are baked." You can freeze them after they are baked and cooled. Wrap them in a plastic freezer bag, then defrost them in a microwave or at room temperature still wrapped.

MAKES 9 BIALYS

FOR THE DOUGH

1	tablespoon yeast	1	cup water, plus an additional 3 to
3	cups all-purpose flour		4 tablespoons if necessary to make
2	teaspoons sugar		a stiff, firm dough
2	teaspoons coarse or kosher salt		

Place all the ingredients in the machine, program for Manual, and press Start. Do not add the extra water until after the first 3 to 4 minutes of kneading. The dough should be stiff but not crumbly. Add more water only if the dough does not form a ball within the first few minutes. While the dough is being prepared, make the filling.

FOR THE FILLING

1	onion, finely chopped (to make about 1 cup)	2	tablespoons vegetable oil
1	tablespoon poppy seeds	1½	teaspoons salt

Place all the ingredients in a small bowl and mix thoroughly. Set aside, at room temperature, while the dough is completed.

TO FINISH THE BIALYS
Flour   Cornmeal

After the final cycle, transfer the dough to a well-floured work surface—one key to the success of bialys is not to skimp on the flour—and punch it down. Cut the dough into 3 equal pieces and roll each piece into a 6- to 7-inch rope. Cut each rope into 3 parts and roll each part into a ball. Sprinkle the balls with flour, cover them with a clean dish towel, and let them rest for 10 minutes.

Select 1 large or 2 smaller heavy baking sheets and sprinkle them liberally with cornmeal. On a floured work surface, flatten each ball of dough into a 4- to 5-inch circle. Place the circles on the prepared baking sheet(s), sprinkle them with flour, cover with the dish towel, and let them rise 15 minutes.

Preheat the oven to 450°F with the rack(s) near the center position. Use your fingers to firmly push in the center of each circle to form a 1/2-inch-deep well. Fill the well with the onion filling. Cover and let rise for 10 minutes while the oven is heating. Just before placing the baking sheet(s) in the oven, use your fingers to push the indented onion-filled area down one more time.

Bake the bialys for 17 to 20 minutes, or until they are puffed up and just slightly golden brown. Eat them hot or warm, or toasted after they have cooled.

Swiss Scones

Gruyère cheese and white wine—two ingredients of traditional Swiss fondue—are the leading taste ingredients in these subtly flavored scones. They're very nice served in a dinnertime bread basket, and are a special treat teamed with scrambled eggs and ham at breakfast.

MAKES 16 SCONES

FOR THE DOUGH

1½	cups all-purpose flour
1	cup unbleached pastry flour or cake flour
2	tablespoons baking powder
½	teaspoon baking soda
1½	teaspoons salt
1	tablespoon sugar
1	stick (4 ounces) unsalted butter, cut into ⅛-inch slices
8	ounces Gruyère cheese, cut into ¼-inch cubes (about 1¾ cups)
½	cup white wine, plus 2 to 3 tablespoons additional wine if necessary
1	tablespoon kirsch (optional)

Place the flours, baking powder, baking soda, salt, and sugar in the machine, program for Manual, Dough, or Basic Dough, and press Start. Leave the lid of the machine open. After the machine has kneaded for 1 minute, add the butter. After 4 minutes, the dough should look crumbly, with no large chunks of butter remaining; if you see any large chunks, let it knead an additional 2 minutes, or until the chunks have disappeared.

Add the cheese and knead for 1 minute. Slowly add the wine and kirsch and knead for 15 to 20 seconds, or until the dough starts to form large clumps. Cancel the machine and squeeze a handful of dough; if it sticks together, it's ready. If it's too dry to stick together, put it back into the machine, press Start, and gradually add additional wine until the dough reaches the desired consistency.

TO FINISH THE SCONES

1	tablespoon milk for glazing

Transfer the dough to a lightly floured work surface; it'll be crumbly. Gather and squeeze it into a mound and divide it in half. Gently pat each half to an 8-inch circle about ½ inch thick.

Transfer the circles to a lightly greased cookie sheet. Using a rolling pizza wheel, baker's bench knife, or sharp knife, cut each circle into 8 pie-shaped

wedges. Leaving the circle intact, separate the wedges slightly, leaving about ½ inch between each. Brush the tops of the circles with milk.

Bake the scones on the middle rack of a preheated 425°F oven for 20 minutes, or until they're golden brown.

Because Gruyère is a mild-flavored cheese, we leave it in distinct cubes in this recipe rather than shredding it and letting it become part of the dough. Your taste buds will perceive more of the cheese's flavor this way.

Breakfast Sausage Scones

People usually think of scones in their sweet incarnation, laced with fruit or nuts and sprinkled with cinnamon and sugar. These scones take a different tack: Studded with sausage, spiced with fennel, and featuring a piquant accent of sun-dried tomatoes, they're wonderful served with scrambled eggs.

MAKES 15 SCONES

FOR THE DOUGH

2½	cups all-purpose flour
2	tablespoons baking powder
1	teaspoon salt
1	tablespoon sugar
1	stick (4 ounces) unsalted butter, cold and cut into 16 pieces
1	tablespoon fennel seeds
⅓	cup (2 ounces) sun-dried tomatoes packed in oil, drained and snipped into a ¼-inch dice

8	ounces sausage, hot or sweet, casings removed if necessary, cooked, drained, and crumbled
1	egg
½	cup milk

Place the flour, baking powder, salt, sugar, butter, and fennel seeds in the machine, program for Manual, Dough, or Basic Dough, and press Start. Leave the lid of the machine open. Let the machine knead for 5 to 6 minutes, or until the dough is a fairly uniform, coarse-crumb consistency. Add the tomatoes and sausage and let it knead till they're incorporated, about another 30 seconds, then add the egg and milk. Let it knead only until the dough starts to come together, then cancel the machine.

TO FINISH THE SCONES

Turn the dough out on a lightly floured work surface and pat or roll it into a 12 × 9 × ¾-inch rectangle. Using a rolling pizza cutter, baker's bench knife, or sharp knife, cut the dough into fifteen 3-inch squares. Transfer the squares to 2 lightly greased cookie sheets, leaving about 1 inch between each.

Bake the scones in a preheated 400°F oven for 15 to 18 minutes, or until they're golden brown. Remove the scones from the oven, transfer them to a rack, and cool them completely.

You may shape the dough into 2 circles and cut the scones in the more traditional wedge shape if you like; it's a matter of personal preference. The main thing to keep in mind is to handle the dough as little as possible; dough that is handled gently will produce a tender scone, while dough that is manhandled will make a more bricklike finished product.

Fresh Basil, Parmesan, and Pine Nut Scones

These scones are flatter and less shaggy than other types you may have tried; they are almost tender biscuits rather than scones. Try serving them in place of garlic bread with a traditional spaghetti marinara.

MAKES 16 SCONES

FOR THE DOUGH

2½ cups unbleached pastry flour or cake flour

1 tablespoon baking powder

1 teaspoon salt

1 tablespoon sugar

¾ cup grated Parmesan cheese

1 stick (4 ounces) unsalted butter, cut into 16 thin slices

¼ cup finely chopped fresh basil leaves

½ cup pine nuts

½ cup milk, plus additional milk if necessary

Place the flour, baking powder, salt, sugar, and Parmesan in the machine, program for Manual, Basic Dough, or Dough, and press Start. Leave the top of the machine open. After the machine has kneaded for 1 minute, add the butter. After 4 minutes, the dough should look crumbly, with no large chunks of butter remaining; if you see any large chunks, let it knead an additional 2 minutes, or until the chunks have disappeared.

Add the basil and pine nuts, then the milk. Let the machine knead for 15 to 20 seconds, or until the dough starts to form large clumps. Cancel the machine and squeeze a handful of dough; if it sticks together, it's ready. If it's too dry to stick together, put it back into the machine, press Start, and gradually add additional milk until the dough reaches the desired consistency.

TO FINISH THE SCONES
Milk for glazing

Transfer the dough to a lightly floured work surface; it'll be crumbly. Gather and squeeze it into a mound and divide it in half. Gently pat each half into an 8-inch circle about ¼ inch thick.

Transfer the circles to a lightly greased cookie sheet. Using a rolling pizza wheel, baker's bench knife, or sharp knife, cut each circle into 8 pie-shaped

wedges. Leaving the circle intact, separate the wedges slightly, leaving about ½ inch between each. Brush the tops of the circles with milk.

Bake the scones on the middle rack of a preheated 425°F oven for 18 to 20 minutes, or until they're golden brown.

Fresh basil gives these scones a delicate green tinge, not exactly the hue you're used to seeing in bread, but not at all unappealing in this case. If you don't have access to fresh basil, substitute an equal amount of pesto, cutting the amount of salt in the recipe to ½ teaspoon.

Hot Curried Ginger Scones

Serve these hot/sweet scones with any kind of mild creamed soup, such as cream of broccoli or vichyssoise, or with a cold grain or pasta salad. Their brilliant yellow color adds snap to any bread basket.

MAKES 16 SCONES

FOR THE DOUGH

1½ cups all-purpose flour
1 cup unbleached pastry flour or cake flour
1 tablespoon baking powder
1 teaspoon salt
2½ ounces crystallized ginger, finely chopped (about ½ cup)
½ teaspoon curry powder
½ teaspoon turmeric

½ teaspoon ground coriander
2 tablespoons sugar
1 stick (4 ounces) unsalted butter
1 to 2 teaspoons Tabasco sauce to taste (1 teaspoon will give you just a hint of heat; 2 teaspoons will be more assertive)
¾ cup milk, plus additional milk if necessary

Place the flours, baking powder, salt, ginger, spices, and sugar in the machine, program for Manual, Dough, or Basic Dough, and press Start. Leave the top of the machine open. After the machine has kneaded for 1 minute, add the butter. After 4 to 5 minutes, the dough should look crumbly, with no large chunks of butter remaining; if you see any large chunks, let it knead an additional 2 minutes, or until the chunks have disappeared.

Add the Tabasco, then the milk. Let the machine knead for 15 to 20 seconds, or until the dough starts to form large clumps. Cancel the machine and squeeze a handful of dough; if it sticks together, it's ready. If it's too dry to stick together, put it back into the machine, press Start, and gradually add additional milk until the dough reaches the desired consistency.

TO FINISH THE SCONES
Milk for glazing

Transfer the dough to a lightly floured work surface. Gather and squeeze it into a mound and divide it in half. Gently pat each half to a 7-inch circle about ⅜ inch thick.

Transfer the circles to a lightly greased cookie sheet. Using a rolling pizza wheel, baker's bench knife, or sharp knife, cut each circle into 8 pie-shaped

wedges. Leaving the circle intact, separate the wedges slightly, leaving about ½ inch between each. Brush the tops of the circles with milk.

Bake the scones on the middle rack of a preheated 400°F oven for 20 minutes, or until they're golden brown.

When you're after a strong, assertive ginger taste, use crystallized ginger instead of ground ginger. It delivers the same hot punch as fresh ginger, but tempers it with the sweetness of the sugar it's crystallized in, making it perfect for cookies, cake (gingerbread), and muffins. It is important to knead it by hand though, because the hard variety can scratch the coating in the bread pan.

Black and Blue Saga Shortbread

One most often thinks of shortbread as a sweet teatime treat. But this lusty version belongs on the buffet table, cut into thin wedges, where guests will find it wonderfully addictive. Teamed with crisp apples and a glass of port, this short-bread also makes a fitting finale to a thoughtfully prepared dinner.

SERVES 10 AT A BUFFET; 10 TO 15 AT DINNER

FOR THE DOUGH

2 cups unbleached pastry flour or cake flour
1/2 teaspoon salt
2 teaspoons sugar
2 teaspoons coarsely ground black pepper

6 ounces Saga blue cheese, pulled into marble-size pieces
1 stick (4 ounces) unsalted butter, cut into 16 pieces

Place the flour, salt, sugar, and pepper in the machine, program for Manual, Dough, or Basic Dough, and press Start. Leave the lid of the machine open. After 1 minute, add the blue cheese and the butter. Knead for 5 to 8 minutes, or until the mixture has formed a ball, then cancel the machine.

TO FINISH THE SHORTBREAD

1/2 cup blanched sliced almonds

Transfer the dough to a lightly greased 9-inch round cake pan and press it firmly and evenly into the pan.

Sprinkle the almonds evenly over the dough. Bake the shortbread in a pre-heated 350°F oven for 55 minutes to 1 hour, or until the almonds and the short-bread crust underneath are golden brown. Allow the shortbread to cool to lukewarm, then slice it into 20 wedges. When they are completely cool, remove the wedges from the pan and serve them at once or store them in an airtight container.

◇

If you're a fan of blue cheese, this is a good recipe to sam-ple different varieties. Try straight supermarket-style blue cheese, then compare that to Saga blue, true Roquefort, Cam-bozola, or Stilton; the differences are subtle and interesting.

◇

Japanese Pancakes

The idea for this recipe comes from the Tassajara Bread Book. *Thinly julienned vegetables are mixed with a thin pancake batter of flour and potato starch (available at Asian food stores), then cooked on a griddle or in a heavy frying pan until golden. The vegetables may be cut up a day ahead and stored in a plastic freezer bag in the refrigerator. The batter may be made one day ahead and combined with the vegetables just before cooking. Be sure to refrigerate the batter. Leftover pancakes can be refrigerated and reheated in a microwave.*

MAKES SEVEN 6-INCH PANCAKES

FOR THE BATTER

1 1/2 teaspoons yeast
1 1/2 cups all-purpose flour
1/2 cup potato starch
2 eggs
1 cup milk heated to 120°F and cooled to lukewarm

1 teaspoon salt
1 tablespoon sugar
1 tablespoon sesame oil
2 tablespoons sesame seeds

Place all the ingredients in the machine, program for Dough or Manual, and press Start. The batter will be thin.

TO FINISH THE PANCAKES

1 celery stalk, thinly sliced diagonally
1 carrot, peeled and shaved with a vegetable peeler
2 scallions, root end trimmed, thinly sliced and cut into 2-inch lengths

2 cups Napa cabbage, thinly sliced from the leafy end
1/3 cup finely chopped red onion
2 to 3 tablespoons vegetable oil

Pour the batter into a large bowl and add all the vegetables. Stir to mix.
Preheat a griddle or frying pan to medium-high and sprinkle with enough vegetable oil to thinly coat the surface. Using a 1/2-cup measure, ladle the batter onto the preheated surface, leaving enough room to turn the pancakes. Cook each side for 2 1/2 minutes, or until the edges are set, the tops are slightly moist, and the bottoms are a rich golden color. Serve the pancakes warm with soy sauce if desired.

 HINT: *You can experiment using other vegetables or precooked meat. Just be sure that the pieces are thinly sliced.*

Yeasted Apple Pancake

This glorious pancake, perfect for Sunday brunch, has batter that is cakelike and very moist. Granny Smith apples, which are available year-round, are best for this recipe because of their assertive taste and the fact that they don't get soft and mushy when cooked. This pancake is especially good topped with Special Syrup (recipe follows).

SERVES 4

FOR THE BATTER

1	teaspoon yeast		2	tablespoons sour cream
1	cup all-purpose flour		1	tablespoon unsalted butter, softened
1/2	teaspoon salt			
2	tablespoons brown sugar		1/2	cup milk, at room temperature

Place all the ingredients in the machine, program for Dough or Basic Dough, and press Start. Mix the batter for 3 minutes, not including the preknead cycle, then cancel the cycle. Let the batter rise in the machine for 1/2 hour. While the dough is rising, you can prepare the apples.

FOR THE APPLES

1	large Granny Smith apple (1/2 pound)		1	tablespoon rum or a flavored brandy
3	tablespoons unsalted butter, softened		3	tablespoons sugar
			1/4	cup chopped walnuts

Preheat the oven to 350°F.
   Peel, core, and thinly slice the apple. In a nonstick pan, cook the apple slices in the rest of the ingredients except the walnuts until tender. Set aside.

TO FINISH THE PANCAKE

Butter and flour an 8-inch cast-iron skillet or baking dish. Stir the walnuts into the apple mixture and spread this into the skillet. When the batter is finished, remove the pan from the machine and, using a rubber spatula, scrape the batter out over the apple mixture, spreading it over the top, and bake for 12 to 15 minutes, or until the pancake is firm to the touch.

Remove the pancake from the oven and invert it carefully onto a serving platter. The apples will now be on top and the pancake a rich golden brown.

Serve the pancake hot from the oven with maple syrup and soft butter. Or, you can make this very special syrup to top it.

Special Syrup

3 tablespoons unsalted butter   3 to 4   tablespoons real maple syrup
2 tablespoons sugar

Place all the ingredients in a small saucepan and heat slowly until the sugar has dissolved. Pour the syrup over the pancake just before serving.

French Peasant Pancakes

This hearty pancake, bursting with flavor, makes an unconventional luncheon or light supper meal. Chopped greens, leeks, shallots, and a touch of garlic are sautéed and then covered with a yeasted buckwheat pancake batter that is fried until golden brown. You can make the pancakes without the bacon if you wish. The batter will keep for one to two days in the refrigerator.

SERVES 3 TO 4 AS A LIGHT LUNCH OR SUPPER; 6 TO 8 AS A SIDE DISH

FOR THE BATTER

1	teaspoon yeast		1	teaspoon sugar
3/4	cup all-purpose flour		1	cup water
3/4	cup buckwheat flour		2	large eggs
3	tablespoons milk powder		1/4	stick (1 ounce) unsalted butter or
1	teaspoon salt			margarine

Place all the ingredients in the machine, program for Dough, Basic Dough, or Manual, and press Start. The batter will resemble thin pancake batter. If your machine is the type with a hole in the bottom, you will need to remove the finished batter to a bowl or pitcher.

TO FINISH THE PANCAKES

2 to 3	small leeks		2	large shallots, finely chopped
4 to 6	slices well-cooked bacon, coarsely chopped, with the drained fat reserved, or (vegetarian option) 2 tablespoons olive oil		1/2	pound greens, such as Swiss chard or spinach, carefully washed and dried and cut crosswise in 1/4-inch strips
1	garlic clove, minced			

Trim the root end and green leaves from the leeks and cut the remaining white sections in half lengthwise. Holding the leeks under running water, spread the layers of the leek, leaving them intact, as you wash them thoroughly to remove any grit. Cut the leeks crosswise into 2-inch sections and julienne the sections.

To make the first pancake, put 2 teaspoons of the bacon fat or the 2 tablespoons olive oil in a 10-inch nonstick frying pan and heat over medium-high heat. Add half of the garlic, shallots, and leeks and sauté for 2 to 3 minutes, or until they just start to turn soft. Add the greens and sauté for 2 to 3 minutes, or until they just start to wilt. Sprinkle half of the bacon over the vegetables. Quickly pour half of the buckwheat batter over the vegetables, tilting the pan to spread the batter evenly. Cook for 4 to 4 1/2 minutes, loosening the edges of the pancake and tilting the pan to spread around the uncooked batter. Lift the edge of the pancake to check that the bottom is deep golden brown and crispy. The top should be set. Loosen the edges again and slide the pancake onto a rimless plate. Add another teaspoon of bacon fat to the pan and tilt the pan to coat. Invert the pan over the plate and flip the plate and the pan together so that the uncooked side of the pancake falls back into the pan. Cook this second side for about 4 minutes, or until it is golden brown and crispy. Repeat for the second pancake.

HINT: *Be sure the leeks and greens are thoroughly washed. These may be peasant pancakes but we don't want them that earthy. Fill a large pot with water, swish the greens around for several minutes, and then let them sit a minute for the grit to settle to the bottom of the pan. Remove the leaves from the pan and wash each leaf under running water, then pat dry.*

Iranian Yogurt Pancakes

These delicious, slightly tart pancakes are good for breakfast or as a light supper meal. Or try them as a dessert or a late-night treat spread with sour cream or homemade Yogurt Cheese and topped with Rhubarb Sauce (recipes follow). The batter can be made the night before, put in a covered container, and refrigerated until morning—just be sure that you use a large enough container to allow for the batter to rise.

These pancakes are best eaten warm, but they can be cooked and reheated in a toaster oven or microwave or eaten at room temperature.

MAKES 12 PANCAKES

FOR THE BATTER

2	teaspoons yeast	1	teaspoon salt
1½	cups all-purpose flour	2	large eggs or egg substitute
1½	cups unflavored yogurt (low-fat works fine)	½	stick (2 ounces) unsalted butter or margarine
2	tablespoons sugar		

Place all the ingredients in the machine, program for Dough, Basic Dough, or Manual, and press Start. The batter will be thin. If your machine is the type with a hole in the bottom of the baking pan, remove the finished batter to a bowl or pitcher.

TO FINISH THE PANCAKES

Preheat a large nonstick skillet or spray an electric griddle with nonstick vegetable spray and set the thermostat to medium-high. Using a ¼-cup measuring cup, pour the batter for 3 pancakes at a time. Cook the pancakes for about 2 minutes, or until the edges lose their shine. Lift the edge of 1 pancake and check that it is golden brown underneath. Flip the pancakes and continue cooking for another 2 minutes. Repeat with the rest of the batter.

Yogurt Cheese

2   cups plain yogurt

Place the yogurt in a fine-mesh strainer or colander lined with a double thickness of cheesecloth. Set the strainer or colander over a bowl and place in the refrigerator. Allow the liquid or whey to drip from the yogurt for 8 to 10 hours. The longer it drips the thicker the consistency of the cheese. Use the cheese as you would sour cream or cream cheese.

Rhubarb Sauce

2½   cups rhubarb, sliced into ½-inch   ¾ to 1   cup sugar
     pieces   3   tablespoons water

Place the rhubarb, sugar, and water in a nonreactive saucepan and cook over medium-high heat for about 5 to 10 minutes, or until the rhubarb has softened and the sauce has thickened. This can also be done in a microwave set on high for 5 to 6 minutes. The cooking times for both methods will vary according the freshness and thickness of the rhubarb stalks. Stir occasionally, especially as the liquid is reduced, and lower the heat if necessary.

HINT: *The secret to successful pancakes of any type is to preheat the griddle or skillet. A drop of water should dance around the surface if it is hot enough.*

Savory Mexican Corn Pancakes

These special pancakes are quick to whip up and are the perfect companion to sausage or bacon. The batter is adapted from the King Arthur 200th Anniversary Cookbook.

MAKES 10 PANCAKES

FOR THE BATTER

1	cup sour cream	1	cup all-purpose flour
1/4	cup corn oil or vegetable oil	1	tablespoon baking powder
2	large eggs	1/2	teaspoon salt
1/4	cup sugar	1	teaspoon freshly ground black
1	cup cornmeal		pepper

You will be using your bread machine only long enough to mix the batter. Place all the ingredients in the machine, program for Dough, Basic Dough, or Manual, and press Start. Mix for approximately 3 minutes, scraping the sides of the pan with a rubber spatula to ensure proper mixing. Cancel the machine and transfer the batter to a clean stainless-steel bowl.

TO FINISH THE PANCAKES

1	medium onion, sliced	4 to 8	jalapeño peppers, chopped
1	large green bell pepper, sliced	3/4	cup grated Cheddar cheese
4	tablespoons salad oil		Sausage, for garnish (optional)
1	plum tomato, chopped		Salsa, for garnish (optional)
1	garlic clove, minced		

Over medium heat, sauté the onion and pepper slices in the oil until tender. Add the tomato, garlic, and jalapeños. Continue cooking for 3 to 4 minutes, then remove from the heat and cool. Stir the onion mixture into the batter and finally stir in the cheese.

Heat a nonstick pan set over medium-high heat. When the pan is hot, using a 1/4-cup measure, drop the batter into the pan and cook the pancakes slowly, 3 to 4 minutes, on each side. Arrange the pancakes on a platter and top them off with sausage and salsa.

Corn Onion Pancakes

These savory pancakes are perfect for a light lunch or supper. Try them topped with sour cream, guacamole, and chopped green onion. They are thin and flexible enough to be rolled like crepes or blini.

The cooled pancakes can be frozen or made ahead and refrigerated. Separate each pancake with waxed paper and store in a plastic bag.

MAKES EIGHT 5-INCH PANCAKES

FOR THE BATTER

1	teaspoon yeast	$1^{1}/_{2}$	cups warm water
$^{2}/_{3}$	cup all-purpose flour	1	small onion, finely chopped (about
$^{2}/_{3}$	cup cornmeal		$^{1}/_{3}$ cup)
$1^{1}/_{4}$	teaspoons salt	2 to 3	dashes of Tabasco sauce

Place all the ingredients in the machine, program for Dough, Basic Dough, or Manual, and press Start. The batter will look like thin pancake batter. Remove the batter from the machine 15 minutes after the first kneading is finished. If you have a baking pan without a hole in the bottom, you may remove the pan and work directly from the pan. Otherwise transfer the batter quickly to another bowl and wipe up any drips.

TO FINISH THE PANCAKES

1	teaspoon garlic oil	$^{1}/_{2}$	cup guacamole, for filling
2	teaspoons olive oil	1	green onion, finely chopped, for
$^{1}/_{2}$	cup sour cream, for filling		filling

Mix together the garlic and olive oils. Heat an electric frying pan to 360°F, or place a large skillet over medium heat, and add half of the mixed oils. Use a $^{1}/_{4}$-cup measure to pour the batter for 2 or 3 pancakes at a time into the hot pan. Use the edge of the measuring cup to quickly swirl and spread the batter. Fry the pancakes for $1^{1}/_{2}$ to 2 minutes, or until the edges have set and they are slightly golden brown on the bottom. Flip them and fry another $1^{1}/_{2}$ to 2 minutes. Pat the pancakes lightly with paper towels to remove any excess oil. Add the remaining oil to the pan and repeat until the batter is used up.

Spread 1 tablespoon of the sour cream in a line down the center of each pancake. Top with 1 tablespoon of the guacamole. Sprinkle with a little of the green onion and roll the pancakes around the fillings. Serve immediately.

Atole Piñon Hotcakes

On Cerrillos Road about a mile from downtown Santa Fe is an unprepossessing building that houses the Tecolote Café, New Mexico's premier breakfast mecca. It's an agonizing task to choose anything else from a menu that features Carne Adovada Burritos: lean pork cooked in chile caribe, rolled in a flour tortilla, topped with red chile and melted cheddar, and served with a side of posole. But I branched out and ordered the blue corn hotcakes—little suspecting that, after one heavenly bite, I would have to rewrite my list of favorite breakfast meals.

Light as a summer breeze, anchored to the plate only with buttery toasted pine nuts (and as much maple syrup as you dare pour before being labeled "piggy" by the people sitting with you), these hotcakes owe their special taste and texture to blue cornmeal, long prized by Native Americans, which is a grain that has come into its own these days. Blue cornmeal is available in health food stores and by mail order (page 301). For this recipe you will need the very finely ground variety that looks like flour.

Tecolote's owner and man of the kitchen, Bill Jennison, generously shared his recipe with me so I can have a taste of Sante Fe whenever I'm in the mood.

MAKES 16 LARGE OR 24 TO 30 SMALL PANCAKES, SERVING 6

FOR THE BATTER

1	tablespoon yeast	1/3	cup vegetable oil
1	cup finely ground blue cornmeal	2	extra-large eggs
2	cups all-purpose flour	4	tablespoons nonfat dry milk
1	tablespoon baking powder	1 1/3	cups water, plus up to an
2	tablespoons sugar		additional 1/3 cup to make a slowly
1 1/2	teaspoons salt		flowing pancake batter

Place all the ingredients in the machine, program for Manual or Dough, and press Start. Allow the machine to knead only until the ingredients are completely mixed. Use a rubber scraper to make sure all the flour is incorporated from the bottom and sides of the pan. The consistency should be thick but flowing batter. Cancel the machine, leave the top closed, and allow the batter to sit for 1 hour.

Alternatively, you can mix the batter the night before, pour it into a covered container, and allow it to rise in the refrigerator.

TO FINISH THE HOTCAKES

1	cup (5 ounces) toasted pine nuts (see the Hint)

Heat a griddle or large skillet, using a small amount of oil or butter if necessary to prevent sticking. Stir the pine nuts into the batter. To pour the batter onto the griddle, use a $1/4$-cup measure for small hotcakes and a $1/3$-cup measure for large ones. Cook the hotcakes for about 90 seconds on one side, then when the upper surface starts to bubble (and the underside is a lovely golden brown), flip them and cook for another 40 to 50 seconds.

Serve them hot with lots of sweet butter and real maple syrup.

HINT: *To toast pine nuts, for each cup of pine nuts that you are toasting, heat 1 tablespoon vegetable oil in a large skillet set over high heat. Add the pine nuts and stir constantly or shake the pan vigorously to agitate them until most turn a golden brown and some just begin to get dark spots. (The nuts will not toast uniformly, which I think adds to their beauty.) Immediately empty the pine nuts into a strainer, cool slightly, and then blot off any excess oil with paper towels.*

It makes sense to toast more nuts than you need for one recipe so you will have them on hand when you need them for another recipe or want to make the original recipe again. Toasted pine nuts should be cooled completely, then stored in the freezer in heavy-duty plastic freezer bags.

You can cook the hotcakes, let them cool completely on wire racks, stack them with waxed paper between each one, and freeze them in a heavy-duty plastic freezer bag for up to 3 months. Place them in a single layer on a baking sheet without defrosting and heat them in a 300°F oven for 15 minutes, or until hot.

Sweet Breads, Dumplings, Biscotti, and Other Desserts

Apple Fig Bread

This bread is folded with a simple technique, which makes you look as if you have mastered the art of fine pastry baking. It makes an elegant appetizer when it is sliced thin and made without the sugar glaze. With the sugar glaze, it is a delectable coffee cake or tea bread.

You can freeze these loaves up to six months after they are cooled by first wrapping them tightly in foil and then placing them in a plastic bag.

MAKES 2 LOAVES, EACH SERVING 6 TO 8 AS COFFEE CAKE OR TEA
BREAD; 8 TO 10 AS AN APPETIZER OR DINNER BREAD

FOR THE DOUGH
1	tablespoon yeast	3	large eggs
3	cups all-purpose flour	1/2	stick (2 ounces) unsalted butter or
1 1/2	teaspoons salt		margarine, softened and cut into
1/2	cup sugar		pieces
2/3	cup plain yogurt		

Place all the ingredients in the machine, program for Dough, Basic Dough, or Manual, and press Start. The dough will look sticky but will not be sticky to the touch. While the dough is rising, make the filling so that it can cool.

FOR THE FILLING
1	cup dried figs (6 ounces), cut into quarters	1/2	cup coarsely chopped walnuts (2 ounces), toasted in a preheated 350°F oven for 4 to 5 minutes
1	cup coarsely chopped, firm apple, such as Granny Smith or Delicious	2	tablespoons honey
1/4	cup water	1/2	teaspoon ground cinnamon

Place the figs, apple, and water in a small saucepan and bring to a boil over medium-high heat. Lower heat to medium and continue cooking for 4 to 5 minutes, stirring constantly, until the water has almost completely reduced and the figs and apple have softened. Remove from the heat and add the walnuts, honey, and cinnamon, stirring until well blended. Cool to room temperature.

TO FINISH THE BREAD
1/2	stick (2 ounces) unsalted butter or margarine, melted	4	teaspoons sugar (optional)
1	large egg beaten with 1 tablespoon water		

Spray a large baking sheet with nonstick vegetable spray. Transfer the dough to a work surface lighted coated with vegetable oil or sprayed with a small amount of nonstick vegetable spray. Divide the dough in half and let it rest for 10 minutes. Using a rolling pin, roll each piece of dough to a 12-inch circle. Spread 2 tablespoons of melted butter on each circle. Place half of the filling in the center of each circle and spread to within 3 inches of the edges. Fold the edges inward, overlapping them to form a 6-inch square. Lift the folded squares to the prepared baking sheet and pat to flatten them slightly. Cover with plastic wrap and let rise for 1 to 1½ hours, or until the dough is slightly risen. The squares will not double in size but will rise and puff more while baking.

Preheat the oven to 350°F with the rack in the center position.

Just before baking, generously brush the squares with the egg glaze and sprinkle each with 2 teaspoons sugar if desired. Bake for 25 to 30 minutes, or until the tops of the loaves are puffed and golden brown.

HINT: *A toaster oven works well for toasting the walnuts and avoids heating up a larger oven.*

Pink Peppercorn and Lavender Shortbread

I have a friend who loves to cook with pink peppercorns. He once told me they would even be great in a dessert, and this recipe proves that he is right. I suggest you serve these unusual cookies to your jaded (culinarily speaking) friends who think they've seen everything.

If you are planning a fancy tea party, or need a treat for a meeting or an unusual hostess gift, think of these. They have a subtle hint of heat from the peppercorns that is tempered by the mild lavender taste. These are cookies for grown-ups. Since vanilla is another important flavor in these cookies, it's important to use real vanilla extract—not the imitation kind.

This shortbread will keep, tightly sealed, for one week at room temperature (in a cool place), or you can freeze it for up to four months in a freezer-strength plastic bag or a plastic container. You should defrost it still covered.

MAKES 12 WEDGES

FOR THE DOUGH

2	sticks (8 ounces) unsalted butter, very soft	1	tablespoon vanilla extract
³/₄	cup confectioners' sugar (unsifted unless it is very lumpy)	3	cups all-purpose flour
		1	tablespoon pink peppercorns, crushed
¹/₂	teaspoon salt	1	teaspoon dried lavender

Preheat the oven to 325°F with the rack in the center position. Select a 9-inch metal pie plate. Glass will also work but the shortbread will not be as crisp.

Place the butter, sugar, salt, and vanilla in the machine, program for Manual, Dough, or Basic Dough and press Start. Allow the mixture to knead until blended. With the machine running, add the flour and allow it to knead until a crumbly ball forms, about 4 to 5 minutes. Add the peppercorns and lavender and allow the dough to knead 2 to 3 minutes more. You can push the mixture together with a rubber scraper.

TO FINISH THE SHORTBREAD

Turn the dough out into the ungreased pie plate and use your fingers to press it evenly over the bottom of the pie plate. Press the tines of a fork around the border to make a design, then press the fork at 1-inch intervals into the surface of the dough. This keeps the shortbread from puffing up while baking.

Bake the shortbread for 30 to 35 minutes, or until the edges are beginning to turn a light golden brown. Remove the shortbread from the oven and use a sharp knife to divide it into 12 wedges, but do not remove them from the pan until they are almost cool.

Cherry Almond Ring

Tart or sweet dark cherries make a wonderful contrast to the sweet almond paste filling in this seductively beautiful pastry. The ring makes a beautiful presentation with the golden brown crust vented to reveal a hint of the filling inside.

The baked ring can be frozen after cooling completely. Wrap it tightly in foil and place it in a plastic bag. Defrost it still wrapped, remove it from the bag, loosen the foil, and reheat it in a 300°F oven for ten minutes.

SERVES 8

FOR THE DOUGH

1	tablespoon yeast		$1/2$	cup sour cream
$3^1/4$	cups all-purpose flour		2	large eggs
1	teaspoon salt		$3/4$	teaspoon finely grated orange rind
$1/3$	cup sugar			or $1/4$ teaspoon orange oil
$1/4$	cup evaporated milk			

Place all the ingredients in the machine, program for Dough, Basic Dough, or Manual, and press Start. This light dough will not be sticky to the touch after several minutes of kneading.

TO FINISH THE RING

3	tablespoons unsalted butter or margarine		1	tablespoon unsalted butter or margarine, melted
$3^1/2$	ounces almond paste		3	tablespoons sliced almonds
1	large egg		2	teaspoons sugar
1	16-ounce can pitted tart or dark sweet cherries			

In a food processor or with an electric mixer, beat together the 3 tablespoons butter, almond paste, and egg until well blended. Drain the cherries in a colander and press gently to remove the excess liquid. If you are using the larger sweet cherries, cut them in half. Check for pits even though the can says "pitted."

Grease or spray a baking sheet with vegetable spray.

Remove the dough from the machine to a work surface and spray the surface lightly with vegetable spray, if necessary, to keep the dough from sticking. Let the dough rest for 10 minutes and then roll it to a 20 × 8-inch rectangle. Spread the almond paste mixture evenly over the dough to within $1/2$ inch of the edges. Sprinkle the cherries evenly over the almond paste. Moisten the edges of the dough and, starting with a long side, roll it up jelly roll style. Seal the seam, using your fingertips or a fork, and go over it several times to be sure it holds.

Place the roll, seam side down, on the prepared baking sheet and form it into a ring. Moisten the ends with a little water and seal them together carefully. Using a very sharp knife or pair of scissors, cut 1-inch slashes ½ inch into the top of the dough every 2 inches. Do not cut down into the sides of the dough or the ring will separate during baking. Cover the ring with a clean towel and allow it to rise in a warm place for 1 to 1½ hours, or until nicely puffed but not doubled in bulk.

Preheat the oven to 350°F with the rack in the center position. Brush the top of the ring with the 1 tablespoon melted butter and sprinkle with the almonds and then the sugar. Bake for 25 to 30 minutes, or until it is deep golden brown. The ring should have a crisp hollow sound when tapped. Cool the ring slightly on the baking sheet, then slide it over a few inches to prevent sticking. Serve warm or at room temperature.

HINTS: *The key to a beautifully shaped ring is to seal all the edges carefully, moistening them lightly with water and going over them several times. The slits on the top are important as vents for the filling inside. It is important to slice the dough down deep enough to expose the filling, but slice it only on the top or the ring will split during the baking.*

If you find that your ring is splitting during baking, next time try baking it in an oven that has not been preheated. Place the pastry in the cold oven, and then set the dial to the required temperature.

Blueberry Twist

Blueberries and a brown sugar and nut streusel filling are rolled and twisted in a rich lemon-flavored dough to form this heavenly pastry. The twisted roll is then coiled in a nine-inch baking pan. The loaf puffs way up out of the pan into a glorious golden dome. The tart blueberries provide a nice counterpoint to the sweet brown sugar and nuts.

This twist can be frozen, tightly wrapped in plastic and sealed in a plastic bag. It will keep for two to three days in the refrigerator because of the high fat content of the dough.

SERVES 8 TO 12

FOR THE DOUGH

1	tablespoon yeast		2	eggs
3	cups all-purpose flour		6	tablespoons (3 ounces) unsalted butter or margarine
1/3	cup sugar			
1	teaspoon salt		1/2	teaspoon lemon oil
3/4	cup evaporated milk			

Place all the ingredients in the machine, program for Dough, Basic Dough, or Manual, and press Start. The dough will be on the firm side and will not feel sticky to the touch.

FOR THE STREUSEL FILLING

1/2	cup light brown sugar, packed		2	tablespoons (1 ounce) unsalted butter or margarine, cut into pieces
1/2	cup walnuts			
2	tablespoons all-purpose flour			
1	teaspoon cinnamon			

Place the brown sugar, walnuts, flour, cinnamon, and cut-up butter in a food processor and process until the walnuts are finely chopped and the mixture is evenly mixed. Or, by hand, place the brown sugar in a small mixing bowl. Chop the walnuts to fine pieces and add them along with the flour and cinnamon. Stir with a fork until evenly mixed. Add the cut-up butter and, using a pastry cutter or 2 knives in a crisscross motion, cut it into the brown sugar mixture. Set aside.

TO FINISH THE TWIST

2	tablespoons (1 ounce) unsalted butter or margarine, melted		1	egg beaten with 1 tablespoon water
1	cup blueberries, fresh or frozen (see the Hints)			

Transfer the dough to a work surface and let it rest for 10 minutes. Roll the dough to a 24 × 8-inch rectangle. The dough should roll easily without sticking, but if necessary, spray a little vegetable spray on the work surface or rolling pin.

Spread the melted butter over the dough to within ½ inch of the edges. Sprinkle the streusel mixture evenly over the butter. Sprinkle the blueberries over the streusel. Moisten the edges of the dough lightly with cold water and roll the dough up tightly, starting with a long side. Seal the seam carefully, pressing it with your fingers. Seal the ends by pinching the dough together.

Generously grease or spray a 9 × 2-inch springform pan with vegetable spray. Line the bottom of the pan with foil and spray or grease it again. Lifting the ends of the rolled-up dough, twist the roll 5 or 6 times. Gently lift and shape the twisted roll into a coil in the pan. Leave about ½ inch in between the coils, for the dough will rise and fill in the spaces. Using a very sharp knife or scissors, cut ½-inch-deep vents every 1 inch around the top of the coil, being careful to not cut down the sides. Cover the pan with plastic wrap and let the dough rise in a warm place for 1½ to 2 hours, or until about a third larger. It will rise to fill the pan while baking.

Generously brush the top of the coil with the egg glaze. Preheat the oven to 350°F with the rack in the center position. Bake for 35 to 40 minutes, or until the top is a deep golden brown and the center is firm and crisp. It is better to overbake, especially if you are using large cultivated frozen berries; otherwise, their extra juice may make the center a little damp.

Loosen the sides of the loaf by running a knife around the edges of the pan, then remove the sides of the pan. Cool the loaf on the bottom of the pan for 15 minutes. Remove the loaf from the pan bottom to a serving plate or cutting board and serve it warm or at room temperature.

HINTS: *Fresh wild blueberries have the most flavor. The large cultivated variety have milder flavor and more juice. Frozen berries tend to be more runny as they are cooked, especially the large cultivated kind. Baking for a longer time to compensate for the added liquid will help. You can create an even more intense flavor by adding ½ cup dried blueberries, which are available in gourmet stores and by mail order (page 301), to the fresh or frozen berries.*

Lining the pan with foil will make removal and cleanup easier.

Raspberry Cream Cheese Breakfast Tart

This delicate buttery pastry is perfect for that special Sunday brunch. You can also make it with blueberry or boysenberry preserves if you wish.

SERVES 8

FOR THE DOUGH

1	teaspoon yeast	$1/2$	teaspoon lemon zest
$1^1/2$	cups all-purpose flour	$1/4$	stick (1 ounce) unsalted butter,
2	tablespoons brown sugar		softened
$1/2$	teaspoon salt	1	egg yolk
$1/2$	cup water		

Place all the ingredients in the machine, program for Manual, Dough, or Basic Dough, and press Start. The dough will be slightly sticky at first, but during the kneading process it will form a ball. While the dough is rising, you can prepare the filling.

FOR THE FILLING

8	ounces cream cheese, very soft	2	egg yolks
2	tablespoons sugar	1	teaspoon vanilla extract

Cream together the cream cheese and sugar until creamy. Add the egg yolks, one at a time. Scrape the bowl after the last egg yolk has been added. Mix in the vanilla. Refrigerate the filling until you are ready to assemble the tart.

FOR THE STREUSEL

$1/4$	stick (1 ounce) unsalted butter	2	tablespoons rolled oats (not
2	tablespoons brown sugar		instant)
2	tablespoons all-purpose flour	$1/8$	cup coarsely chopped nuts of
1	teaspoon ground cinnamon		your choice

In a mixing bowl, cut the butter into the brown sugar, flour, and cinnamon. Do not create a paste. Stir in the oats and nuts.

TO FINISH THE TART

3	tablespoons raspberry preserves

Preheat the oven to 400°F with the rack in the center position. Lightly grease a 9-inch fluted tart pan with a removable bottom. Place the pan on a baking sheet to make it easier to get in and out of the oven and to prevent oven spills.

When the dough cycle is completed, remove the dough and let it rest, covered with a clean towel, on a lightly floured work surface for 5 minutes. Roll out the dough to a 10-inch circle. Line the tart pan with the dough. Place spoonfuls of the cream cheese filling over the dough, using a rubber scraper or the back of a spoon to spread it out evenly. Place the raspberry preserves on top of the filling and spread them out in a thin layer. Sprinkle the streusel over the top.

Bake the tart for 20 minutes at 400°F, then lower the oven to 350°F and continue baking for 10 to 12 minutes. Cool the tart in the pan for 10 minutes before removing the sides. Serve warm or at room temperature.

Cardamom Circle Twists

We offer a choice of sugar or nut topping for these beautiful, sweet twists of flavored dough, which are also delicious plain. I think they are great for morning coffee. They are not too sweet for dinner rolls and make a great addition when you are serving a variety of rolls.

The cooled twists can be frozen, tightly wrapped in plastic and stored in a plastic bag, then defrosted while still wrapped.

MAKES 14 TWISTS

FOR THE DOUGH

$^2/_3$ cup unsalted butter or margarine, cut into pieces
$^1/_2$ cup milk heated to 120°F
1   tablespoon yeast
3   cups all-purpose flour
$1^3/_4$ teaspoons salt

$^1/_4$ cup sugar
1   egg
$^1/_2$ teaspoon freshly ground cardamom (use a pinch extra if it is already ground)

Add the butter to the heated milk to cool it slightly. Place all the ingredients in the machine, program for Dough, Basic Dough, or Manual, and press Start. The dough may look a little sticky but it won't feel sticky to the touch.

TO FINISH THE TWISTS

1   large egg beaten with 1 tablespoon water
$^1/_3$ cup finely ground almonds or walnuts (optional)

$^1/_3$ cup sugar (optional)

Grease or spray a baking sheet with nonstick vegetable spray.
Turn the dough out on a work surface. Use a little vegetable spray if it sticks, but it should work fine without any spray. Divide the dough into about twenty-eight 1- to 1½-inch balls. Cover the balls with plastic wrap and let them rest for about 10 minutes to make them easier to roll out.

With the palms of your hands, roll each ball to a 10- to 12-inch rope. Twist 2 ropes together and squeeze the ends. Form this twist into a circle, pinch the ends together, and smooth the seam. Repeat with the rest of the ropes. Place the twisted circles on the prepared baking sheet, cover them with plastic wrap, and let them rise for 1½ hours until slightly puffed and rounded but not doubled in bulk.

Preheat the oven to 400°F. Brush the egg glaze over the twists, then sprinkle them evenly with either the nuts or sugar or both, if desired. Bake the twists for 10 to 12 minutes, or until golden brown. Lift one side of the twists to check that they don't get too dark on the bottom.

HINTS: *Halfway through the baking time, rotate the baking sheets to bake the twists evenly.*

For the maximum flavor, buy cardamom pods to peel and grind yourself, as this spice loses its flavor rapidly.

Cranberry Orange Relish Sticky Buns

The tartness and color of the relish filling contrasts beautifully with the sweet sticky buns. This recipe is easily made with the dough from your machine and store-bought cranberry orange relish. The sticky buns can be frozen, tightly wrapped in foil in a plastic bag.

MAKES 9 STICKY BUNS

FOR THE DOUGH

1	tablespoon yeast	¹/₂	stick (2 ounces) unsalted butter or margarine
2³/₄	cups all-purpose flour		
¹/₄	cup sugar	1	large egg yolk
¹/₂	teaspoon salt	1	tablespoon orange peel or
³/₄	cup milk heated 120°F and cooled to lukewarm	¹/₄	teaspoon orange oil

Place all the ingredients in the machine, program for Dough, Basic Dough, or Manual, and press Start. The dough will look light and sticky.

TO FINISH THE STICKY BUNS

3	tablespoons unsalted butter or margarine, melted	²/₃	cup light brown sugar
		¹/₃	cup coarsely chopped walnuts
1	cup cranberry orange relish		

Spray a work surface and rolling pin lightly with nonstick vegetable spray or sprinkle them lightly with flour. Turn the dough onto the prepared surface, cover it with a clean towel and let it rest for 10 minutes, then roll it to a 16 × 10-inch rectangle. Spread the dough with 1 tablespoon of the melted butter. Spread the cranberry orange relish to within ¹/₂ inch of the edges. From a long side, roll the dough jelly roll fashion. With a sharp knife, cut the roll into 9 slices.

Add the remaining 2 tablespoons of melted butter to a 9-inch round pan and tip the pan to coat the bottom and sides. Sprinkle the brown sugar evenly over the bottom of the pan, then sprinkle the walnuts evenly over the sugar. Arrange the slices of rolled dough on top of the sugar and nuts. Cover the pan with plastic wrap and let the dough rise in a warm place for 1 hour, or until doubled in bulk.

Preheat the oven to 350°F and bake the sticky buns for 20 to 25 minutes until they are golden and crisp on the top.

HINTS: *The walnuts will be extra flavorful if you toast them in a preheated 350°F oven or toaster oven for about 5 minutes, or until they just start to brown.*

For easy cleanup, soak the pan in warm water for 10 minutes.

Millie's Hamantaschen

The Jewish holiday of Purim has always been my all-time favorite because (1) I get to dress up as a princess, not just act like one, and (2) my mom, Millie Apter, makes the best hamantaschen in the world.

These triangular-shaped cookies get their name from the tricorner hat worn by that depraved villain Haman, who set out to rid Persia of Jews but in fact ended up dangling himself, thanks to the brave Queen Esther (the very first radical feminist, if you ask me). She blew the whistle on him in a time when women were supposed to be showpieces, not mouthpieces.

These plum pockets are traditionally filled with lekvar, which is a thick fruit butter made with prunes or apricots, or a filling made with poppy seeds, apples, raisins, and almonds. Lekvar is available in specialty food stores and by mail order (page 301). The poppy seed filling comes in cans, but the homemade kind (recipe follows) is so much better. Whichever filling you choose to make, remember there is a lovely custom associated with Purim called shalach monos in which you deliver gifts (usually in the forms of fruits and cookies) to your friends, family, and neighbors. Hamantaschen are perfect for this. Versions for yeasted and nonyeasted dough follow.

MAKES ABOUT 20 COOKIES

FOR THE YEASTED DOUGH

2½	teaspoons yeast		1	tablespoon vegetable oil
3½	cups all-purpose flour		3	tablespoons honey
¼	cup sugar		¾	cup water
1	teaspoon salt		3	large eggs plus 1 egg white
½	stick (2 ounces) unsalted butter, softened			(reserve the yolk for the egg glaze)

Place all the ingredients in the machine, program for Dough, Basic Dough, or Manual, and press Start. If the dough is dry and crumbly, add a few more teaspoons of water until the dough forms a discrete ball.

At the end of the final cycle, remove the dough to a lightly floured work surface. Cover it with a clean towel and allow it to rest for 20 minutes. Line 2 heavy baking sheets with parchment paper or foil.

TO FINISH THE HAMANTASCHEN

3	tablespoons vegetable oil	1	egg yolk beaten with 2 table-
1½	cups filling: either commercially prepared prune or apricot lekvar or Poppy Seed Filling		spoons milk

Divide the dough into 2 equal pieces and, working with 1 piece at a time, roll it out to a ¼-inch thickness. Using a 4-inch cookie cutter or wide glass, cut 10 circles. Brush the circles with a light coat of oil and place 1 generous tablespoon of filling in the center. Imagine the circle as a triangle and bring 3 of the "sides" up to meet in the center, forming a Y-shaped seam. Pinch the edges together to seal (some of the filling will seep out during baking). Place the triangles on a prepared baking sheet, 2 inches apart, cover them with a light cloth, and allow them to rise in a warm place for 45 minutes, or until doubled in bulk. Repeat with the remaining dough.

Preheat the oven to 350°F with the rack in the center position. Brush the tops of the cookies with the egg glaze and bake for 15 to 18 minutes, or until they are deep golden brown. Cool on a wire rack before enjoying.

FOR THE NONYEASTED DOUGH

3½	cups all-purpose flour	3	large eggs plus 1 egg white
2	teaspoons baking powder		(reserve the yolk for the egg glaze)
1	teaspoon baking soda		Finely grated rind of 1 lemon
1	scant teaspoon salt	3	tablespoons lemon juice
¾	cup sugar	1	teaspoon vanilla extract
¾	cup vegetable oil		

Sift together the flour, baking powder, baking soda, and salt and place them in the machine. Add the other ingredients program for Manual, Dough, or Basic Dough and push Start. Allow the machine to knead the dough until it forms a discrete ball, then remove the dough to a floured work surface.

TO FINISH THE HAMANTASCHEN

2	tablespoons water	1	egg yolk beaten with 2 table-
1½	cups filling: either commercially prepared prune or apricot lekvar or Poppy Seed Filling		spoons milk

Preheat the oven to 375°F with the rack in the center position. Line 2 heavy baking sheets with parchment paper or foil. Cut the dough into 2 pieces and, working with 1 piece at a time, roll it out to a ¼-inch thickness. Use a 2½-inch cookie cutter or a floured glass to cut rounds. Brush the edges of the circles with water and place 1 generous tablespoon of filling in the center. Imagine the circle as a triangle and bring 3 of the "sides" up to meet in the center, forming a Y-shaped seam. Pinch the edges together to seal (some of the filling will seep out during baking). Place the triangles on a prepared sheet, 1 inch apart. Repeat with the rest of the dough.

Brush the tops of the cookies with the egg glaze and bake for 17 to 20 minutes, or until they are deep golden brown. Cool on a wire rack before enjoying.

Poppy Seed Filling

1 large Granny Smith apple, peeled	$^1/_2$ cup chopped almonds
1 cup poppy seeds	$^1/_4$ cup raisins
1 cup whole milk	Finely grated rind of 1 lemon
$^1/_4$ stick (1 ounce) unsalted butter	$^1/_4$ cup sugar
2 tablespoons honey	

Grate the apple, either by hand or in a blender or food processor, and set aside. Place the poppy seeds in a blender or food processor and blend or process until they form a thick, crumbly paste. Add the remaining ingredients except the apple and process or blend until smooth. Place the mixture in a heavy-bottomed saucepan and bring to a boil. Lower the heat and continue cooking, stirring frequently, until the mixture is thick. Cool, then stir in the apple.

Baci Biscotti

There is nothing quite as magical as the combination of chocolate and toasted hazelnuts. The pinnacle of this union is celebrated to perfection in Perugina's classic confection known as Baci. Dare I go one step further and use these sweetest of kisses as an ingredient in my favorite cookie? My theory is that since one thing Italian is good, then two things are Bellisimi! *You be the judge.*

MAKES ABOUT 75 BISCOTTI

3   ounces unsweetened baking
    chocolate, coarsely chopped
8   ounces Baci (15 candies)
3   extra-large eggs
1¹⁄₃ cups sugar
1   cup (8 ounces) hazelnut butter
    (available in health food stores, or
    made by placing 1 cup toasted,
    skinned hazelnuts in a food
    processor and processing until
    smooth)
3   cups all-purpose flour
1   teaspoon baking powder
¹⁄₂ teaspoon salt

Preheat the oven to 350°F with the rack in the center position. Line a heavy-duty baking sheet with foil and lightly oil or spray the foil with nonstick vegetable spray. Melt the chocolate either in the microwave or in a small bowl set over a pan of gently simmering water. Use a small, sharp knife to cut the Baci into fourths (from top to bottom).

In the bowl of an electric mixer set at medium speed combine the eggs and sugar and beat until smooth and slightly thickened. On low speed add the chocolate and hazelnut butter (with its oil) and mix until completely incorporated.

Sift the flour together with the baking powder and salt and mix into the egg mixture. Finally, with the machine on the slowest speed, add the Baci. Mix only until the Baci are distributed. The dough will be shiny and oily.

Place the dough on a clean work surface and divide it into three equal pieces. Roll each piece into a 15-inch log, about 1¹⁄₂ to 2 inches in diameter. Place the logs 3 inches apart on the prepared pan and bake in the preheated oven for 30 minutes.

Remove the pan from the oven and reduce the temperature to 325°F. For easy handling, cut each log in half while still on the baking sheet and remove to a cutting board. (The long logs are not firm and will break if you try to move them without cutting.) Use a sharp knife to cut each log into 1-inch pieces. Place the cookies back on the baking sheet on end at least 2 inches apart (you'll have to use two baking sheets or repeat the operation twice) and place them in the oven for an additional 15 minutes. Cool completely before serving.

Date Turnovers

*Date turnovers are enjoyed by many Middle Eastern cultures. They are indi-
vidual rich, yeasted pastries with a spicy-sweet date nut filling. You can freeze the
cooled turnovers in plastic bags, then defrost them still wrapped and refresh
them by placing them on a baking sheet in a 325°F oven for ten minutes.*

MAKES 2 LARGE TURNOVERS

FOR THE DOUGH

½	stick (2 ounces) unsalted butter or margarine	3½	cups all-purpose flour
1¼	cups evaporated milk, warm	1	teaspoon sugar
1	tablespoon yeast	1½	teaspoons salt

Add the butter to the warm milk to cool it slightly. Place all the ingredients in
the machine, program for Dough, Basic Dough, or Manual, and press Start.
The dough will be firm and not sticky after several minutes of kneading.

FOR THE FILLING

½	cup water	½	teaspoon ground cinnamon
1½	cups (11 ounces) chopped dates	¼	teaspoon ground cloves
½	cup dark brown sugar, firmly packed	1	tablespoon lemon juice
1	cup (4 ounces) walnuts, chopped into ¼-inch pieces		

Add the water and dates to a medium saucepan and bring to a low boil over
medium heat. Reduce the heat to medium-low and simmer for 7 to 8 minutes,
or until the liquid is reduced. Stir as needed, especially toward the end, to keep
the mixture from scorching. Remove from the heat and add the brown sugar, walnuts, cinnamon, cloves, and lemon juice. Stir the mixture until well blended.

TO FINISH THE TURNOVERS

¼	stick (1 ounce) unsalted butter or margarine, melted	2	teaspoons sugar
1	egg beaten with 1 tablespoon water		

Remove the dough from the machine to a lightly oiled work surface and divide
the dough in half. Roll each half to a 12- to 14-inch circle. Brush each circle

with the melted butter to within ½ inch of the edge. Divide the filling between the 2 circles, placing it on one half of each circle and keeping it within ½ inch of the edge. Moisten the ½-inch edge lightly with water. Fold the other half of each circle over the filling, sealing the edge carefully by pressing it between your fingers. Fold the sealed edge inward, gathering the dough as you go to form a neat edge. Using a pastry scraper or large spatula, lift the turnovers to a baking sheet (you should be able to fit both turnovers on the same baking sheet). Cut 4 vents in the top of each with a sharp knife or scissors.

Cover the turnovers with plastic wrap and let them rise for 1 to 1½ hours until nicely puffed but not doubled in size.

Brush the egg glaze over the tops of the turnovers and sprinkle them with the sugar.

Preheat the oven to 350°F with the rack in the center position and bake the turnovers for 20 to 25 minutes, or until they are a deep golden color. Rotate the baking sheets once halfway through the baking time so the turnovers bake evenly.

HINT: *Egg glazes create darker crusts, so be sure you consider that when you are checking for doneness. A slight golden color may be deceiving in terms of doneness.*

Apple Dumplings

Whole apples are slightly poached in an apple cinnamon syrup and filled with cinnamon and sugar. Then they are wrapped in a rich, sweet thin dough and baked to a deep golden color. The reduced apple cinnamon poaching syrup is drizzled over them and a dusting of confectioners' sugar completes this luscious dessert.

The apples can be precooked, wrapped in dough, and refrigerated until you are ready to bake. Don't forget to reserve the reduced poaching liquid. Baked dumplings can be reheated in a microwave but do not overcook them or they will get soggy; it takes forty-five seconds for one dumpling and about three minutes for four dumplings.

SERVES 4

FOR THE DOUGH

1	tablespoon yeast	1	large egg
2¾	cups all-purpose flour	6	tablespoons (3 ounces) unsalted butter or margarine, cut into small pieces
⅓	cup sugar		
1	teaspoon salt		
½	cup milk heated to 120°F and cooled to lukewarm	¼	teaspoon orange oil

Place all the ingredients in the machine, program for Dough, Basic Dough, or Manual, and press Start. The dough will be firm. While the dough is being made, poach the apples so that they have time to cool.

FOR THE APPLES AND SYRUP

4	medium-sized tart, firm apples, such as Cortland, Empire, or Granny Smith	1	cup sugar
		¼	stick (1 ounce) unsalted butter or margarine
1	cup water	¼	teaspoon ground cinnamon

Peel and core the apples. Add the water, sugar, butter, and cinnamon to a large saucepan and stir over medium-high heat until well mixed and the sugar has dissolved. Add the apples and continue cooking for 10 minutes, turning the apples occasionally so that they cook evenly. Remove the apples from the syrup and cool them to lukewarm. Reserve the syrup in the pan.

TO FINISH THE DUMPLINGS

½ cup sugar
1 teaspoon cinnamon
1½ tablespoons unsalted butter or
   margarine, cut into 4 pieces
1 egg beaten with 1 tablespoon
   water

1 tablespoon confectioners' sugar,
   for garnish
4 scoops vanilla ice cream, for
   garnish (optional)

Remove the dough to a work surface that has been lightly oiled or coated with a light film of nonstick vegetable spray. Divide the dough into 4 sections and roll each section to about a 7-inch square or circle. Each piece of dough should be big enough to completely wrap an apple with a ½-inch seam allowance.

Mix together the sugar and cinnamon. Place an apple in the center of each rolled-out piece of dough. Fill the hollow in the top of the apple with the cinnamon sugar mixture, then dot it with a piece of butter. Moisten the edges of the dough with a little water and fold the pieces of dough around the apples, making sure to seal them carefully. The seam at the top must be carefully sealed or it will open up while baking.

Preheat the oven to 400°F with the rack in the center position. Grease or spray an 8-inch baking pan with vegetable spray. Carefully lift the wrapped apples into the pan and brush the egg glaze over them. Bake the apples for 30 minutes, or until the crust turns a deep golden color.

To serve, place each baked apple in the center of a small plate or shallow bowl. Reheat the syrup so that it pours easily and drizzle it over the apples. Dust with confectioners' sugar and place a small scoop of vanilla ice cream beside the apples if desired.

HINT: *When you dust the apples, place the confectioners' sugar in a small strainer and, using the back of a spoon, press it through while shaking the strainer back and forth over the apples. This will give it a light delicate look and eliminate lumps. There are also special shakers made for this purpose.*

Almond Honey Katahs

The special technique in this recipe of layering and folding the dough produces a pastry of unparalleled lightness that simply melts in your mouth. The taste of the honey butter glaze keeps dancing around in memory long after the last bite has disappeared. We always thought that the Armenians were the masters of handling bread doughs, and this pastry confirms it. Lynne has adapted their technique to the bread machine and has supplied detailed instructions for hand-forming the pastry.

These katahs are memorable eaten warm from the oven and are also delicious at room temperature. They may be frozen, after baking, tightly wrapped in a plastic bag.

MAKES SIX 5- TO 6-INCH KATAHS

FOR THE DOUGH

1	tablespoon yeast		$^1/_2$	stick (2 ounces) unsalted butter or margarine
$3^1/_2$	cups all-purpose flour			
1	teaspoon salt		$^1/_2$	cup warm water
$^1/_2$	cup evaporated milk		1	large egg
$^1/_4$	cup vegetable shortening		2	tablespoons honey

Place all the ingredients in the machine, program for Dough or Manual, and press Start. The dough will be smooth and firm after several minutes of kneading but will still be light.

FOR THE FILLING

$^1/_2$	cup light brown sugar, firmly packed		$^1/_2$	teaspoon ground cinnamon
			$^1/_3$	cup currants
$^3/_4$	cup finely chopped almonds (4 ounces)		3	tablespoons unsalted butter or margarine, melted

Place the brown sugar, almonds, and cinnamon in a small bowl and stir with a fork until well combined. Add the currants and stir until evenly mixed.

Spray 2 large baking sheets with nonstick vegetable spray and set aside.

Remove the dough from the machine and divide it into 12 balls. Let the balls rest for 10 minutes, covered with plastic wrap. On a lightly floured surface, roll each ball to a 6- to 8-inch circle and pile the circles in 3 stacks of 4. Keep the stacks covered with plastic wrap. Take one stack and roll it to a 15- to 16-inch circle. The stack will roll out easily if you keep working from the center out. If at any time the dough begins to resist you, let it rest for 5 to 10 minutes and try again.

Spread this circle of dough with 1 tablespoon of the melted butter. Sprinkle with ½ cup of the filling. Cut the circle in half, and starting with the cut edge roll the dough and the filling together into a long rope and twist it several times.

Coil this twisted rope on a prepared baking sheet by holding on to one end and coiling the rest of the rope around it. Let the end you are holding onto stick up through the center about 1 inch. Now, using the heel of your hand, flatten the coil, pressing the tail end into the center, to a 5- to 6-inch diameter. Continue with the remaining stacks of dough and filling, reserving any leftover filling for the topping. Be sure to leave at least 2 inches between the katahs on the baking sheets. Cover the baking sheets with plastic wrap and let the dough rise for a few minutes while the oven is preheating.

TO FINISH THE KATAHS

¼ stick (1 ounce) unsalted butter or margarine, melted

2 tablespoons honey

Preheat the oven to 350°F with the rack in the center position.

Mix together the melted butter and honey and generously brush it over the katahs. Sprinkle them with the remaining topping and bake for 15 to 18 minutes, or until they are well puffed and golden. Remove them from the sheets and cool on wire racks.

> HINT: *When you are working with any type of fancy pastries that are this labor-intensive, bake them carefully, 1 sheet at a time, in the center of the oven and rotate the baking sheet front to back at least once. This will prevent hot spots in your oven from making the pastries black on the bottoms or tops.*

Wine Biscuits

Biscotti di vino *are hard Italian "biscuits" made with wine, and often served with wine. Semisweet and very peppery, these biscuits can be served with a mild cheese after dinner, or before dinner with a robust red wine, one that can stand up to their assertive spiciness.*

MAKES 4 DOZEN BISCUITS

FOR THE DOUGH

2¹⁄₂ cups all-purpose flour
2 teaspoons coarsely ground black pepper
6 tablespoons sugar
1 teaspoon salt

¹⁄₂ cup plus 2 tablespoons dry red wine
2 teaspoons baking powder
¹⁄₂ cup vegetable oil

Place all the ingredients in the machine, program for Manual, Dough, or Basic Dough, and press Start. Leave the lid of the machine open. Check the dough after 2 minutes; it should be well combined and should have formed a ragged ball. If it hasn't, let it mix 1 additional minute, or until the desired consistency is reached. Cancel the machine and transfer the dough to a lightly oiled work surface.

TO FINISH THE BISCUITS

Preheat the oven to 350°F. Divide the dough into 48 pieces. Roll each piece into a log about 5 inches long and about the width of your little finger. Join the ends of the log together to form a ring 1¹⁄₂ to 2 inches in diameter. Put the rings close together on an ungreased baking sheet; they won't expand appreciably and so can be set close together.

Bake the biscuits for 30 to 35 minutes, or until they're a light golden brown. Remove them from the oven and transfer them to a wire rack to cool completely.

The biscuits that result from this recipe hark back to the European definition of the word rather than our American definition. In Europe, biscuits are crisp crackers or cookies; in this country, they're soft, baking powder rolls. The word biscuit comes from the Middle French biscuit, *"twice cooked," which refers to the way this type of hard, durable cracker was baked.*

Macadamia Nut–White Chocolate Biscotti

An indulgent extravagance of flavors and textures is in store for you here. If you can't find macadamia nuts, you can substitute toasted whole almonds or pecans. Be sure to use real white chocolate (made with cocoa butter) for this recipe.

MAKES ABOUT 40 BISCOTTI

3	extra-large eggs	8	ounces white chocolate, chopped
1	cup sugar	1/2	cup unsweetened dried coconut,
3	cups all-purpose flour		toasted
1/2	teaspoon salt	1 1/2	cups unsalted macadamia nuts
1	teaspoon baking powder		

Preheat the oven to 350°F with the rack in the center position. Line a heavy-duty baking sheet with foil. Oil the foil or spray it with nonstick vegetable spray.

FOR THE DOUGH

Place the eggs and sugar in the machine and program for Dough. Press Start and allow the machine to knead for 3 minutes, not counting the preknead cycle. In a small bowl, mix together the flour, salt, and baking powder. With the machine still running, add this mixture and knead until a ball forms.

Add the chocolate, coconut, and macadamia nuts and knead for an additional 2 minutes, until these ingredients are incorporated. You may have to use a rubber scraper to push them down the sides of the machine and to encourage them into the ball. It is better to do too little kneading and finish by hand than allow the nuts to get crushed.

TO FINISH THE BISCOTTI

Remove the dough to a very lightly floured work surface. Dust your hands with flour and form the dough into a thick log. Cut the log into 3 equal pieces and roll each into an 11 × 1 3/4-inch log. Flatten the tops slightly with your fingers. Place the logs at least 2 inches apart on the prepared baking sheet. Bake for 30 minutes.

Remove the baking sheet from the oven and lower the temperature to 325°F. Use a very sharp knife (a serrated one is good for this) to cut the logs on the diagonal into 3/4-inch slices. Lay the slices on the baking sheet (or on a very large wire rack, if you have one) and return them to the oven to toast for 10 minutes. They should look dry. Cool them completely on a wire rack, then store them in airtight tins.

Quitza Bernardo

The divine inspiration for quitza came from my determination to combine two of my favorite dishes: pizza and quiche. This rich dessert sports a rich, creamy, rum-enhanced custard studded with bits of marrons glacés (candied chestnuts) in a brioche crust. Warm from the oven or at room temperature, it makes a fabulously indulgent ending to a meal, or the high point of a dessert buffet table.

I love it when there are kids in my cooking classes. One particularly helpful young man at Bristol Farms in Anaheim Hills, California, accompanied his mother, who was the class assistant. Bernardo knew where every utensil was kept; he could scout out any ingredient and deliver it with dispatch. And he paid rapt attention during class. Since he was instrumental in scouting out the candied chestnuts for this dessert, I am naming it after him.

This dessert is best made in a springform pan. The thirteen-inch conical springform made by Kaiser is perfect for this.

SERVES 12

FOR THE BRIOCHE DOUGH CRUST

1	tablespoon yeast	1½	teaspoons salt
3¼	cups all-purpose flour	1½	sticks (6 ounces) unsalted butter,
½	cup sugar		melted and slightly cooled
3	tablespoons nonfat dry milk	3	extra-large eggs

Place all the ingredients in the machine, program for Dough or Manual, and press Start. The dough will be extremely sticky at first, then slightly less so as the kneading progresses. Some will continue to stick to the bottom of the pan. Don't be tempted to add more flour—this is quite a loose dough. It will firm up when chilled.

At the end of the final knead, place the dough in a well-oiled 2-quart bowl, cover it with plastic wrap, and refrigerate it for at least 24 hours, or as long as 36 hours.

Generously butter a 13- or 12-inch springform pan with 2-inch-high sides. On a lightly oiled work surface, roll the chilled dough into a 16-inch circle. Fit the dough into the pan, pushing the excess up the sides to the top. Form a fluted crust by pinching the edge between your fingers. Allow the crust to rise, uncovered, in a warm place until puffed.

TO FINISH THE QUITZA

6 extra-large egg yolks
2 cups heavy cream
2/3 cup brown sugar
1/3 cup dark rum

1 10-ounce jar candied chestnuts in syrup, broken into pieces, syrup reserved

Preheat the oven to 425°F with the rack in the center position and make the filling.

In a mixing bowl, whisk together the egg yolks, cream, sugar, and rum. Prick the bottom of the crust all over with a fork. Pour in the filling, sprinkle on the chestnuts, and drizzle the syrup over the surface. Bake for 15 minutes and then reduce the oven temperature to 375° and bake for another 30 minutes. The quitza is done when the filling quivers yet no longer rolls when the pan is jiggled. Allow the quitza to cool for 15 minutes before removing the springform sides. Cut it into wedges and serve it warm or at room temperature.

Strawberry Rhubarb Pie

The crust of this pie stays crisp and dry until you cut into the tangy, sweet strawberry rhubarb filling. The juices then soak into the sweet rich dough to give you a taste something like a cross between a pie and a cobbler. The crust is about double the thickness of a traditional pie crust and airier. Pliable and understanding, this dough is a great alternative for the cook who is intimidated by crusts that are hard to roll out or that fall apart. In fact, since as the crust bakes and rises it can cover up a multitude of visual sins, feel free to play with it.

This pie tastes best the day it is baked. Cool it for at least fifteen minutes before cutting. Try it with ice cream.

SERVES 6 TO 8

FOR THE DOUGH

1	tablespoon yeast		1/2	cup milk
2 3/4	cups all-purpose flour		1	large egg
1/3	cup sugar		6	tablespoons (3 ounces) unsalted
1/4	teaspoon orange oil or the finely			butter or margarine
	grated rind of 1 orange		1	teaspoon salt

Place all the ingredients in the machine, program for Dough, Basic Dough, or Manual, and press Start. The dough looks firm and will not be sticky to the touch.

FOR THE FILLING

8	ounces fresh, thin, tender rhubarb,		2	teaspoons cornstarch
	cut into 1/4-inch slices		1/4	teaspoon nutmeg
1/2	cup sugar			
1	tablespoon water			

Place the rhubarb, sugar, and water in a small heavy-bottomed saucepan and cook over medium-high heat for about 10 minutes, or until the liquid is reduced and the mixture is thickened to an applesaucelike consistency. Stir constantly for the last few minutes. Remove from the heat and add the cornstarch and nutmeg, stirring until well mixed. Cool to lukewarm.

TO FINISH THE PIE

1	pint fresh ripe strawberries, hulled		1	egg beaten with 1 tablespoon
	and sliced			water

Remove the dough to a lightly floured work surface, divide it in half, and let it rest, covered with a clean towel, for 10 minutes. Roll each section of dough to a 12-inch circle. Butter or spray a 9-inch pie plate with nonstick vegetable spray.

Fold 1 of the circles in half and lift it into the pie plate. Open up the folded dough and spread it so that it drapes over the rim of the pie plate about 1 inch. Spread the cooled filling over the bottom of the lined pie plate. Cover the filling with the sliced strawberries. Moisten the edges of the dough with a little water.

Fold the second circle of dough in half and lift it on top of the fruit. Spread out the dough and pinch the edges to seal. Fold this pinched seam about 1/2 inch toward the center. Using the tips of your fingers, poke down and under a bit. Don't worry if it looks a bit messy; it will even out later as it rises and bakes. With a sharp knife or kitchen scissors, cut three 3-inch slits in the top piece of dough. Let the pie rise in a warm place for about 1 hour. There will only be a slight rounding.

Preheat the oven to 400°F with the rack in the center position. Bake the pie for 20 minutes and then generously brush it with the egg glaze. Bake the pie for 10 more minutes, or until it is a deep golden color.

Hints: Don't shortcut precooking the rhubarb and reducing its juices or you will have too much liquid on your hands after the pie is baked.

Glazing the pie after baking it first will help prevent the crust from becoming too brown. If the crust looks like it is getting too brown, cover the top of the pie loosely with foil.

Sfinci

On St. Joseph's Day, Cindy's grandmother would head down to the basement to her favorite enamel stove to fry up these sugar-coated melt-in-your-mouth pastries to celebrate this saint's day. Cindy regarded it as a special treat to go over and help her grandmother dredge the sfinci in sugar. This is Anna Salvato's Old World Sicilian recipe. Enjoy.

MAKES 14 SFINCI

FOR THE DOUGH

1	tablespoon yeast	1	tablespoon sugar
4	cups all-purpose flour	2	teaspoons salt
2	cups water	1¼	cups raisins

Place all the ingredients except the raisins in the machine, program for Dough or Basic Dough, and press Start. Add the raisins during the last 3 minutes of the kneading cycle.

The dough will be sticky, so do not be alarmed if the dough is not a perfect ball of dough. During the first few minutes of mixing you may have to encourage the mixing with a rubber spatula.

TO FINISH THE SFINCI

4	cups corn oil or vegetable oil, plus an additional 2 tablespoons for your fingers	2	cups sugar mixed with 1 tablespoon cinnamon

When the dough cycle is finished, remove the pan from the bread machine so that you can work directly from it.

In a heavy frying pan over medium-high heat, heat the 4 cups oil to 375°F. While the oil is heating, cover a cookie sheet with paper towels to drain the sfinci on.

When the oil has reached frying temperature, oil your fingers and reach in and grab a small handful of dough. Stretch out the dough a little so it is not a ball and place it into the hot oil. You can fry up to 3 or 4 balls at a time. Turn them over as they begin to brown and fry them on the opposite side. Remove them from the oil, let them drain for a few minutes, then dredge both sides in the sugar and cinnamon. Repeat this process until all the dough is used up. Serve hot or warm.

Mail-Order Guide

Boyajian, Inc.
385 California Street
Newton, MA 02160
(617) 527-6677
Citrus oils, flavored olive oils, caviar, smoked salmon, extra-special maple syrup

Cardullos Gourmet Shoppe
6 Brattle Street
Cambridge, MA 02138
(800) 491-8288
Exotic and hard-to-find ingredients, spices, sauces, seasonings, and chocolate

Chef's Catalogue
3215 Commercial Avenue
Northbrook, IL 60062–1900
(800) 338-3232
Baking pans (Kaiser La Forme conical springform), rolling pins, timers, pizza pans

Gluten-Free Pantry
Beth Hillson
P.O. Box 881
Glastonbury, CT 06033
(203) 633-3826
Wheat and gluten-free mixes, recipes, and newsletter

The King Arthur Flour Baker's Catalogue
P.O. Box 876
Norwich, VT 05055
(800) 777-4434
Excellent free catalogue showcasing a wide variety of flours and grains, sourdough starters, grains, spices, yeasts, oils, specialty baking equipment, tools, professional quality unusual ingredients, baking books, Lora Brody's Bread Machine Boost®

Williams-Sonoma
P.O. Box 7456
San Francisco, CA 94120–7456
(800) 541-2233
Top-quality baking equipment (Kaiser La Forme pans) and ingredients, Boyajian flavored oils, caviar, packaged sourdough starters, smoked salmon, Lora Brody's Bread Machine Boost®

Index